Also by Gail Godwin

THE MAKING OF A WRITER, VOLUME TWO

RANDOM HOUSE

New York

THE
MAKING
OF A
WRITER

VOLUME TWO

Journals, 1963–1969

GAIL GODWIN

EDITED BY ROB NEUFELD

Published in the United States by Random House,
an imprint of The Random House Publishing Group,
a division of Random House, Inc., New York.

RANDOM HOUSE and colophon are registered
trademarks of Random House, Inc.

Grateful acknowledgment is made to Alfred A. Knopf, a
division of Random House, Inc., for permission to reprint
excerpts from *Dream Children* by Gail Godwin,
copyright © 1976 and copyright renewed 2004 by Gail Godwin.
Reprinted by permission of Alfred A. Knopf, a division of
Random House, Inc.

LIBRARY OF CONGRESS CATALOGING-IN-PUBLICATION DATA
Godwin, Gail.
The making of a writer : volume two /
Gail Godwin ; edited by Rob Neufeld.
p. cm.
Includes index.
ISBN 978-1-4000-6433-5 (hard)
EBOOK ISBN 978-0-6796-0438-9
1. Godwin, Gail—Diaries. 2. Novelists, American—
20th century—Diaries. 3. Fiction—Authorship. I. Neufeld, Rob. II. Title.
PS3557.O315Z468 2006
813'.54—dc22   2005044929

Printed in the United States of America on acid-free paper

www.atrandom.com

2 4 6 8 9 7 5 3 1

FIRST EDITION

Book design by Gretchen Achiles

To

Kathleen Krahenbuhl Godwin Cole

(1912–1989)

Mother / Writer

PREFACE

❧

*O*ur hope from the beginning of this project has been to trace through these early journals the "soon or never" trajectory in the life of an aspiring writer.

"When, when will mine eyes find the light?" Prince Tamino beseeches the priests in *The Magic Flute.* "Soon, soon, Youth, or never," comes the ominous choral reply. Which pretty much sums up the tension in Volume 2 of *The Making of a Writer:* "Am I going to get to do what I want to do more than anything? Or will it be a case of my having wanted what could never be?"

This second and final volume of *The Making of a Writer* contains entries from journal notebooks dating from July 23, 1963, to July 6, 1969. The journals in Parts 1 through 5 were written in England; those in Parts 6 through 9, in Iowa City, Iowa.

Volume 1 of *The Making of a Writer,* published in 2006, opened in the summer of 1961, when, at age twenty-four, after two staggering personal and professional failures (one of each), I started over as a waitress in order to earn money to travel abroad and become a writer. Volume 1 broke off in midsummer of 1963, in London, on a note of reassertion and resolve, although with no concrete "proof" of my having yet accomplished anything.

Volume 2 of *The Making of a Writer* continues in the London of 1963–1965, when I am asking myself whether or not I have overstayed my time in this fascinating city, then suddenly changes gears with a precipitous marriage to an English doctor met in a fiction-writing class. Volume 2 ends in Iowa City, with me as a soon-to-be published novelist.

Apropos of the "soon or never" cusp, I remember a poignant walk I took with my mother on a visit to Asheville, North Carolina, from Iowa City at the end of the summer of 1968. I was thirty-one, twice divorced, and had been a student in the Iowa Writers' Workshop since the spring of 1967. Now I was working toward a doctorate in literature and supporting myself on a teaching fellowship while yearning (a feeling often closer to despairing) for the day when I would be a "certified" writer, i.e., published. At the end of that summer semester, having passed my Old English exam, I boarded a Greyhound bus and went home to my best friend, my mother, Kathleen. As far back as I remembered, both of us had yearned to be novelists.

I say "be novelists," as distinct from "write novels," because, at the time I am speaking of, the day of the walk, we had completed seven novels between us: three each and a shared one, entitled "The Otherwise Virgins." She wrote the first version, and after shopping it around for several years, bequeathed it to me when I was a junior at Chapel Hill. "I still think it's a damn good story," she said. "Take it and see what *you* can do with it." I kept the plot and the three women's points of view, updated the college campus from post–World War II to post–Korean War, added my own quirks and sensibilities—and got off to an inauspicious start by sending it to the same agent who had rejected the first version and remembered the plot and the title. This shared novel, along with our other unpublished novels (including two later ones she wrote), is now in the Southern Historical Collection in the Wilson Library at the University of North Carolina at Chapel Hill. I still think "The Otherwise Virgins" is a damn good story. I wish I had a hungry young writer to whom I could say: "Take it, with my blessing, and see what *you* can do."

Now, on this afternoon walk, through neighborhood streets of my mother's childhood and mine, we were again talking about the elusive and inexhaustible subject of writing.

On the bus trip from Iowa I had read Colin Wilson's funny, short autobiographical novel *Adrift in Soho,* which chronicled the apprentice years of some young would-be writers, artists, and anarchists hanging out with one another in post–World War II London. And now Mother was reading it, and on our walk she was telling me all the things she was enjoying.

"And you know what I love most?" she said. "Some of them are so close to what they want to do, and they don't know *how* close. But we do."

Gail Godwin

CONTENTS

Part one

THE DRAMATIC SELF

London

JULY 23, 1963, TO SEPTEMBER 30, 1963

*I*n the summer of 1961, twenty-four-year-old Gail Godwin dispatched herself to Europe to become a writer. Having shed both a marriage and a journalism career, she hung her financial well-being on the promise of a job with a soon-to-open U.S. Travel Service office in London.

For two years, Gail negotiated foreign cultures and demanding relationships while hungrily educating herself and recording her emotional and intellectual progress. The first volume of Gail's journals (published in 2006) revealed how she'd found her voice and purpose, distinguishing herself from her influences. The second volume now shows how she built on that self-confidence to publish her first stories and novels.

Fittingly, Volume 2 opens with Gail parked at her desk in her familiar Chelsea boardinghouse, reading her previous journals. "I have only to reread them to pick out the inconsistencies and to recognize the few true aspirations that thread through page after page," she writes.

Using herself as a laboratory of introspection, and her relationships as opportunities to understand others, Gail follows the model of one of her heroes, Carl Jung, whose Memories, Dreams, Reflections recorded his inward explorations. What Gail comes up with is distinctive, and is encapsulated in the title of this journal part, "The Dramatic Self."

The dramatic self is, in one sense, the posing self, the one that is on stage in society. In another sense, it is the self that experiences the most essential dramas—meaningful interactions based on one's natural agenda. Finally, there's the dramatic self that is separate from the person and belongs in the world of literature, the one that is re-formed to sound true in stories.

Reading about Gail's adventures and misadventures shows how her literary sphere of existence was as prominent as her social one. While her coworkers, fellow tenants, and boyfriends provide community, they stand in opposition to her aloneness and imagination.

Through it all, the psychology, politics, and nuances of male-female relations preoccupy Gail. Although any subject would do for a writer striving

to develop her art, gender relations were particularly pertinent at the time.
Gail was in the thick of the matter. "I want to . . . exploit, define, name, place
this ever-shifting contest between men and women," she wrote on August 13.

The dilemma for Gail was how to have her enlightened perspective
correspond to happiness in personal relationships, in which egos often
foiled idealism. On August 13, Gail wrote that she wanted to convey,
among other things, "the feeling you get while living through a happy
moment—when you refer back to the past when you had anticipated this
moment, and when you look toward the future when you won't have it any
longer." She wanted anticipation and reflection to be part of the mo-
ment—yearning, experience, and loss, all one.

JULY 23, 1963

More and more I believe in these journals. They are my "thinking out"
grounds where I can record and measure my deviations. I have only to
reread them to pick out the inconsistencies and to recognize the few
true aspirations that thread through page after page. It is difficult to
label oneself "faithful" when, upon rereading two years' worth of self-
reflection, one finds agonizings over B., Niels, Antonio, James, Jim
Jensen, Henry, and Gordon! On the credit side, I know for certain that
this urge to understand/write is no fly-by-night whim. I know how
Gordon feels when people say: "Oh, Bisley! Yes, I'm a pretty good
marksman myself. I'll have to come out with you one Sunday and shoot
a few bull's-eyes!"[1] I feel the same impatience with people who say:
"Oh, yes, writing. I'd like to write if I only had the time. My life would
make one *hell* of a story."

Pat Farmer wrote her après-honeymoon letter to Doreen[2] "and every-

---

1. The National Rifle Association of Great Britain is located in Bisley. Major shooting meets
took place there.

2. Doreen, Gail's immediate supervisor at the U.S. Travel Service office, is a complex character: a disorganized boss, a thirty-plus unmarried woman who dreams of finding the right
man, and a former "air hostess" who has adopted the calmness of that job title.

body" from Mexico City. She obligingly described the wedding—sending clippings—and the honeymoon, showing a color photo of herself among Mayan ruins. Mr. Miller couldn't wait to read the letter. He always liked her. "Well! Is that from you-know-who? She finally made it. See, there's hope for you girls yet!" Pat wrote about how she and Pepe went skin diving and horseback riding. Then she put in the paragraph about how happy they were, adding that it was somewhat of an adjustment, etc., etc., but that it was surprising how much you could get out of a situation where you worked very hard to make the other person happy, etc., etc. She then mentioned that she was trying to get a job with USTS-Mexico. Doreen read the letter and then expounded upon how ecstatic Pat must be.

After Doreen left, Dorothea[3] observed: "I think it's interesting that she wants to work again." Then we both exchanged knowing looks, and she said: "My God, by the time we're thirty-five we're going to be goddam sages." So the balance is restored in the office, or should I simply say the dialectic has swung? Dorothea admits taking refuge from the realization of a bad marriage through hard labor. "By the time I've prepared a meal and cleaned the house and washed up and ironed, I don't have time to think about myself. I'm too tired. Of course I realize that there might be a lifetime of this."

After spending the better part of the past three days with Gordon on the shooting range at Bisley, sailing in Henley,[4] drinking in various pubs, and then last night at the horse show, I have come to the conclusion that I still love him, but in a modified way. I think I will value him for the efforts I am making to win him! We passed two people in the White City Stadium[5] and he said: "Were those men or women?" I said,

3. Dorothea was a coworker at the U.S. Travel Service office whose marriage of respect and affection, but not passion, provided one of many models for Gail. Dorothea and Gail shared many confidential observations.

4. The Henley Sailing Club was formed in 1896 at Cordery's Boatyard in Shiplake, about thirty miles west of London, on the river Thames. In 1962, the club was expanded to include a bar. Gail met Gordon Wrigley in April 1963. He was a research engineer, specializing in ceramics, and the great-nephew of the founder of the William Wrigley Jr. Company, famous for its spearmint gum. As he admitted to Gail, Gordon had a habit of analyzing and categorizing people.

5. White City Stadium was built in 1908 for the Olympics. In 1927, it was modified to accommodate greyhound racing. In 1947, it began hosting horse shows. The stadium was demolished in 1985 for a complex of BBC buildings.

sort of off the cuff: "Why, the one that looks like a man is a woman; the one that looks like a woman is a man." "What makes you say that?" he asked. "Well, you should always know that things are the opposite of what they appear." (Canting unforgivably!) "Smart girl." Did he really think so? I also learned about his experiences on the convoy going to the U.S. during the war. He said he even made himself a survival kit. There was something in this story about the calm, almost detached way he went about things. I saw the war from a little boy's eyes. And the way he'd watch the laggers-behind get sunk by the German U-boats. All this—the years in Canada and Trinidad—shaped him, too. But I think he was born with this dogged, plodding, stubborn way of doing things.

But, today in Gill's bookstore, several incidents combined and made me see the kind of man that is possible: I saw a book I wanted, [the latest volume of] Simone de Beauvoir's autobiography,[6] about her writing and her life with Jean-Paul Sartre. And I thought, Wouldn't it be nice if someone knew me so well they would know this is the book I want and bring it home? I know that I am capable of such consideration toward someone else. Then I thought of the possibility of, say, Gordon bringing me that book. It was impossible. (1) He doesn't go into bookstores. (2) He doesn't know who Simone de Beauvoir is. (3) He doesn't know what I read, in spite of the fact he's always inspecting book titles. Somehow I remember Doug[7] and me in the bookstore in Detroit one evening while we were killing time before seeing *Spartacus*. I was in heaven—thousands and thousands of glossy new books, two floors of them, and some strange new symphony playing. I asked Doug if he would buy me *Jacob's Room & The Waves* by Virginia Woolf, a $1.75 paperback, and he grudgingly assented. The music grew on me. I went up to the man at the desk and asked him what it was. "Oh, that's Beethoven's *Pastoral*, I think," he said. And when we were back in Florida I bought it and began playing it more and more to assert my aesthetic independence from Doug.

6. Gail was reading *The Prime of Life*, the second volume of de Beauvoir's memoirs; it documents de Beauvoir's unmarried relationship with philosopher Jean-Paul Sartre as well as her responses to the rise of Hitler and the onslaught of World War II.

7. Douglas Kennedy, Gail's ex-husband, a photographer on the *Miami Herald*.

JULY 27–28 · *After midnight*

I read an article by Marya Mannes[8] today. I'm one of those women whose composition is balanced peculiarly between woman-ness and creativity.

JULY 30

Dorothea: "I think I attribute that sick feeling I have every morning to the leftover anxiety from unremembered dreams."

AUGUST 7

It is with immense relief that I close the door to my room on the top floor of a Chelsea house,[9] settle into a comfortable bed, and listen to the sounds of the night, the muffled hum of traffic down by the embankment, the toned-down rock and roll of a German radio program (bringing back the night in the East Berlin police station, fall 1961).[10] True, time is the villain and we are trapped in him. True, love is sometimes not returned. True, friends are sometimes false. But to be aware of this—all of it—and still want to go on living, that is the triumph. It is the reward. Go on, French voices; and there is Rachmaninoff in the background. Thomas Wolfe called loneliness a brother and I think he was right. And I have not read Rimbaud or Baudelaire nor have I even begun to put down what I will put down on paper.

8. Marya Mannes wrote feature articles and art criticism for *The New Yorker* and for *The Reporter* (a leading political and cultural magazine that ran from 1949 through 1968). She often cautioned against the suppression of women's creativity in the United States, and made an envying comparison to Soviet women in order to goad her compatriots into relaxing their gender biases.

9. Gail rented a room in a boardinghouse run by Mr. and Mrs. West, a couple declined in fortune, who missed the days of British colonial nobility. Except for a period living alone in her own apartment, November 1962 to May 1963, Gail had stayed with the Wests and their collection of boarders in three different houses. Her 1983 novella "Mr. Bedford" is based upon her time with the Wests.

10. Gail wrote an article chronicling her journey to Berlin and her interrogation by East German police; it appeared in the *Asheville Citizen-Times* in November 1961.

But first, the bad dream and then the realizations that came unexpectedly out of a weekend that, from all outward signs and from everybody else's viewpoint, was pleasant, restful, and full of good fun.

This morning, the alarm awoke me at eight. Then I dozed and dreamed that I was standing in some sort of a gymnasium watching some performance or other. Gordon came in with John[11] and Sally Milner, the very attractive, upper-class English girl who works at USTS. He said to me, "Oh, hello, nice to see you," in that cordial way he has. Then he transferred his entire attention to the performance on the stage. I kept watching him for some assurance that we had meant something to each other. Finally I asked him, "Gordon, aren't we going camping together?" And he answered very surely, very unembarassedly, with the same detachment that he used the day Bobbie[12] and I turned up at the same time in his flat when he was sick, "No, I'm afraid I can't. I'm taking Sally." Then I turned to Sally and said, "But how? You've just come back from three weeks' vacation." She replied, "Yes, but you see, in this life, some people get three weeks' vacation and some don't get any at all. And usually the people who get three get offered more." So I took my sweater and handbag and said, "Well, in that case, I'll be leaving." I walked out of the gymnasium, feeling Gordon's eyes on me, thinking: He'll be sorry. Then I got outside and thought: It hurts as much as it possibly can—ever. Then I turned around and went back in and caused a scene. Gordon remained smiling and unperturbed. I said: "I'm just in the same category with Bobbie." He answered: "That's okay. I like having her around once a week or so."

I awoke feeling beaten. I lay at the foot of my bed, saying "Oh, no!" Then I got up and went to the washbasin to wash away any visible traces of the ordeal I'd just been through. I looked surprisingly normal to myself in the mirror. I thought: It cannot get any worse. Then, and this is very important, I was overcome by an almost beautiful kind of relief: I recognized my plight and accepted it, knowing that I was going to live

---

11. John was Gordon's roommate.

12. Gordon was also seeing a younger girl named Bobbie, with whom he went on camping trips.

it out—like you wear out a pair of shoes or write out a journal. There was a basic sense of continuation of life, a celebration of change.

AUGUST 8 · *Thursday*

I just thought: If I wanted to get rid of Gordon, I would simply hand over my stack of journals from 1961 onward. By the time he read through the first one, he would be shocked. I cannot forget Gordon's statement re Ingmar Bergman: "I don't understand mad people and I don't want to."

> *With so much sunshine in my memory, how could I have bet on nonsense?*
>
> —ALBERT CAMUS, *NOTEBOOKS, 1935–1942*

Sometimes small things, past happenings, flash across my memory and I am astonished by who I am and what I have done. The dangerous thing is to judge myself by the standards of other people.

AUGUST 9

Just like old times again—me, myself, and I—with diversions of catching 19s and 22s[13] to work; Robin and Henry came for lunch to dredge up old times, which are better left undredged. Next week: a press party for the governor of Florida.[14] Fall is coming and again there are many possibilities.

I don't know whether I am becoming eccentric or losing my mind or whether I really am right. Robin[15] came to dinner at my invitation and expense, spent two hours talking to the Portuguese woman in a variety of French-Spanish-English. I could not join in, but sat and smiled for a

---

13. The 19 and 22 London bus lines served Chelsea.

14. Cecil Farris Bryant was the governor of Florida at the time.

15. Gail met Robin in January 1963 at the travel office. He was an exuberant friend who, however, grew sour when people didn't play along with his larks.

few hours. At 10:30, I went out for a walk. When I came back, Robin had been looking for me, and we went to a pub where there were two old friends of his who just got married. They had much to talk over. At intervals, Robin would say: "Gail is bored. I've behaved badly tonight. She gave me a meal and then I spent two hours talking to somebody else." When we left the pub, Robin said: "Why can't you make the effort to talk to people, etc." He was incensed. I tried to explain that he hadn't introduced me. He said he had. We parted none the unhappier for parting.

AUGUST 11

I have often wondered how big an indulgence this journal is—especially when I am recording the comings and goings of men. *Gianni Schicchi*[16] is playing . . . I have a Madeira hangover. Last night I sorted out my writing and did a little bit of revision.

TO BARBARA'S IN Hampstead for coffee and pancakes. Now, there's an interesting girl. Very selective, good taste, fighting her South African origins a little too fiercely. We listened to Negro spirituals, drank coffee, looked at her brass rubbings, and discussed things one ought to discuss. That's the point about Barbara. One feels one is doing so many worthy things. I am sure the man who marries her will do so because he thinks she is the type of girl one ought to marry.[17]

AUGUST 13

One would have a great advantage over his dark devils if he could predict *when* which of them were due to turn up. I *think* I have a special cycle—of course, Hilda[18] would chalk it up to my astrological chart. At

---

16. In *Gianni Schicchi*, a comic opera composed by Giacomo Puccini, the title character falsifies a will for a disinherited family and, in doing so, sneakily bequeaths valuable property to himself, thus providing a dowry for his lovesick daughter. In Godwin's novel *Violet Clay*, Minerva, the owner of a woodland retreat, tells Violet how she'd sung Schubert songs and the daughter's aria from *Gianni Schicchi* at her parents' parties.

17. In December 1964, Gordon, who had moved to Rugby, became engaged to Barbara.

18. Hilda was a palmist in London whom Gail had seen from time to time.

certain times, I am obsessed with the passing of time, wrinkles, aging, becoming unattractive to men. It is at these times that I tend to be possessive, shortsighted, a real "leaner." At other times, time is relatively unimportant. Just living, hearing airplane sounds, going out, chatting with the Wests, etc., is enough. And then there are periods like tonight—INTERIM periods, mid-swing between cycles. I am not terribly upset or intense about anything. People seem fairly remote. I have written well today. I wrote last night—suddenly I am not tired after dinner. I bought a £3 tome on Thomas Wolfe, which I could not afford. Tonight I am going to enjoy my dinner, do my exercises, write the final paragraph of "Bay Bridge,"[19] maybe set my hair, and read *The Window of Memory*,[20] which is an academic study of Wolfe and how he wrote.

A man was in today from the Pennsylvania Tourist Board. He pointed out a town called Intercourse, Pa., on the map.

LATER FINISHED "BAY BRIDGE." It is exciting to see yourself progressing in the work you want to do. I am learning to convey feelings through the use of words—or the careful nonuse of them. The scene where they are crying at the drive-in is exactly as I want it—the sudden shift from him to her of possession of the upper hand.

THERE ARE CERTAIN things I still want to convey, especially in "Bright Eyes," which will be the longest story in the volume: (1) the feeling of knowing you have lost, but being grateful for the quality of awareness which allows you to experience such a degree of pain; (2) the feeling you get while living through a happy moment—when you refer back to the past when you had anticipated this moment, and when you look toward the future when you won't have it any longer; (3) the feeling of sex when you love somebody—but doesn't everybody try to describe this

19. "Bay Bridge" was a story based on Gail's first love, who had joined the Air Force and then come to "claim her," she says, in 1955. Their engagement was broken when Gail reconnected with her father, who sent her to Peace College. The story has been lost.

20. In *The Window of Memory* (1962), Richard Kennedy reconstructs Thomas Wolfe's development as a writer, beginning in 1928, at which point Wolfe had written more than half a million words and published nothing. Though Gail could strongly identify with Wolfe's desire to encompass the world and his recognition of epic material in his hometown (Asheville, North Carolina—also Gail's), she did not share his epic style.

sooner or later?; (4) the feeling of frustration when you are trying to become a complete, integrated person and everyone else seems so far ahead; (5) the feeling of that awful unquiet shadow that suddenly appears over a day and for no reason at all.

"Bright Eyes" will be the main story, and yes, I have been lazy in describing him.[21] I will have to go back and try again.

Then "Bay Bridge"—the beginning of womanhood.

Then "Mourning"—the ending is weak.

Then "Wesley Phipps"[22]—the room scene is weak.

Then "The Happy Couple"[23]—to fill up space. Is that right?

Other things that I want to do: exploit, define, name, place this evershifting contest between men and women.

AUGUST 14 · *Wednesday*

Gordon and John and I had dinner at Barbara's. She really laid on a spread. I begin to like her. She is good-natured, quiet, calm, courteous; and she appreciates good things. A description of the contents of her bed-sitter in Hampstead would be an adequate description of her. She read DHL's poem "Snake"[24] aloud, and it was beautiful. Not many people can read poetry aloud. John made a chart entitled "Ball Pressure" for measuring the attributes of women. You get 10 or up to 10 points for each attribute and the highest score is 100. He lists: (1) personality, (2) character, (3) overall appeal, (4) facial beauty, (5) body beauty, (6) compatibility, (7) conversation (you can lose 10 points here), (8) intelligence,

---

21. "Bright Eyes" portrayed a preacher on a soapbox at Hyde Park Corner in London, and the memories of a disastrous affair his screed arouses in a passing American girl.

22. "Wesley Phipps" was a short story that Gail wrote about a man who returns to his family's business after a year of dreaming. The story is lost.

23. Gail based "The Happy Couple" on a sinister young American couple whom she'd met in London. The husband kept giving away the wife's secrets.

24. In D. H. Lawrence's poem "Snake," the poet feels honored by a snake's use of his water-trough, but then throws a log at it in a fit of revulsion, thus revealing the beast's godliness and his own pettiness. In 2003, the poem appeared in *Snakes: An Anthology of Serpent Tales* (edited by Willee Lewis) along with Godwin's piece "My Snakes." There, Godwin shares with Lawrence, and evidently with Barbara, too, a reverence for the animal, which she relates through a series of vignettes—from her reading of Kipling's *The Jungle Book* to a shared admiration of a large garter snake with her late companion Robert Starer.

(9) sex appeal, (10) cleanliness. Alden[25] is back from driving a tractor in Denmark. He walked into the office and there was immediate joy from me. He is so alive, so aware, yet so beautifully detached. As John says: He just floats around the world minding his own business. And Gordon says: "He'll be a good doctor. He won't make any money because he'll go around saying, 'Ah, that's okay, never mind the payment, let's just have a drink instead.' "

AUGUST 18 · *Sunday*

I can quite see how, in about ten years' time, I come home from a Sunday afternoon walk, look in the mirror, add up my assets and liabilities, and then put a bullet through my head after the manner of MWG.[26] I am certain I know something of what he felt. I must put all of this down before I can even hope to go out tonight. I want to understand these huge inferiority complexes of mine. How, in crowds and on buses, passing my reflection in shop windows I feel so ugly, so inadequate. Naturally, I realize that this is not the whole truth. As Alden (happy boy!) says about himself: Some people have told me I'm handsome, others that I'm homely as hell. So I just accept the supposition that I fall somewhere between those two extremes and that some people are going to go for me and others aren't.

But anyway, to try to define the indefinable. Today is like fall. I am visited with all the end-of-summer sadness, the vestigial back-to-school eagerness. I awoke at 1:00 p.m. feeling that nothing was real, that all my senses had tricked me, and that I did not know another human being and never would.

---

25. Alden James, a Canadian, had come to London to study medicine. He was a friend of Robin's, and a man's man, riding motorcycles, camping out, smoking cigars, doing the Hemingway thing, including expressing anguish over women.

26. Mose Winston Godwin, Gail's father, committed suicide on January 9, 1958, twenty years after Gail's mother had divorced him, and three years after he had reentered Gail's life in a supportive way following her high school graduation. "Mourning," one of the stories Gail noted on August 13 that she was developing, reflects on this subject, as does Gail's novel *Violet Clay*, in which the heroine's uncle, Ambrose Clay, commits suicide.

AUGUST 22

> *I may remark ... that though in that early time I seem to have*
> *been constantly eager to exchange my lot for that of some-*
> *body else, on the assumed certainty of gaining by the bar-*
> *gain, I fail to remember feeling jealous of such happier*
> *persons—in the measure open to children of spirit. I had*
> *rather a positive lack of the passion and thereby, I suppose, a*
> *lack of spirit, since if jealousy bears, as I think, on what one*
> *sees one's companions able to do—as against one's falling*
> *short—envy, as I knew it at least, was simply of what they*
> *were, or in other words of a certain sort of richer conscious-*
> *ness supposed, doubtless often too freely supposed, in them.*
> —HENRY JAMES, *NOTES OF A SON AND BROTHER*[27]

YOU DO GET bogged down in him.

What he was after was the apprehension of that "condensed and heightened form of reality" he called legend.

> *But Wolfe's work is not important merely because it can be*
> *read as social history. He raised his autobiographical hero*
> *above the level of realism to become an archetypal figure en-*
> *gaged in the quest for self-discovery and forced constantly to*
> *readjust his focus on life as he went along.*
> —RICHARD KENNEDY, *THE WINDOW OF MEMORY*

Write simple sentences. Report. Don't moralize. No pretensions. I am always afraid I am going to bore people and that is why I sometimes go to the clever-arty extreme.

---

27. James's autobiographical work *Notes of a Son and Brother* was published in 1914. James died in 1916.

—

A SENSE OF FRUSTRATION BECAUSE:

I have "Bay Bridge" finished but it is lacking in something;
I need to put some good hard labor into "Wesley Phipps";
I need to finish "Bright Eyes" and I'm scared of the
    Hyde Park scene.[28]

The Moviegoer was based on an outline of [Søren Kierkegaard's] *Sickness unto Death.* I must write about going to the movies alone and why it is so good.[29]

AUGUST 23

Today, a well-dressed middle-aged couple came in. I immediately detected "Deep South" accent and asked where they came from. "New Oah-leans," they said proudly. "We live right behind the Cotton Bowl stadium." I asked them if they'd read Walker Percy's *The Moviegoer.* They exchanged looks and their faces closed to me. "I just don't understand how anyone can read that book," she said, more to him than to me. It turns out they had met Percy and his wife for tea. "He hasn't been well." She went on to say that none of her friends had been able to make "head nor tail" of the book and that Percy certainly hadn't done himself proud. "I can't imagine where he got his ideas," she said. "From the gutter probably. Now if you want to read a book that will give you a picture of the real South, go and get *Lanterns on the Levee*[30] by his uncle, William Alexander Percy. I want you to write that down. It's been so nice talking to you."

28. "Sometimes crazed people," such as the street preacher in "Bright Eyes," "make the kind of sense for which you haven't got the courage," Gail notes.

29. Gail has a passion for the movies, and many are cited throughout her journals. Walker Percy's novel *The Moviegoer,* published in 1961, became a celebrated example of southern existentialism.

30. In his autobiography *Lanterns on the Levee* (1941), William Alexander Percy—Greenville, Mississippi, poet and lawyer—depicted the erosion of southern aristocratic values in the tide of business corruption. While fighting the Ku Klux Klan, W. A. Percy maintained a belief in white racial superiority and paternalism. He adopted his young

—

THERE IS A NEW form in writing. It is often in the present tense, it has a wide scope, yet it is disciplined and concise and easy to read.[31] Big theme for a big story: ties based on conscious relatedness may someday replace those of blood and soil. This is what has bothered me for so long, my "homelessness." I consider my home the place I am and the people whom I admire and with whom I associate.

AUGUST 24

Saw *Chips with Everything* with Barbara. She lacks a certain vitality. I enjoyed the play. The main character, an upper-class son of a general "toughing it" in the ranks of the RAF, reminded me of Paul T. in Miami.[32]

AUGUST 25

A colorless, seasonless Sunday. I am sure the weather is like this in purgatory. Wrote all morning and afternoon. Then went to see Bardot in *Warrior's Rest* with Andrew and Anne Rose.[33] American voices dubbed in, so that a French girl, lounging in the ruins of Rome (or somewhere), is able to say: "Still carryin' the torch?" And at the end the hero, with three days of beard stubble, comes to Bardot, dressed in black and pale, wandering among the ruins of an old church. "I give up!" he cries. "I want to join the human race. Make me live. Marry me! Marry me!" The music swells. Bardot looks heavenward. He kneels and buries his unshaven face in her lap. Her platinum-tipped fingernails grip his scalp. She has got her man.

---

cousins, Walker Percy and Walker's two brothers, when their mother died driving off a bridge. Walker Percy's *The Moviegoer*, set in New Orleans, presents a stockbroker—Binx Bolling—who, despite his urge to do noble things, cannot connect to noblesse oblige. His sense of unreality is moored in movie watching.

31. The year 1963 saw the publication of Sylvia Plath's *The Bell Jar*; John Updike's *The Centaur*; J. D. Salinger's *Raise High the Roof Beam, Carpenters and Seymour: An Introduction*; Mary McCarthy's *The Group*; James Baldwin's *The Fire Next Time*; and Joyce Carol Oates's first book, *By the North Gate*.

32. Paul Trinchieri was a friend who introduced Gail to opera.

33. Andrew Baker was a fellow boarder in the Chelsea house. Artistic, music-loving, enamored of James Bond movies, in debt to his housemates, he inspired the character of Alexander in Gail's novella "Mr. Bedford." Anne Rose was his girlfriend.

I am about to write the ending to "Ambrose." I undress, putting on lace pajamas. I see my naked body in the mirror and I think: I want to be undressing to get into bed with a man.

After she leaves Father Flynn, she returns to school, stopping at the ABC store...[34]

I write and write and write. Stayed home with a cold. Writing and dozing, having disturbing dreams. The only reality I have is the writing. I expand my perception as I write. I know my stories are on the side of people now. Just stay away from the sentimental. USTS provides me with a practical place to go in the daytime. I could become so *lost* in my dreams.

The dream I had, while living with Doug, about my father coming to see us on an empty bus. Doug wouldn't let him in—so he got back on the bus and drove it away.

The Honeymoon

—

The jet plane—the girl and her husband sitting on the plane. She is dressed in a black wool dress, black hat, pearls, new everything—underwear, etc. She is slightly displeased with him because he has on an old ankle-length overcoat. His reason is that he only visits his parents in Canada once a year and buying a new overcoat would be silly. She gets a little nauseated on the plane. They talk, mostly about the wedding and their various friends' reactions to their gifts, etc. From time to time, she returns to her book. She is reading _____ (something he would call intellectual).

THE FEELING HERE THAT COMES OVER HER: THE DULLED RELISH OF POSSESSION. She tries to pinpoint just

---

34. Here, Gail begins to work on the story "Mourning," alternately titled "Father Flynn" and "Ambrose," based on her reaction to news of her father's suicide.

when the change took place, goes back over the wedding, the words. A friend had told her, "I never saw such love in anyone's eyes as yours."

The relatives meet them at the Detroit airport. His mother and father are old. The sister is not chic and her dress is too long. The girl feels the sister eyeing her as she walks ahead up the ramp.

Now the details, the details—

The bedroom—all his old pictures and things representing a time when she was not there. Hockey picture taken in 1936! She was not even born. The striped pajamas. The newness of everything, her luggage. The stifled lovemaking at night. Parents in the next room. "I'm doing all right by you, aren't I?" The strangeness of the contents in the medicine cabinet, Canadian labels.[35]

She could still recall her feeling back when, in stores, she would say ". . . for my husband." But when he took her up to his old office and introduced her as "my wife," she felt embarrassed, as if they were perpetrating some kind of fraud.

The tenuousness! The just-missed element of it all! Somehow, the way it could have been must be brought out, too.

They were hardly twenty thousand feet in the air on the Miami–Detroit flight when Evan[36] intimated to the man sharing their triple seat that they had just gotten married.

The point of this story is to show the horror of a simulacrum of marriage compared to the validity of a true marriage. They are not

---

35. Gail will make great use of surveys of room furnishings throughout her fictional career. See Clare's reading of her stepfather's house in *A Southern Family* (chapter 3), Emma's view of Tess's houseboat in *Queen of the Underworld* (chapter 5), John Empson's apartment in *The Perfectionists* (chapter 5), and the Eastons' bedroom in "Mr. Bedford." On September 3, 1961, Gail had made this note: "Marya Mannes says to look around a man's apartment to determine what he is." (*The Making of a Writer: Journals, 1961–1963*).

36. Evan is also the name of the husband in "Gull Key," Gail's 1962 unpublished novel.

truly married. There was none of the waiting, the drifting into the love of a real marriage.

> *She had very sincere eyes. The pastor had looked at her, taking her at eye-value, saying, "Yes, I think you mean it."*
>
> *The Canadian TV—the Vikings—Evan's mother's story of her marriage. "I never took my ring off."*

Show the way something could be by writing HOW IT ISN'T.

> *On the way home they begin planning the redecoration of their house. She is impatient, clinging to the prospect of varnishes and baseboards, paint and nails. They would build a fortress around themselves, and when it was acceptable, beautiful, stylish and clean, maybe then the awaited guest (love) would come—*

AUGUST 28

Somehow, in spite of the bad taste in my mouth from several insincerities (what is the word I want?—sort of a blemish on the day), I feel that I am a lucky person in that people usually give me the benefit of the doubt. It looks as if I'll be going to the U.S.A. in October whether I planned it or no. Mr. Miller called his bank manager and told me, "We'll see that you get home."

One hundred and fifty thousand Negroes peacefully demonstrated in D.C., and the Wests and I watched on Telstar and felt involved.[37]

AUGUST 29

Something of the glamorous days returns tonight, wafted along on a cloud of hair spray, listening to the BBC. I have a few good years left of

---

37. The August 28, 1963, March on Washington culminated a summer of thousands of civil rights demonstrations and was timed to influence Congress to vote for the Civil Rights Bill. Some counted the number of participants at five hundred thousand, the largest political demonstration in the United States up to that time. An estimated 25 percent of the demonstrators were white.

being a handsome desirable. My hair is growing out—I remember standing in front of the bathroom mirror in the hotel in New Orleans, waiting for Cliff to come, and before a mirror in a motel in Pompano Beach while A. snoozed on the double bed.[38] He is the only lover I ever had who dared to steal one of my journals. What a good one he threw into the sea!

"One of those very unfortunate things has happened. The cellist has broken a string."[39]

I WANT TO redo "Roxanne"[40] in the third person.

After Ginny met Ruth Day at the Embassy party in Copenhagen, she got a big kick out of writing letters home to South Carolina.

And another story, which I will enjoy doing: "A Shipboard Romance."

Both these stories can be short novels—worked on simultaneously to fit my dichotomous work-system—"Roxanne" when I am feeling the civil liberties pangs; "Shipboard Romance" as an outlet to get in those dissertations about the lonely woman's search for the perfect man.

AUGUST 30

Otherworldly music coming over the radio—I got so imbedded, I had to return to the sanctuary of all Chelsea escapists—the cinema. Saw *North by Northwest* again. The last time was with Doug. What impressed me was how much detail I didn't notice last time. Walked home in the rain—stupid me—whet the sinuses. Gordon is on his way back to London. He will actually be back on Sunday night and barring the unfore-

38. Cliff and A. were two former love interests, one a ship's captain Gail had known in 1959, the other a fellow reporter on the *Miami Herald* in 1960.

39. During a BBC music program, a cellist had broken a string.

40. "Roxanne" was a novel that Gail had been writing for two years, based on her friend Lorraine O'Grady. A light-skinned African-American, Lorraine confronted Gail's southern heritage and its racial divisions. They first met at Ambassador William Blair's reception for Marian Anderson in Copenhagen, October 1961, and then became each other's confidante and opposite.

seen (a beautiful girl in Jersey; an accident) he will appear at Grosvenor House for the reception for Chief Spotted Back of Nebraska.[41]

AUGUST 31 · *Portrait of 5:30 on a Saturday afternoon*

I have finished ironing and I've drunk my badly made tea (too strong). Andrew and Anne Rose have returned from the Kenya Coffee shop, where they go every Saturday afternoon, he to show her off and she because he says they're going. I go up the carpeted steps to where Mrs. West sits in the little kitchen, beginning to piece together her creative meal, which Andrew will scorn. Anne Rose will be delicately noncommittal and Gian Carlo will fall in with the majority because he is a foreigner.

I stand in the kitchen talking to Mrs. West for a time. I say: "This is your best time, isn't it? When you're sitting there preparing the evening meal." I say this for an attempt at "reading" her, trying to bridge the gap, as usual. "Well," she laughs, "if you really want to know, I'd rather be off on that island with Princess Margaret. With the Greek millionaire."

"Who, Onassis?"

"No, the other one. The one who was married to Bettina, the beautiful one, you know?"[42]

"Oh, yes." I don't. I go to the sink, balancing my ironed clothes on one arm, the hanger digging into my arm, and wash out my teacup to get rid of one encumbrance. I had planned to drink the second cup leisurely in my room, but now I have gulped it all down nervously while talking to Mrs. West.

"No, Gail, there are a lot of things I'd rather be doing; but I think the thing is, if you know you have to do something, then try to enjoy it."

"I couldn't agree more," I say. "You know, I think it takes a real tal-

---

41. Mrs. Frank Morrison, wife of the governor of Nebraska, led a tourism and trade promotion group from her state to Europe. Chief Spotted Back Hamilton, an Omaha Indian and performer of ceremonial songs, was one of twenty-nine in the entourage.

42. Bettina (Simone Micheline Bodin Graziani), a Givenchy model and worldwide celebrity in the 1950s, had been the mistress of Prince Ali Khan, a jet-setting Ismaili Muslim.

ent to overcome everydayness. Not many people can do this. Oh, a lot can handle their big moments, but when it comes to getting the best of the everydayness, they're real flops." I know I am on the right track to her now. I make a move to leave the kitchen while I'm ahead. But these leavings are always awkward. Sometimes she says something as I reach the door and then I must turn back and prolong the conversation.

"You know, Gail, I'm reading *The Ambassadors* and . . ."

"Do you like it?"

"I think it's . . . well . . . you've read it, haven't you?"

"Yes." The first twenty pages.

"Well, I think it's *fan*tastic." Here she screws up her face in that special way of hers.

"Yes."

"I really shouldn't say this because I haven't gotten into it yet, but his choice of words . . ."

"Yes . . ."

"And you know, Gail, I get the funniest feeling . . . No I won't say it. I'll finish it first."

"No, no. Say it now and then we'll compare it later."

"Well I feel that the whole thing is . . . I can't express myself very well . . . a sort of satire. No, that's not the right word."

"Irony?"

"Yes! Well no, not exactly. It's as though all the characters are engaged in a high form of comedy. Like he's poking fun at them."

"And like they're poking fun at themselves."

"Yes!"

"I think this is why he's great," I say. Oh, I'm onto it now. "He offers something for people on all different levels. The people who don't see the irony can be content with modeling their lives on the civilized, striving for the morality of his characters. Whereas people like you can go one step further and see the comedy." (Always before, I had been one of those people who believed in James as a purveyor of incommunicable moral solitude.)

"I think that you can say this of real people, too," I continue. "Civilized, aware, intellectually honest people are forever playing a game.

Watching themselves trying for various effects, eliciting various responses in other people."

"Yes, I think you're right." She's peeling a carrot.

"The thing is, to recognize that you are playing a game. When you lose sight of this, it's dangerous."

"Yes."

"But weren't they remarkable brothers. Look at William, what he did. And the father was a scholar——"

"I know. What a family."

At this point Mr. West in his checkered sport coat enters the kitchen. "What family? Yours?"

"No," I say. "The James brothers."

"Oh! Jesse James."

"No, silly!"

I laugh. Mrs. West laughs from the mouth, not from the stomach. A half laugh.

"William and Henry." I say.

He pats me. "Oh, really?" As if to say, I knew, but I'm pretending I didn't know. Mrs. West and I both know that he meant Jesse.

"Ah, spoken like a true American," I say, cheerfully leaving the kitchen. All the way out this time.

Mrs. West from her table gives a throat laugh. A little more natural than the mouth laugh.

I start upstairs with my clothes.

"Gail and I were talking about *The Ambassadors,* the book I'm reading," I hear her begin.

"Say, Gail," Mr. West calls after me. "You know whose picture is going to be on the new ten-thousand-dollar bill?"

"No, whose?" I start back to the kitchen.

"Mine." He laughs, standing there in the door. Mrs. West in the background laughs. What kind of laugh was it this time?

I laugh, so he can see me, and then flee, laughing again after I am out of their sight so they can hear me and think I think it is still funny.

They hear and begin laughing together. This time it is the combined laughter of the two feeling appreciated.

SEPTEMBER 1

I do not understand Doreen. She knew the thing started at 2:30, so she shows up when the party for Chief Spotted Back is almost over. "I got tied up," she says sweetly. Gordon gets back tonight late and if all goes right he should show up at Grosvenor House tomorrow evening.

Describe moments like now when I am in a state of suspension. I pick up half a dozen books. A spy story in the O. Henry Award volume: no. Doris Lessing's *Daily Telegraph* story on her father: no. Kierkegaard: no. I think: I want some maxims. I want someone to tell me how to live. Then a swatch of music, a lighted window—a square of light across the way; the thought of going home. October air and leaves and the inevitable afternoon boredom I will feel. I need that change. And it's a good life. Living in London and going home once a year.

SEPTEMBER 3

It's 8:30 p.m. and the sky is dark. Color: indigo? Cobalt? No, a pearly luster. I am reminded of Gaert[43] and the long nights in Copenhagen when we played *Carnaval*[44] and shared wishes. "What would you wish for, Gaert?" "I think ... I think I would wish for the secret of the blue color." So much comes to me through the crack under the door. Quick! Catch it before it is gone. Isaac Stern and Brahms's Violin Concerto in D[45]—Shelley Burman[46] trying to force-feed me a three-month survey course in "Culture."

43. Gaert, a friend of Gail's in Denmark, often provided good company. Blond-haired and soft-voiced, he aspired to be an artist.

44. *Carnaval*, a piano composition by Robert Schumann, had appealed to both Gail and Gaert for its virtuoso variations that break away from a courtly theme. The music opens Gail's novel *Violet Clay*.

45. In Gail's unpublished novel "Gull Key," Bentley Lewis prepares dinner for her new husband, Evan, to the music of the Brahms concerto. The Rondo finale matches Bentley's excitement as she prepares to reveal to Evan the beginning of her locally set novel, *The Lighthouse*.

46. Shelley Burman had been the chief resident surgeon at Chapel Hill University Hospital with whom Gail had had a stormy relationship (see "The Angry Year" in *Mr. Bedford and the Muses*).

Gordon showed up on time at Grosvenor House, wearing a kilt and appearing a little nervous. We did not come together like a clash of symbols, rather we "meshed," simply took up where we left off. As if I had just come back from a trip to the ladies' room. I look back upon last night today and have a distinct feeling of being "let down." Why? Simply because I expect to walk all my life to the accompaniment of stirring background music? He was as easy as one could want. He mixed with the Nebraskans (a constant rose blush upon his face) and he spoke softly and meaningfully to everyone. I knew I could leave him and not worry about him getting self-conscious or "feeling stranded." He never "gets bored"—I think this is one of his greatest merits—he finds something of interest in every human situation, even when Maggie Bruce-Adams got on his nerves when we went to the Captain's Cabin (a restaurant) afterward. Henry and Bob Briggs are "city dwellers" to him. He behaved admirably, just almost losing his temper when we found the police had towed his van away for being an obstruction. I made a big thing of being calm myself. "I'm glad I'm with you," says he, squeezing my shoulder as we go by Trafalgar Square on a no. 53 bus to pick up our confiscated vehicle.

SEPTEMBER 4

One month from today—October and homecoming. Today I caught several faint footprints in the sand, as Father Webbe[47] would say. I am sitting in the fishbowl looking out at weary rain-conditioned faces moving up and down Vigo and around the corner to Sackville Street. The newspaper seller stands against our plate glass window to get out of the rain. He calls, *"Evening Standard,"* sounding like a primeval beast in pain. I am sinking into everydayness.[48] Then I see the vision, only for a minute. I think (something along these lines) I am seeking a way to celebrate the

---

47. Father Gale D. Webbe had been rector of St. Mary's Episcopal Church in Asheville and prepared Gail for confirmation when she was eleven. In his book *The Night and Nothing*, he wrote about man's connection beyond his self with eternity. Shortly, Gail will find this book, just published, in Hatchards Bookshop.

48. "Everydayness is the enemy," Binx Bolling says in Walker Percy's novel *The Moviegoer*, which Gail had read five months previously. That idea is one aspect of existentialism that strikes Gail; yet she seeks something more meaningful than momentary purpose in life, something more in the form of a design.

life I have been given. Therefore the outside forces (meaning in this case the surface qualities one judges in other people, meaning the synthetic "second life" we have created ourselves—a life of shorthand pads and PROs[49] and consumer ratings—meaning all this) do not really matter. The difficult thing is staying out of the involvement with these things.

The other thing is this: As I see this pattern more clearly, I will be able to write about it. It will seek its proper subjects. The theme will be there. "Wesley Phipps," for instance. I had a nostalgic feeling (quite different from a conviction). I put it down. Then I tried to go back and work it into something "meaningful." But that was not the right way round. I must distinguish between evocation and edification.

SEPTEMBER 7

Gothic-type Sunday morning. The damp gray sky comes into my open window. With cold, clammy fingers, I write about a short experience, listening to "Alexander's Ragtime Band" on the Light Programme.

I was lying here about six last evening trying to talk myself out of going to the party. I wanted to go because of the slim chance that a new one would suddenly catch my eye from across the room. But I had about decided to stay home. It was safer—more uncomplicated. Then Andrew burst into the room after his return from the Kenya Coffee shop. "Gail, I've got you a man. I'm telling you, he's got everything. Now shut up, don't ask me anything." I gradually wheedled out of him that his name was Barry. He was a stockbroker with pretty teeth. He drove an Alfa Romeo. He wouldn't give Gordon the time of day on the street. All this sounded pretty phony to me. Plus the fact that he had just been jilted by a model at Yves St. Laurent.

But let's do this in scenes. He came to the house, and when I walked into the room, I liked him on sight. He was smiling. Andrew was right about the teeth. There was also a certain nobility. I also knew at once he was Jewish. We immediately began talking of Barry Goldwater. I had

49. PROs are the records of the British Public Record Office.

said: "At present, all the southerners are for another Barry." He leaned forward and said: "What's that? Did you say, 'I love you, Barry'?"

By the time we left for the party, we were friends. He told Andrew in an aside, "She's a very sweet girl"—what else could I be after an Yves St. Laurent model?—"but I think she looks sad."

I remember one scene in particular. We were driving around Bayswater, looking for Pembroke Villas. We were rumbling (in the way Alfa Romeos rumble) up a hill lighted by orange streetlamps. There was a pub on the corner with red and blue lights above the Watneys sign. The radio was playing a catchy tune. He was at the wheel, now with his horn-rimmed glasses on, confident and lighthearted. I began thinking once again of those memorable words of Camus: "With so much sunshine in my life, how could I have bet on nonsense?" I was thinking: Extraordinary things do go on happening to me. How did I think I would stay in a rut? Here is a man, quite presentable in his envelope, with a worldly style and nobody's fool—yet no phony. He exists positively enough to blot out Gordon for the moment, which is all I can ask. There is none of this subterfuge. We have plenty on which to dwell. He knows he is attractive to women and therefore can bet on romance. Romantic things happen to romantic people.

The party was packed with all the old hot-air kids. Sheila grows more hysterical each time I see her.[50] Barry and I left and came back to my place. I made coffee for him and we had a conversation bordering on the aggressive. Every time we tried to play false, wham—a barrier went up and we recognized it and stopped. He told me about the model, Christina ("I walked the streets in Paris for two days in the rain"), enjoying the pathos. And then about romance: "I'd rather be hurt in romance than have no romance at all. Then I can always say: 'I'm seven feet tall and no coward in love.' " And about women: "I think they all go through a wanton period when they sleep with everybody, trying to find something or forget someone or make up for something. Then they realize it's not doing them any good and they clamp down."

50. Gordon had said that Sheila and her roommates lived on hot air, not with a sense of independence and a vocation (see *The Making of a Writer: Journals, 1961–1963*, entry for May 13, 1963).

—

BARRY GOLDWATER (as I call him) left, kissing me in a brotherly way on the mouth and saying: "We'll have dinner together next week." It is nice to have a Jewish man again.

7:00 p.m.

"When the golden sun sinks in the hills . . ." (radio).[51] Cooler now when I sit in the window. Summer is truly over. Andrew and Anne Rose and I went to see *Smiles of a Summer Night*—truly engrossing. The characters are involved in a love dilemma, everyone in love with everybody else. But what is different is the manner in which Bergman chooses his scene. This time: eighteenth-century Sweden. Summer night when the sun never sets. Everyone wins in love—according to their own manner of winning. The cunning lover cannot expect to win the prize that an innocent would win.

The sun. Not much. But orange and just barely warm on my face. Something super-real about now. The tang in the air. The plane overhead. Andrew hates the sound of planes droning, refrigerators humming in empty houses, and tractors in fields: "They remind me of my own loneliness too much."

I make a vow: I will not accept less than life. I will seek the treasure of the serendipiter.[52] I will not rest until I find ultrasupersonic understanding with someone—

SEPTEMBER 9 · *10:40 p.m.*

I heard "Pomp and Circumstance," cried my eyes out about my father, wrote some on the sly, and am now back knowing what I must do.

51. "When the golden sun sinks in the hills" is the first line in the song "Little Grey Home in the West," which had a "There's No Place Like Home" theme and was a favorite during World War II.

52. "Serendipiter" was a current term; in 1961, Gay Talese had published *New York: A Serendipiter's Journey*, based on articles he'd written for *Esquire* about the city's unnoticed denizens.

SEPTEMBER 11

In twenty-three days, I go home. I'm going to buy clothes for this winter, see a Broadway play, walk all over New York with John Bowers,[53] and talk to everybody.

On Saturday, a work morning. Go somewhere, anywhere, in afternoon. To the Ionesco play?[54]

SEPTEMBER 13 · *Friday*

The interminable week is over. Funny dreams lately.

Wednesday night's was as follows:

It is fall. There is a lot of color and the air has a dreamlike, crisp security. The time is a holiday—possibly Labor Day Weekend. The chipmunk[55] is giving a weekend party at his house. I am supposed to sleep there Saturday, Sunday, and Monday nights, work Tuesday, and then return to Blowing Rock for Tuesday night's festivities (a feeling of liquid warmth pervades the dream). I work a hundred miles away from the Rock—only it's London. I am still with USTS. Also, I am expecting Gordon back this same holiday and I am glad I will have an excuse not to see him because he has been away camping with another girl. A letter comes from him. I am surprised and pleased, but when I open it, I find the writing almost indecipherable. Yet I think: Good. I'll take a long time reading it because I'll have to go slowly. The script is tight and small. He starts off with phrases from songs. And I think: He's trying to get in the habit of writing by saying anything that comes into his head. But that is all right, too. There are many, many arrangements to make in this scene but I don't seem to be worried about them as I had been in

53. John Bowers, a writer living in Greenwich Village, was a friend and confidant.

54. Alec Guinness was appearing at the Royal Court in Eugène Ionesco's *Exit the King*, for which he received the London Theatre Critics Award for best actor.

55. "The chipmunk" was the assistant manager at Mayview Manor, the Blowing Rock, North Carolina, resort at which Gail worked in the summer of 1961 to earn money for her passage to Europe. He was young, rich, and eager; and Gail came to appreciate his intensive campaign to win her approval.

past dreams. My entire family is there and I am thinking: Strange, I do not resent them. I am changed and for the better. Mr. Cole comes riding by in a shiny new truck with the children in it. They are laughing. I think: Funny, I do not mind the truck now either.

This next bit is confused. There is some little person there that I love. It has certain aspects of Franchelle and certain of Rebel[56] and certain animal characteristics. It is very small. The only thing is, it has testicles. They are warm and (I think) furry. I think: I must pick it up with one hand while it is still small enough. It is still growing, apparently. I begin to lift, not thinking I'm going to accomplish it. But I do. Then someone or something comes into the picture and indicates that he would not mind holding this little person for a while. I let him. He cuddles it and begins licking it as a cat would.[57] I think: It is good. Because they both have testicles. The testicles are touching. There is also something about my taking a shower.

The element of security pervades the entire dream. I am loved and I love; I am invited to parties. I am able to accept responsibilities. But the little creature must indicate some aspect of myself I cannot completely get hold of. Once before I dreamed of a furry, lovable creature (more like a dog). I was leading it by a rope. Then it began to get bigger. I was afraid and panicked. I sicced my dog on it. My dog tore it to pieces. The little creature looked up at me as it was torn to bits, not understanding. In this new dream I wasn't afraid. Does that mean whatever this furry creature represents is becoming less of a threat?

GOT OUT MY old writing tonight. I am good. I have to persist.

SEPTEMBER 17

Today I had my own little epiphany. I had been sitting at one of the big tables in the Embassy library rereading an article by Marya Mannes en-

56. Franchelle, Rebel, and Tommy were Gail's siblings by her mother and stepfather, Frank Cole.

57. In her 1987 novel *A Southern Family*, Gail describes Lily and Ralph Quick's acquisition of a female puppy to start Ralph's "clan of dogs." One puppy licks Clare, the heroine, and is

titled "Pardon Me if My Brain Shows." (This morning I received a letter from Stella[58] saying she was marrying Don Trapp, the one she really wanted. There was a paragraph in there to me about being myself, not trying to change myself to be popular for the world.) After I finished the article, I walked out into the smoky autumn sunshine, consciously praying as I walked down the steps of the Embassy. I said: "Please. Let me be honest." Sometime during the walk back to the office, I saw it all just for a minute, and of course it flashed past—like the flock of pigeons over Grosvenor Square—at the moment that I gained my resolve. It left an imprint this time, as it hadn't many times before. There had been (before) just a disquiet, knowing that there had been something better, but I hadn't remembered what it was.

Walking back down Grosvenor Street—under the temporary structure for a building which has been the same ever since I first walked down that street—I saw the large portion of hours I have spent trying to be things other people wanted me to be. I saw myself at the rugby dance Saturday night—trying to pretend I loved twisting; trying to fake it that I was a golden girl. I saw myself fawning in front of the Wests, compromising, saying I liked people I didn't like, making their standards mine. I saw myself in all the many clothes I've worn that I didn't like but were "in style." I saw myself fitting my conversation to Doreen's pace, and wondering if Dorothea thought I was bright. Trying to squeeze myself in to fit their patterns, trying to spread myself out to fit their image. From now on, I plan to say what I mean. If I feel it will be awkward or will not accomplish any purpose, I will not speak at all. But under no account will I be a chameleon.

Today I began a book of short stories and suddenly became impatient with the author because he was explaining to me. I didn't want to hear what everyone's motives were. I wanted to watch [the characters] working and playing at life and then (as I do in the daytime) try to fig-

---

chosen for liking the family rather than necessarily for being liked. "Better take love where you can find it," Ralph, the stepfather, says.

58. Stella Anderson, Gail's good friend from Chapel Hill, North Carolina, arrived in London to stay at the Wests' boardinghouse in September 1962. The character Arden Speer in Gail's novella "Mr. Bedford" is based partly on her.

ure them out. Also I was angry with him for giving me no new images. I then turned to John Updike as to an old friend.

"Burton received the silver." That is all. This is about a clerical man at the dentist's. If John Updike had been afraid the public would not understand, he could have added, disastrously, "as he would the Holy Communion wafer." Thus spoiling everything.[59]

SEPTEMBER 19

Another wasted night. Early to bed. Insomnia. At 4:00 a.m., Chelsea Old Church clock strikes. I have never gone so long at a job without a break. I need to unwind among people I feel perfectly safe with, people who have known me from the cradle up and who can always be depended upon to open the door, no matter what disgrace I am coming from. In London, or indeed anywhere except Asheville, I have no one person who will take me as I am. That, I suppose, is what B. meant when he said last fall: "I have no one, no one in the world, who will let me be what and where I have to be."

If I put the detail in my stories that I do into my letters to Mother, I would be made.

SEPTEMBER 24

What is existentialism?

Many of us had our first news of this philosophy from some rather bizarre and bohemian settings in Paris after World War II.

"This new philosophy . . ."

"But it's not. It's very old."

59. John Updike's story "Dentistry and Doubt" had been published in *The New Yorker* and included in his first book of short stories, *The Same Door* (1959). Burton, an American minister especially sensitive to moral dilemmas, reflects on such subjects as the value of pain and the competitive birds he sees in the dentist's backyard. The short work proved to be a big inspiration, Gail says, for her story "An Intermediate Stop" (the others being Bishop John A. T. Robinson's controversial *Honest to God* and Gail's memory of a charismatic Scottish preacher who had led a retreat at Peace College during her junior year). Burton's meditations also resonate with Father Walter Gower's in Gail's 1991 novel *Father Melancholy's Daughter:* "He recognized . . . that in his very thinking of his own humility he was guilty of pride, and his immediate recognition of it as pride was foundation for further, subtler egotism."

—

MODERN SOCIETY BECOMES a kind of bureaucratically organized flight from the self, a flight into which everybody can easily drift. More than a century ago, Kierkegaard railed against the depersonalizing forces of modern society far more powerfully than do Riesman and Whyte.[60] Same line of criticism developed more subtly by Ortega y Gasset, Jaspers, Marcel, and Buber.[61]

Kierkegaard insisted on the necessity of faith as a vital act beyond reason. Beyond this message as a Christian apologist, Kierkegaard brought to the attention of philosophers and psychologists the fact that human existence can never be totally enclosed in any system. To exist as an individual is to strive, change, develop, stand open to the future, and be incomplete—while a system, by its very nature, is closed, complete, static, dead.

Life is lived forward and understood backward, says Kierkegaard. If we were ever to understand it completely, we would have to be already dead, without a future and with no untried and novel possibilities before us.[62]

Our lives become meaningful to the degree that we bind together tomorrow, today, and yesterday in an active whole.

60. The malaise that people felt, as reflected in unfulfilling relationships and questions about identity, gained credibility in David Riesman's *The Lonely Crowd* (1950) and William Whyte's *The Organization Man* (1956).

61. Karl Jaspers, author of *Reason and Existence* (1935), was a major proponent of the idea that a complete system of philosophy isn't possible, since things are always in the process of becoming. Gabriel-Honoré Marcel, author of *The Mystery of Being* (1951), also attacked reductionism, and related the method to modern, bureaucratic society. He focused on interactions and moments of decision, donning the mantle of Søren Kierkegaard and Jaspers. Martin Buber was an earlier, theological Jewish writer whose landmark book *I and Thou* (1923) broke down the division between subject and object, and shaped a philosophy of transformation.

62. Gail has embraced aspects of existentialism that she can wed to her own views, and that emerge in future works. Her attraction to José Ortega y Gasset's ideas about "transmigrations of the soul" into the feelings of others was prefigured in her childhood writings—for instance her composition "The Autobiography of a Tin Cup," told from the cup's viewpoint, and fulfilled in such passages as Violet Clay's reimagining of her uncle's suicide in *Violet Clay*. The fluidity of past, present, and future is a recurrent theme in Gail's work. "The human mind . . . is a chronic time traveler," Margaret muses in *Evensong*, and it has the ability to pull the human body along "like a wagon, with its entire load of sensory equipment." The open-endedness of one's fate finds witty expression in *Queen of the Underworld*, in which Don Waldo Navarro, an exiled Cuban author, reveals that the title of his memoir, *Destinos y Desatinos*, demonstrates that the mere addition of the letter *a* turns destinies into blunders.

SEPTEMBER 25 · *11:20 p.m.*

Going home in one week and one day. The most I can expect is that it will clear the air. I will break away from the horrible routine of USTS. Next spring, I must return to the U.S.A. Otherwise I see myself living safely in England, uninvolved in the history making of my own country, subjecting my heritage to one abortive romance after another with Englishmen who cannot understand or appreciate my way of being.

NINETY THOUSAND COPIES of the Denning Report come out at midnight.[63] People have actually been queuing outside the stationery store since afternoon!!

SEPTEMBER 28 · *Saturday*

A peculiarly annoying day. I wish I could identify this anxiety that follows me periodically like a black cloud. Woke up at 7:30 a.m., feeling about a thousand years old. Faced the mirror and felt "the panic"—the lines encroach and, what is more, there are already gray hairs. (Yet the girl at the Chelsea Public Library asked whether I was over twenty-one.) Went to the hairdressers and had my hair straightened—then took a taxi to the Guildhall for the Lord Mayor's election and left my Jung book in the back of the taxi. Hell.

The election was colorful, objectively interesting, and packed with history. Mr. Haydon[64] volunteered information and introduced me to a former Lord Mayor with steel blue eyes and a wry smile who pressed some dried flowers into my hand "to keep you from getting the plague." But, sitting in the Guildhall, facing the sun-touched bronze figure of

63. Conservative sexual mores took a hit when John Profumo, British secretary of war, was exposed having an affair with bombshell Christine Keeler, who'd also slept with a Soviet naval officer. Lord Denning's report gave details.

64. Mr. Haydon visited the offices of USTS and called himself "the Alchemist." He belonged to the Guild of Goldsmiths. He had invited Gail to the Lord Mayor's swearing in and the luncheon to follow in the Guildhall.

Churchill, all I could think was: Where is Gordon now? Is he at Bisley? Why didn't he call and tell me what had been decided? How he would enjoy this election! He takes such objective interest in everything. Also, I knew Mr. Haydon probably faced a lonely evening (that's why he reads and travels so much) and I hate to feel I am prolonging the agony or abetting other peoples' loneliness. I think the kind of person who does not show his loneliness is most pleasant to be with. Not that Mr. Haydon pressed me; it was his very carefulness not to press that showed how lonely he must be. He has learned just how little you may demand of others.

Then home on the bus—the usual sense of release as soon as I was out of his company—and to the Chelsea Public Library. But oh, Christ, prevent me from becoming one of these solitary-intellectual types, wandering the smoky streets with an armload of psychology books— a type I am fast becoming.

Ah, God, all those books on personality and finding God; and all the people, on their knees, searching the shelves for weekend comfort. One day I am going to write about this awful loneliness, describe it—the weekends especially. It's like this all over the world: Chapel Hill, Miami, London. The only times I have not been a victim were in situations where I have been working very hard (Blowing Rock) or doing some-thing physical, or during those (brief) times—when?—when I have been spending time with someone I loved. But usually then I was sim-ply putting off my inadequacies until a later date. As with Shelley B., I would shortchange my classes, my studies, even my loyalties, to be with him. Then, in turn, after the weekend, I would be left to cope with my own deficiencies.

After dinner

It is almost nine. *Gianni Schicchi* on the radio. Paul T.[65] We merge our pasts with our futures.

65. Paul Trinchieri, Gail's opera-loving friend.

How sick, disgusted, and confused I am. Finished my short story "Mourning" with no flourishing sense of triumph, hitting the typewriter key with a bang like the pianist's final chord. I doubt my powers, my reality in this world of other people. It seems that I delude myself in every relationship I have. I project my own inadequacies and fears and worst faults on the Wests, on Doreen. I am so filled with panic. God, look at the facts. I am twenty-six years old, with no visible achievement in either of the fields about which I spend the most time thinking. I have not sold one written word. I have not been or become suitable to be loved by the sort of person I find suitable. And the one book that had some of the answers, I left in a taxi.[66] Christ. Help me. I don't think I can get much lower.

SEPTEMBER 30

The end of a terrible, trying month, full of self-doubt, brash actions, and much struggling and growing. That is one month I wouldn't repeat even if it meant being five years younger-looking. Bach choir singing. And if I didn't have these notebooks in which to pour out my fears, I'd probably be much worse off. I was thinking of what it is everybody fears. It isn't poverty—that is a challenge. It is boredom, monotony, everydayness. That is the killer. That's why I go to so many movies. That's why I hated the *Miami Herald.* That's why I couldn't stand Key Biscayne longer than five months. That's why I kept moving around, and why I have always gotten tired of things quickly. I burst in with no restraint, take my fill, and then go on to something else.

Now that I know my conscious enemy, what can I do about it? What steps does one take?

Let the subconscious work on this awhile—

66. Gail is referring to Carl Jung's *Memories, Dreams, Reflections.*

Hiatus

Gail Writes About a Gap in Her Journal

OCTOBER 1, 1963, TO NOVEMBER 16, 1963

———

I went to the U.S. for the first two weeks of October 1963. There is no record in my journal. The following hiatus, from October 1 until the November 17 entry, is a mystery to me. That's a month and two weeks of silence.

Perhaps I kept a travel journal of the two weeks in America, but I don't recall doing so. I do recall isolated events and the mood of that trip, and perhaps that offers some clues.

I was very much divided, baffled, and uncertain about whether I had hit a dead spot in my life or had taken a serious wrong turn at some point in the past year. Had I stayed in England too long? Where was the jolt or the bolt from the blue that could set me on my road again? What *was* my road?

Anyway: the visit home. Asheville in October was as seductive as ever. The air, skies, colors, mountains. I enjoyed my family, snuggled into the old smells and conversational cadences. My baby brother Rebel was five then, and would crawl silently and stealthily from his room to mine; we'd lie there hugging until his father woke and dragged him away. This was sometimes repeated three times a night.

The big difference in Asheville 1963 was that B., though still there, was not there for me anymore. Stella [Anderson], who had just gotten engaged to Don Trapp, came into Asheville from her home in Brevard and we went to "look at" B.'s new wife. Stella said someone told her that the wife was working at, I think, the Chamber of Commerce as a greeter. Stella and I went in and pretended to be looking for various tourist attractions. The young woman was very warm and helpful and beautiful. A real beauty! A stone in my heart!

Then Stella and I went back into the October sunshine, and she lectured me from the pedestal of her new happiness that I need only be myself and all would follow.

But what was "myself"?

I flew down to Raleigh and spent a week with my uncle William, the bachelor judge.[67] He took me around to see all his cohorts and our relatives.

And then it was over and I flew back to London, which was already smoked up and chilled with early dusks and oncoming winter. "Go-or-stay, go-or-stay" was the indecisive mantra to which my shoes marched—from and to the bus stops, to and from work.

I resolved to go back to America "in the spring." But then I'd pause and cross-examine myself: Go back to what? You don't even have the hope of a job there. Go back to whom?

And so on, into the fog season. London still had pea-soupers, though they would soon be extinct.[68]

Then Kennedy was shot. The November 22 entry in my journal is short. I was stunned. No details, but I can still relive them. It's dinnertime at the Wests'. Most of the "inmates" are at the table. Andrew, who has been listening to the BBC in his room, comes running up the stairs: "I say, Gail. Your president has been shot." We bolted our dinner, and Andrew drove me to the American Embassy on Grosvenor Square. A huge crowd was gathered, listening to transistor radios for word of the president's condition. "Don't worry, Gail," said Andrew. "The Americans can fix anything."

But they couldn't fix that.

---

67. William Godwin, Gail's father's older brother, was a Selma, North Carolina, district judge.

68. Five years later, the Extensive Clean Air Act in Great Britain marked the end of the London fog that coal burning had produced for many years.

In the weeks that followed, priorities shifted. My turmoil over an evasive Englishman whose habits I deplored seemed, in retrospect, some sort of aberration on my part. Come spring, I decided, I would definitely go home. If I was to be a tragic failure, let me at least do it on my own turf, where the air was finer and I would not need a special visa to work.

Part two

BROTHERS AND LOVERS

London

NOVEMBER 17, 1963, TO MARCH 23, 1964

Gordon Landsborough[1] (drinking his Bell's whiskey at the London Scottish Football Club after London Scottish lost to Richmond): "You know, I've found many times that people who aren't very intelligent are endowed with a distinct cleverness, a kind of shrewdness, but that isn't the word I want . . ."

Gordon[2] (seizing the description, seeing perhaps himself?): "Could that word not be 'common sense'?"

Landsborough (as an almost imperceptible flicker of disappointment flits across his sharp countenance): "Well, common sense, yes, but that isn't quite the word I meant. It's a sort of canniness that usually causes them to succeed. And then you find some person really brimming over with intelligence (here there is the unmistakable love-of-excellence light in his eyes), but they lack that shrewdness and are complete failures in the world." He left soon after this.

Sunday afternoon

It is raining, mid-November. Leaves are scattered across the enclosed courtyard. The remaining plants in the yellow flower boxes are flattened by the rain. Inside Andrew's "hut," Chopin is playing on the BBC. Andrew fumbles through his bookshelf. "Read Thomas Hardy. *The Well-Beloved.*[3] Everyone should read one of his at least. No, I don't re-

1. Gordon Landsborough was a publisher of action novels and military histories who had an office near the U.S. Travel Service office. He took an interest in Gail's work—particularly her first novel, "Gull Key" (unpublished)—and recommended her to an agent, Ursula Winant.

2. This Gordon is Gail's soon-to-end romantic interest, Gordon Wrigley.

3. *The Well-Beloved* (1897) was Thomas Hardy's last published novel, a satirical fable about a sculptor who seeks a series of idealized women. Its setting is an unspoiled island off the southern coast of England.

member what it was about, but I remember liking it. Look, can you lend me four shillings? I'll go out and buy some cigarettes and chocolates. Would you like some chocolates?"

"I used to know Rowntree—he was from York, too,"[4] Andrew says, apropos of the after-dinner mints.

A pause. *The Well-Beloved* begins: "The peninsula carved by Time out of a single stone, whereon most of the following scenes are laid, has been for centuries immemorial the home of a curious and well-nigh distinct people, cherishing strange beliefs and singular customs, now for the most part obsolescent." The cadence of the words blends with the watery London Sunday where there is a strange sense of being nowhere at all.

Andrew (changing over from radio to record player): "Here, listen to this. It's Italian pop. The composer had gone on his honeymoon and fell in love with a waiter in the hotel. Some trouble developed and so he wrote this song to the waiter." It is a catchy tune. Life is not so bad after all, at least for the duration of an LP disc. Then it is over. Andrew is sitting in his straight-backed gilded chair: "You know, life is fucking awful, any way you look at it. When you think of it, you're bloody lucky just to have made it to another weekend. That's why I really can't take this idea of security seriously." He goes out and comes back much happier with a pack of Herbert Tareytons and some expensive after-dinner mints.

Something thrilling about driving through the rain in an open sports car. You are in motion against the elements. Petticoat Lane.[5] "You kill yourself for a parking spot on the other side of Bishopsgate, get out and walk through the rain, spoil your clothes, work up a bad temper to mill about in a throng of subhumans bartering for plastic balls, colored shoelaces, and toy submarines." Onward Sunday Anxiety. Waiting for the curtain to go up on the cinema at Warner's, we listen to the live organ playing "Dancing in the Dark." Andrew: "Think how many of us would be put at ease if they would fasten a little brass cross on the front of the curtain. That would make everything all right."

---

4. Rowntree was an established candy manufacturer.

5. Petticoat Lane Market, a bazaar of stall merchants, grew out of the garment district in East London. It was two blocks east of the local traffic artery, Bishopsgate, and people had to park on the other side.

—

IMAGINE A ROOM still filled with the <u>idea</u> of someone who is no longer there. And imagine that the idea is more comfortable than the actual presence of the person. Robin lying across the single bed, the first three buttons of his gray-green shirt undone. He has a broad, hairy chest. On the table at the foot of this bed, under the lamp, is an eight-by-six-inch matte-finish photograph of Robin in the throes of the London Scottish vs. Cambridge match. He has a murderous look as he bears down upon his opponent. "Yes, I do believe in love," he is saying. "But I think it's a compromise, like they all say. For instance, if you and I were married, or living together (this hastily appended), I would do things that would drive you up the wall. And you would certainly irritate the hell out of me at times. But that doesn't mean you don't like the person. Oh, I'm sleepy. What is that perfume, De?[6] The one I bought for you in France? I'll have to remember that. Come here and kiss me."

NOVEMBER 19

Two American girls overheard in a pub:

"Listen, did . . . When you were going with David, did he ever tell you he loved you?"

"No."

"Ah! Just as I thought. See!"

"Why, does Jack never say it either?"

"No. It's just the same as you. Saturday night I made such a fool of myself. For the millionth time. Let me tell you."

"Do you have a match?"

"No. Yes. Wait, let me look. No."

"I'll be right back. I want to hear this."

"Yes, I want . . ."

"Now. Where were you Saturday night?"

"I made an absolute ass of myself. I want to tell you from the begin-

---

6. De was Gail's scent of choice after she'd interviewed Deeda Blair, the American ambassador's wife, whose signature perfume it was, in Denmark.

ning. Maybe you can help me. We started out completely impersonal, you see. I hadn't seen him for two weeks and I felt 'on top,' so to speak, because I was safe in the knowledge that he had called twice and I had been out each time."

"Yeah?"

"So, we were standing at the bar of the rugby club, talking about something 'safe,' I forget what. I was so proud of myself. I had gotten through the entire game without making one allusion to 'us.' Then he began speaking of going sailing the next day and I immediately felt left out. I said, 'Oh, take me with you.' 'Well,' he said, 'if I go. Of course, I might not go.' 'Then let's do something,' I persisted. 'I know, we could drive to Cambridge. I've never been to Cambridge.' 'I like Oxford better,' he said. 'Well! Then let's drive to Oxford.' It seemed settled. Then, some minutes later, I brought it up again: 'When we go to Oxford tomorrow . . .' Then he said: 'I'm not sure. I have a lot to do.' 'Why don't you like me?' I asked. 'I like you,' he replied, 'but I don't love you.' 'Oh, that's lovely. That's flattering. Why not?' 'I don't want to love anyone. I stop myself before I ever do.' 'Well, do you think you ever could love me?' 'I don't know. I want to be friends with you.' 'But I don't want to be friends!' 'Why not?' 'Because I think I could love you.' 'Oh, that would be a waste if we couldn't be friends.' 'Look, could you ever love me?' 'I don't know. Yes. Maybe. I was having such a nice evening. Look at all these people. It's times like this when people begin thinking of themselves. It's the one time they should be detached, outside it.' 'Don't you miss me?' 'Of course.' 'But you can get along without me?' 'I can get along without anybody. I don't want to be tied down. If I did get married, it would be to some bloody insignificant little woman.' ' But why!' 'Housekeeper.' 'Then why don't you sleep with me?' 'I can't sleep with people I respect. Just those I know there's no danger of my getting close to. I could never sleep with a woman before I married her.' 'But if you're not going to marry me, why can't you sleep with me?' 'Because I'm still working on it.' 'On what?' 'Marrying you.' 'Well, how long will you be working on it?' 'Probably till you marry someone else.' 'God. Why don't you tell me yes or no? Let me be free!' 'I don't know. And you're free.' It went on and on like this."

"God, it sounds just like the conversations I had with David. Only with us it went on for three years and I used to throw up afterward."

"What finally happened?"

"I wrote him that I was marrying George in London. I was so tired of emotional things. I just wanted to be a housekeeper, a simple woman. He wrote back and said for me to name the day and place, anywhere in Europe, and he'd be there."

"What did you do?"

"I wrote him back and told him to go to hell. Then I married George. David was married this past summer."

"Oh, how awful."

"But it doesn't bother me. Really. It bothers me a lot more when other men I know get married."

"Then what do you think is the best thing to do with these men who are so . . . detached? Give them up?"

"Yes, I think so. I think there isn't any other way, really. You see, it's a condition they have. It wouldn't end with marriage. The difference was there at the beginning only you didn't see it or didn't want to. I don't think you have a choice, really."

Jung's two essays.[7]

Middlemarch.[8]

Expanding a small item of observation into a meaningful moment.

NOVEMBER 22

Kennedy is dead. The statesmen have paid their tributes and everything seems ephemeral. People are already speaking of LBJ—the new president. It has been organized hour by hour who shall view the body. The headlines are worded. Life goes on. One commentator said: "This nation still lives."

7. Jung published *Two Essays on Analytical Psychology,* an overview of the new study of the unconscious, in 1917, and revised it several times subsequently.

8. Jane Clifford, an English professor, the protagonist in Gail's 1974 novel *The Odd Woman,* consults George Eliot's novel *Middlemarch* for clues to how an intelligent woman might define herself.

NOVEMBER 26

Events both personal and international have skimmed off the non-valid from my life and I'm going to try and record what does matter and what I must do. I got back my faith in a surprisingly easy way, through typing (because I said I would) an extremely tedious and wordy MS of Robin's, due for publication in his *Marine* magazine. The combination of doing something for somebody else plus sticking to it when I was about to despair—or procrastinate—did the trick. A much saner person, I went down to the kitchen to get a glass of milk. I feel the same fire to live, absorb, learn, move, and do that I'd felt in Copenhagen, awake night after night, listening to the electric trains shuttle into Klampenborg station, knowing the ocean was outside also.

A lot of the sentimental is tied up in my grief over John Kennedy's assassination. I don't really deserve to eulogize or call it "grief." I didn't even go out and vote three years ago on Key Biscayne. Doug didn't either. Afterward, we sheepishly discussed it, justified it by saying we didn't want either candidate. But even then I felt the charm and the new life of the administration of JFK. They were fascinating to read about, young, interested in the arts and the intellect, rich and fashionable. And these three years, for me, have been an era when I dared to move, do new things, go and live in Europe, take chances, burn bridges, aim high. Now that era is over and I feel it is time for me to go home again. Dorothea (when she was at Radcliffe, she campaigned for him as senator) feels it worse. The best thing that came out of her grief was when she said: "We can carry it on a little bit simply by refusing to hate. Every time you start hating, just remember . . ."

Though somewhat garbled, these touchstones emerge. Not only from this crisis, so much bigger than my little personal grievances, but also from recent events on a smaller scale, i.e., the beagling meet on Saturday with Landsborough and Gordon. It was an epitaph to a really wasted (and unrequited) passion, resulting in a confident hatred of such apathy in myself.

I do not need to see Gordon again.

DECEMBER 5

A moment out for a progress report. Tonight the house was still, the Wests having gone out in full plumage to the premiere of the film made from Lampedusa's *Leopard*.[9] Sat in front of the fire and read (Ashmore's *An Epitaph for Dixie*),[10] but couldn't really concentrate as long as anyone else was in the room. Well-organized, very English Daphne was sitting in the yellow chair pasting on her new false fingernails.

Riding to work in the morning, I am pleased to find I am facing outward again. I am not in love with anyone and I depend on no one for the completion of a happy day. Sometimes I have double glimpses of myself, however, and it almost kills me. I see the mortal and the eternal standing in each other's skin. Most of the time they are merged in a fairly acceptable whole. But tonight, for instance, as I was bending over to move the heater, the one slipped awry. The eternal (which is neither man nor woman but a little of each; which concerns itself with large rather than petty matters; which has a deep and genuine desire to help humanity) was separated from the mortal, a twenty-six-and-a-half-year-old female, no longer in the blossom, yet in the late bloom, who fights a losing battle with the destroyers of skin tissue and hair color, who cares about appearance and the mating ritual.

Glimpses such as this are soul-rending. How I loathe the thought of dying.

9. Luchino Visconti made a classic movie based on Giuseppe Tomasi di Lampedusa's novel *Il Gattopardo* (*The Leopard*), the story of the passing of an era in Sicily as modern Italy absorbed traditional society.

10. In 1958, when *Epitaph for Dixie* by Harry S. Ashmore was published, northerners had a bias against southerners that was closer to abolitionist feelings than to twentieth-century ones; and Ashmore was in a perfect position to know. Born in Greenville, South Carolina, he became the editor of two Southern newspapers—the Charlotte *News* and the Arkansas *Gazette*—then left the business to campaign for Adlai Stevenson, the Democratic presidential candidate criticized by northerners for opposing the abrupt imposition of civil rights laws on the South. By 1963, Barry Goldwater, Arizona Republican, had begun to win over long-standing southern Democrats. It is in this light that Gail's mother had liked Goldwater. Many northern Democrats were patronizing toward southerners.

DECEMBER 6

Letter from Frank and Kathleen really putting me in my place for joining the mass hysteria. Saw George (the ex-USTS chauffeur) in the pub.
I went over and kissed him. He looked frightened to death. Then, recov-
ering, he told me he'd found a £20-a-week job as chief mourner at a
Shepherds Bush mortuary.

DECEMBER 9

This weekend, Beckenham, Kent. Remodeled coach house and Robin's
amazon family slightly tipsy and strong. Franco–Anglo Saxon blood
(Challis and Jones special mixture) high in their wide cheeks. Robin's
red, square hand around mine. He, his mother, and I listen to "Have
Some Madeira, M' Dear," a song from a 1957 hit revue. The last time I
heard it was in Shelley B.'s little house in Chapel Hill. The song bridged
two times and I saw that I had done what I would have wished to do five
years ago.

Later, lying in front of the dying fire. He is so easy to be with, so big,
so comfortable. I always remember I am in the presence of a man.

The dialectic shifts. Dorothea thinks Robin is boring. And Andrew.
Just in the heat of my hate-Andrew swing, Andrew comes out with:
"What's the answer?" On TV is a cad who has returned to his loving and
broad-minded wife. Daphne has gone to get the milk. "I know the answer," says Andrew. "It's to try to get a little more and a little more unselfish as you go. But you can't do it out of do-goodishness and you can't
do it because you've heard happy people are unselfish people and you
want to be happy. It's damn difficult to get less selfish."

DECEMBER 16

If I am destined for another bout with the Diary, with catalogings of
self, then at least let it simply aim to describe what is in the process of
going on rather than to draw any sweeping conclusions. Conclusions

look so silly when you read them over later. Whoops. Here come the carolers. The first note of "Silent Night" sounds, the doorbell rings, the needy box is extended. Salvation Army. Oxfam. Veterans. Lorraine came, typical to fashion at 11:00 p.m., into Southampton.

We talked and I found—after she'd recounted all her recent experiences—that she was still acting out the same patterns and hadn't changed at all in spite of the fact that she kept telling me how much she had changed. I found myself angry at her upon her arrival and whenever we were with other people. I do not admire her—perhaps we are too much alike in some ways—but I like being with her. Perhaps it's because of the freedom we give each other for self-exploration. We can be selfish to a greater extent because we recognize the other doesn't regard this as a fault. Thus I like to listen to her for hours and offer my suggestions because I know my turn is coming and her suggestions will help me as much as mine help her. Because—this is it—we are alike and while we can't see ourselves properly, we can damn well spot the faults in the other. Thus when she tells me: "You have a great capacity for guilt. You look for situations which will make you uncomfortable, and if you can't find any you create a nice guilt-triggered situation."

I can look back and see the Shelley B. and Frank Crowther[11] Rathskellar scene plus all the numerous triangles I have contrived and then have been beaten by. The John Bowers and Lorraine situation in N.Y.: I promised them both all of myself in one day and ended up slighting each.

I fit myself into scenes where I'll come off badly or won't measure up. (Robin: "You're your own worst enemy.") The party I gave Saturday night. I knew the Wests wouldn't approve and I knew I'd have to be a policeman about the furniture, carpets, etc.

Of course, one of the biggest bad showings was my 1962 October homecoming when I was considering marrying B. and arranged it so I'd spend the first weekend with Uncle William and the second with L.! I was miserable at both places and lost B.

11. Frank Crowther was a bookish friend from Chapel Hill who took a civil service job at the USTS in Washington. He was one of the Chapel Hill friends who continued to keep in touch with Gail.

Then at work: Doreen provides a wonderful weapon with which I can castigate myself as often as I like. I know where she stands on most things, so I know how to deviate and thus rouse her ire. I am remembering that dream I had about the dog. He was my watchdog, my guilt complex, my conscience. I saw something strange, something I didn't understand, and so I sicced him on to it—only to find it was innocent with bewilderment when it looked up, dying, at me.

I MET ANOTHER ONE. I'd say this one rates about 90 percent. I think I spoiled it by being aggressive.

DECEMBER 17

Back into the whirlpool. Measuring life in terms of a particular appointment with a man. But maybe it is not too late. Maybe I still have an hour or so in which to assert the truths formed in the noninvolved weeks of November. I get off the track when I get all perturbed about time (Robin calls it "your forty-years-from-now depression"), when I start trying to be what I think everyone thinks I ought to be. This new one is no sluggish Gordon. He saw something he liked Saturday night and came back Sunday to follow it up. "He's definitely courting," said Lorraine. And if he is, he has already fashioned the image that he will worship. Why not just drift along and be soft and loving, and not give any great exhibition of intellectualism to scare him off.

DECEMBER 22

"No wonder you drive men away," says Lorraine. "No matter how much they like you, you finally exhaust them. You force them to become involved in your own cataclysmic little dervish. I don't know why I've stayed as long as I have. You're not easy to be a friend to. You seem to lack the power to love. In Copenhagen, for instance, I gave you my number and you didn't telephone. Then, when I saw you in Drop-In, you said, 'I didn't think you really meant it.' I found you a place to live because I knew how it was to be alone in a new country. When I left Copenhagen, you didn't even go to see me off. That hurt. Then when you wrote to say you'd be in N.C., I telephoned you from Boston. I arranged to come down to see you in N.Y. And what did you give me? We had one hour alone together in Penn Station. One hour! And then you ask me after I've scarcely gotten off the boat: Why do you keep up with your friends—to use them? If that were so, why did I not break off from you long ago? But in spite of everything, I haven't because I like you. And it hurts me to hear your friends speak of you: 'Gail's all right, but . . . ' You constantly embark on this self-defacing scheme and pretty soon they are going along with all the bad things you say about yourself."

AND EVEN WITH THE New One, Andy [Hurst]. He is doing everything. He is pursuing. He is admiring. All I have to do is shut up and consider him. But there is this perverse longing to berate myself.

Eight hours later

Almost midnight and I have got to get this all down—all or nothing. Lorraine came at three and Andy and Steve showed up promptly at five. I served them very bad tea. The fire was blazing and Lorraine and Steve (Andy's older brother—the most adjusted artist I have ever seen) held the floor. Subjects: Cairo—Alexandria—*The [Alexandria] Quartet*—was it or was it not great?—Cuban agriculture—Czechoslovakian commitment to the Communist line—the Danes and their Viking gods. (Here Lorraine gave me a plug: "You know, Gail said to me in Denmark, 'The Danes do have a religion. They have their Viking gods.' ") Steve: "Don't you feel at some times that some figure is messing up your life? Some sort of god or something?" Andy: "Yes, I think Diana, the goddess of chastity, has been interfering with yours lately." Steve is more practical, less sensually attractive, more intuitive and better-read. Andy is shyer, quiet. They seem to get along beautifully and to complement each other. Andy has the sense of humor. Both are

Oxford educated. They are neither insular nor "boned up" in only one subject.

Do Jack Malone's[12] typing.

CHRISTMAS NIGHT

Alone and comfortable in a warm room. Lorraine is out with her policeman—the Buckingham Palace Guards winked at her from under their great fur hats. Her travel adventures put Fielding and Frommer to shame. Frowsy[13] has lost Birgit. The Christmas card said: "No I am not married damn! Birgit has found another and told me goodbye. It has been a lousy year."

Lorraine and I have spent a great deal of time lying on this bed talking.

Re Andy: "When they like you, there is none of this plotting and scheming."

Dorothea has quit USTS and is leaving Griffith.

JANUARY 1, 1964 · *1:30 a.m.*

This is the quietest and soberest New Year's I've spent in several years. Green Street last year, Copenhagen the year before, Miami, Miami, Miami before that. I'm home in bed, not drunk, not depressed, and not expecting any more from this life than I've got. Perhaps the highlight of this evening was when Andy's brother Steve said: "I want you to meet Christine and see what you think. Because I'd accept your judgment."

12. Jack "Tucson" Malone was a homeless man who was writing his memoirs at the post office. Gail typed them for him on the IBM Selectric at the U.S. Travel Service. Selections from them were published in *The Daily Mail.*

13. "Frowsy" was the son of Gail's former landlord, Rolf Høiass, a widower, and lived in the Høiass house near Copenhagen during Gail's three months there at the beginning of her time abroad. Frowsy proved to be a good friend with a mischievous sense of humor, and Gail never tired of him, though the tension in the household was high.

JANUARY 2

I never thought I'd be glad to see Doreen back, but I will be. Dorothea half-dead with cold and husband trouble. Out of the hell, Andy's voice on the telephone asking if he can meet me next door at the pub tomorrow night. As if he were afraid ever to ask me for the same day.

Said Dorothea: "You want lots of men and a man senses this. As for me, I'm just the opposite. And, you know, people were always asking me to marry them."

Andy's mother wrote a note to thank me for my note. I feel a rightness about that family. They appreciate the qualities I have been taught to appreciate.

JANUARY 3

Andy standing over the stove in the small kitchen, turning the sausages with his thumb and forefinger. I glimpse the gold signet ring on his little finger and this symbolizes, somehow to me, the unobtainable.

Steve is talking to me. He is telling me he has written a novel and is writing another. He is describing a Cornish dissenter in the art class.[14] Andy stands, shoulders hunched, neck bent forward in his usual stance. Something princely about the shape of his head with close-cropped reddish-gold hair. In this kitchen, there is physical magnetism and the intuitive interplay of two minds—it takes both of them to provide this. Steve has read the Updike story that I gave them and says the man is deadly accurate.[15] I think: This is the first time I can remember giving somebody a story and having them read it so quickly. Then Andy pipes up. He has read it, too. Last night before he went to sleep. So many thoughts come crowding in now. So Andy has read it. What is more, he saw things in it that I liked. The very things that made me like the story.

14. Steve Hurst, a sculptor in metals, taught an art class in London.

15. "Still Life" by John Updike, which appeared in *Pigeon Feathers* (1962), describes an American art student's miscalculation of the mind of an English girl who is his classmate.

He got the tone of the afternoon at Oxford, the presence of things. I am thinking: I must not underestimate this one. Then we laugh some more and Steve goes to drill a hole in a pipe for one of his metal sculptures. Andy begins kissing me in his way that can mean anything. It is his way and I am sure he has looked at many more girls in this blinking, breathless way.

JANUARY 10

After a quiet dinner with Eva from Liechtenstein and a cozy chat with the Wests ("Do you want to know something about Panama, Gail?"), I retired to my room to plow on through Jung's *Two Essays*. Andy rang at 9:30, first speaking to Mrs. West. He was home alone and had gone to sleep after washing his own supper dishes.

The first night I met him, he went to sleep. My first impression of him when Robin brought him to my party at 21 Old Church Street was that he was a good-natured, athletic chap. By the end of the evening, we were paired off. Lorraine and Charlie were upstairs in my room. Robin had taken Anne Jeffries back to Golders Green[16] in Charlie's car. The drunken Irish rugby players had been persuaded to leave. I was fed up. I brought my coat down by the fire in the living room and got under it and went to sleep. Andy—who was no more than a pointed chin and large gray-sweatered shoulders—tried to kiss me. I wouldn't let him. He persisted. So I turned my back and went to sleep. Then he stretched out, his arms spread-eagled, and went to sleep half on the chair, snoring. He said later that, at the end of the party, I accompanied him to the door, kissed him, and said I liked his sweater and I hoped he wasn't bored.

WHAT COMES OUT of this hazy first part of the winter is simply this: I am learning how to live and I perhaps never would have learned had I stayed at home. Nothing is a matter of either/or but—as Father Webbe

16. Golders Green is a nineteenth-century suburb that developed into a wealthy Jewish neighborhood in the 1950s.

says—both/and. The important thing is, Mrs. Luxon[17] in her womanly wisdom remarked: Be yourself, but be polite. That was B.'s parting advice at the airport: "If you're in any situation that frightens you because you feel inferior, just be courteous." And Andy's observation: "She was one of those nervous English girls, who, if you paid her a compliment, would get so embarrassed she would answer something gauche." Then there is Lorraine's advice: "Be honest with yourself, enough so to admit your basic dishonesty."

JANUARY 12

Yesterday was one of those days when almost all the pro- and anti-elements were present, given to me (as to any heroine) to do with as I pleased. First of all, this question of nervousness. What is at stake? Am I proceeding cautiously down the same wrong road again? As Steve said, "What worries me is, do you think we're doomed to keep repeating certain patterns all our lives?"

They came to lunch—the Hurst brothers—the beginning of twelve hours à trois. I resent Steve's presence, and yet I know he is an admirer and helps ease the tension. Why do I resent him? Because he takes part of Andy from me. They have known each other twenty-seven years, have grown up together, and understand each other as only brothers can. What is that understanding like? I don't know. Someday I'll ask Rebel and Tommy. I would think, however, it's something sacred and inviolable. I would never try to turn one against the other. Like, when we were eating, I teased Andy about something and he made a "hen" noise to Steve. "You'll have to excuse our mystical signals," he said. "Downright childish, if you ask me," Steve answered. How much do these brothers talk? A lot, I think. I would be flattering myself if I thought they kept me untouched in their morning conversations. I know the

17. Ermina Luxon was the wife of Norval Neil Luxon, dean of the School of Journalism at Chapel Hill. Gail stayed for a while in their home after having had a run-in with the dean of women and being put on probation for having kept a dog in her room.

treacheries women friends are capable of working upon a man. Perhaps Andy and Steve are "working as a team." Perhaps Andy has said to Steve: "Find out for me." Thus when Steve dances with me at the Hampstead dinner party and we discuss what we always end up discussing—"How to find someone who understands"—I should guard my tongue. He is convincing himself that Christine is the girl for him. "But are you looking for a girl with an absence of negative qualities rather than a presence of positive ones?" I asked. "You may be right," he answered. "Well, there's a big difference," I said. We were sitting in the rugby stands—the "Andrew Charles Brunel Hurst fan club"—his mother and her friend on the other side.

"How long have you known [Christine]?"

"Six months."

"How often have you seen her?"

"About once a week."

"Does she have a lot of other boyfriends?"

"Yes. No. I don't know. She's so elusive."

"Well, I don't want to discourage you, Steve, but I truly believe that if something doesn't happen in three months, it's not going to happen at all."

"Maybe you're right. Sometimes I grab Christine so that she's only a quarter of an inch away and I say: 'Listen to me. We're not communicating.' Then it's all right, for a minute."

"But is that enough? Listen, do you sometimes spend a whole day with someone waiting for that Moment, which never comes?"

"Yes! Yes I do."

Also he said, "I'll tell you something: I've never been attracted to Andy's girls. But I find you exciting."

What were "Andy's girls" like? Were they like Margaret—an obviously "old friend"—her brother was A.'s best friend at Oxford. Why did I not like her? Her fiancé, a thin-lipped boy, who lisped and restored houses and wore slim-fitting Chelsea boots and had been to Dartmouth, obviously liked me. The minute she came up to us, talking through her teeth, undulating her stomach, I hated her. Why? She was pretty. She had a good face, which she knew how to arrange, and excellent legs, which she exposed to her own advantage, sometimes showing halfway up the thigh. She was feminine and asked questions about Andy. Yet I knew she was thinking: I am a success. Her perfume was good, so was her dress, and I just can't see why she's marrying Christopher. He got quite high and was sitting opposite me with his face flushed. "What will you do when you leave here?" he said. "Go back to the States." "And what will you do there?" "I don't know. I'm not sure." "Well, it all sounds damn dilettantish to me," he said. I was surprised at such frankness. No doubt the U.S. was good for him. "What do you mean by that?" I asked. "I meant sort of easygoing." "Thank you," I said, "I'll take that as a compliment." "I didn't mean it either way. Just as a fact." Then he said, "What are you looking for?" "What does every woman look for?" "I'm asking you." "Well," I said, "ask Margaret." "Margaret?" he said. "Well"—she recrossed her legs on the Greek divan and looked prettily puzzled—"I don't know. Why, I guess, a home, security, children." "And what are you looking for?" he demanded of me. I said, "Oh, a good man, I suppose." "Ah! I was waiting for you to say that!" "Okay. I've said it."

At one time, sitting at Andy's feet by the fire, watching the small female terrier repulse the advances of a male collie, listening to Margaret's fragrant, refreshing, Andy-captivating conversation, I actually fought down the impulse to run from the room, to taxi back to Old Church Street, bury my head in the pillows, and cry, saying, "Enough, enough. I am not loved, but at least I am alone in my shame." But I sat by the fire, the pasted social smile intact. Later I told Andy about the smile. Why? "Sometimes I just want to be in someone's arms and be myself but instead I paste on the smile and sit erect."

"That's not my problem," he said. "Mine is simply learning to do the things most people take for granted: going into a shop and ordering something. I freeze. I feel like a mouse."

That's because he never developed a persona, as Jung would say. Anyway, he began looking at his watch and saying, "It's about time we were making a move." Then I became angry and said, "Well, let's leave this very minute and take you home. I wouldn't want you to be anywhere you didn't want to be." Then he took off his watch and began winding it and it almost drove me crazy, the steady persistent sound of it. Then I said, "Well, tell Steve and let's go," and he said, "No, I don't like to force Steve's hand. I certainly wouldn't want him to come up to me when I was engrossed with someone and say: 'Let's go.' " So then we sat together on the low divan and I said, suddenly seized with a little tenderness: "You're very tired, aren't you? You work hard during the week, not so much physically, but just sustaining a monotonous mental frame of mind. It's a drag, isn't it? And then when the weekend comes you have to recover." I don't know what I said, really, but he put his arm around me and said, "How very intuitive of you to see that. Something I didn't see myself." And then I said, "I enjoyed watching you play today. I love watching you." And he said, "I'm so glad." In the car coming home, I sat in the front with Steve and Andy, and some boy sat in the back of the van. Nobody talked much. I thought: Well, the day is over, all days are over eventually, and I'm glad to have had it. The first time I felt this sadness was the day and night in Greenville when Kathleen and I went down on the train[18]—I must remember these things for my children. I'll spend my Sunday reading, sleeping, something, and will see Andy next weekend since his mother invited me down in front of him. (She likes me. Why?) When they stopped at the door, I said, "Please don't anybody get out, as the weather is too awful for politeness." Then Andy said from the back in the extra-loud voice he uses when he gets nervous, "Listen, are you doing anything tomorrow evening? I mean, if you aren't, perhaps you could come around for dinner." "I thought you were going to do your correspondence course," I said. "Well, I am," he said, "but I like to have something to look forward to."

JANUARY 13 · *Monday, 11:05 p.m.*

Laughed myself sick in a Peter Sellers movie only to have the evening shattered by a look in the bathroom mirror. *What kind of truth is this?* I think it said. *You can't trade in your youth anymore.* So, what now? I

---

18. See Gail's story "Over the Mountain," published in *Antaeus* no. 49/50 (Spring/Summer 1983) and anthologized in *Evening Games: Chronicles of Parents and Children*, edited by Alberto Manguel (Penguin Books, 1986).

swear to God, I'll sit up all night until I come to a decision. It's one life, my life, and one-third used up. Is it me who wanted to write books? Do I still? Am I escaping a commitment by saying, "Oh, I wasn't good enough." Do I really want to make a man happy, raise children? Or am I simply frantically chasing around to collect the bits and pieces to put together an acceptable background for my middle age? Do all twenty-six-and-a-half-year-old divorced women go through this? Studying themselves in the mirror, building up false hopes one day, being overly critical the next? The days are going by and I spoil two-thirds of them by fearing that things that have not happened will probably not happen. If I am not meant to marry and have the shared joy that was in last night's walk down the river path, then all the working toward it in the world won't help.

JANUARY 14

Culinary Festival w. Peter Perry[19] and Doreen. When I got home there was a message to call Putney before 11:30. Andy wanted to know if I could see *Billy Budd*[20] on Monday evening.

JANUARY 22

Thus after the second gentle weekend in Oxfordshire, I began constructing my barricade so that Andy could not hurt me. There are ways to do this: Faults are always easy to find. By the time I returned home from work tonight, I had decided that I could live without him. And there on the desk in the hall was a letter in his handwriting. It was a thick letter and I knew it was a Dear John, saying that I would not do. But no, it was a newspaper clipping of a review of *Billy Budd*, Benjamin Britten's opera, which we had seen on Monday night. Then there was a short

---

19. Peter Perry worked as a liaison between travel agents and news sources.

20. Benjamin Britten's opera *Billy Budd* opened in its revised and now classic form on January 9, 1964, at the Royal Opera House, Covent Garden.

note saying simply: Here is a review of what we saw; I'll get this in the post now. He also added he had only had to walk two miles the previous night. He didn't know that I followed him up Old Church Street and saw him just after he'd boarded the bus. His face was pink and he sat on one of the side seats. Apparently, the no. 11 bus only took him to the bridge.

I want so much to get down the impressions of the weekend. Very much like the last. The high point being when Steve and I met Andy coming back from his squash game and I watched him run on ahead in the mist in his white shorts and Oxford Cambridge shirt.

And yet I had begun plans to hurt him, knowing how much rugby means to Andy, by making sure he knew that I knew that Robin was selected for Southern Counties.

My friend Peter Perry gave me good advice tonight upon my request. He said: You're delightful company and damnably attractive and a joy to be with—but you could be a little more thoughtful. Then I said: How can I practice? Whereupon he drew a cat on the back page of a book and said, "What will you think of when you see this cat in six months?" "Why, our discussion on thoughtfulness, of course," I said. "All right, then," said Peter.

MR. HURST SAYING, "How about a spot of sherry" or "Have you ever read anything by a man called Marmaduke Pickthall?"[21] Mrs. H. in the kitchen telling me the story of her marriage. It was not a case of love but, as she says, it has worked out well.

JANUARY 24

I was just thinking as I rode no. 19 to work how glad I was for the experience of Gordon. Nobody could have been more indifferent. Thus I'm surprised when someone shows a real thoughtfulness. (Andy saying at

---

21. Marmaduke Pickthall, a writer admired by D. H. Lawrence, translated the Qur'an into English. Tracing his ancestry to a knight in William the Conqueror's service, Pickthall became a British Muslim.

Billy Budd, "Well, Gail, the first time I saw you, you were wearing what you have on now.")

At work today I saw over a hundred people, talked to them, was either loved, agitated, or faintly amused by them, but when I went back into the stockroom to fish out a dusty brochure on Mississippi, I suddenly thought I should no more be doing this job than raising skunks. (Though that, I think, might be more interesting.) However, most people manage at some time or other to get into a job that is totally unsuited for them for at least a while (Andy selling Hoover vacuum cleaners, D. H. Lawrence teaching, etc.).

The only justification for writing in these journals is putting in the details. We ate with Steve's unrequited love, Christine, and her shrill roommate. Andy thinks I drink too much. ("You're a very capable young lady, but I'm worried about your tummy.")

We had ham, baked potato and salad, cheese and apples, and cider or beer to drink. From the way Christine acts—completely casual, pulling up her tight sweater-dress to expose her knees, scratching a shapely leg with her fingernails absentmindedly—she doesn't have anything to lose with Steve. Also, on the bookshelf by her bunk bed (top deck) she has a small framed picture of a really superb-looking brown-suede-shoes-and-cable-knit-sweater type.

Have been rereading "Gull Key."[22]

BACK ALONE AFTER *West Side Story* (with Robin in his white raincoat). I love excellence. Excellent writing, dancing, talking. The fog was so thick that I had to walk slowly down Old Church Street, and when I looked back I couldn't see the lamppost behind. This scene will stay behind like a dream and linger with me the rest of my life. Two couples were dining at L'Aiglon. A policeman was standing alone outside no. 21. When I approached, he looked at his watch.

---

22. "Gull Key" is a novel that Gail had completed in 1962. It concerns a woman negotiating a marriage that is going wrong and, at the same time, developing herself as an artist by relating to her environment. Though confined to a Florida island community, the woman senses an outlet in its historic lighthouse. The manuscript is now part of the Gail Godwin Papers held in the Southern Historical Collection in the Wilson Library at the University of North Carolina, Chapel Hill.

JANUARY 26 · *Sunday*

Surely there must be some use in trying to convey such a Sunday. I used to be ashamed of journals and think: I ought to be sitting at that type-writer churning out something "worthwhile."

GORDON CAME BY last night and entertained Mrs. West with stories of a Russian friend he had and how they went out to dinner together out of reach of the MI5. I listened to the story with interest. Mrs. W. said: It is always so good to see him; we like him so much. And I was able to answer: Yes, so do I. He's living in Rugby with a cousin.

MRS. HURST TOLD me how she'd said to Mr. Hurst about me: "She's not going back! I'm determined that one of them will have her."

BIG USTS AD IN the color section of *The Times*—silhouette of the Unisphere against a fiery red N.Y. skyline.[23] The office will go haywire tomorrow. I will give the Greyhound addresses a hundred times—tell a hundred people that we are all out of the "FLY All the Way" folder. Interspersed will be trips to the bathroom, varied by use of the stairs vs. the lift. Then there will be lunchtime, prowling about Hatchards[24] for something to save my soul, assuage my guilt, make me better, etc. The inexorable creeping toward 5:30—the same bus trip home, meal, and then finding some way to spend three hours until it's time to go to sleep. Then Tuesday—Wednesday—Thursday—Friday.

Am I in a temporary trough? Should I get out of this airy-fairy land and go back to the land of the living? Is it the land of the living or the land of the live-it-uppers? Will I regret leaving England? Probably yes. But then, is it right to stay here doing the same thing for much longer?

23. The Unisphere was the 140-foot-high, stainless steel model of Earth that symbolized the 1964–1965 World's Fair in New York City.

24. Hatchards was a bookstore on Piccadilly, one block from Gail's office on Vigo Street.

I don't think I can stand this job more than three more months. If it weren't for Andy and something to do after work, I couldn't stand it. Let's just hope some dear old subconscious signal comes through.

Andy and I had dinner with a Jewish South African architect named Zackie Blacker and his soft-spoken, very natural English wife. What I like about certain English hospitality is its very simplicity. People converse while unraveling old sweaters and use the yarn for reknitting.

JANUARY 30

Tonight I had gone into the ladies' room of the pub next door, and just as I was shutting the bathroom door, it came to me. I cannot remember what the voice said, but I remember a feeling of well-being, of everything being all right; of a promise, of faith in myself.

Other flashes come and go. I must keep these journals to preserve what little integrity I have. It is a razor's edge. So much of what can be learned I am finding in Jung's books. There's a case. A man is besieged by his own "otherness," yet by describing it in symbolic language he contributes to mankind rather than just sorting himself out. He was an exception.

How much of this present relationship with A. belongs on these pages? I want to describe something about it. He is very different from me. We went to an Italian restaurant for lunch and he told me about his difficulty in doing the things most ordinary mortals do—picking up a telephone, etc. Later, that evening, he said he had worried that he had been a "moaner."

Deadly dinner with Andy's law firm, but he doesn't like them either. Tomorrow we go up to Oxford and I'm going to relax and not worry about anything. I can't do any more than be myself and be courteous.

FEBRUARY 3

Andrew Baker[25] came by to bring his beautifully mounted photo of Justice Walk[26] for me to send to Stella. It was shades of old times as we sat in his shed in the garden of no. 21—now inhabited by Neil, the Oxford graduate from Tregunter Road who barely makes a living and has both whips and crucifixes hanging on his wall. Neil is a good man. I am slowly learning to recognize genuine people. The conversation leapt. We kept up with each other—one took up where another left off. I came away both laughing and wiser, suddenly comparing something (what?) about the evening with echoes of Andy and his mother talking. I can hear Andy's word patterns: "Well, I mean, crikey, if she didn't want . . ." His mother: "Quite!"

This weekend was my third at Oxfordshire with the Hursts. I like the bed and hot water bottles and the church part. I like to take Communion in that Norman church, and I liked going to the Cotswolds with Andy and walking beside the Windrush [River] and having him say "I've got to take care of you." And I liked the old ruins of Minster Lovell—Andy's arm still encircling me—and the sunlight on the mossy gravestones and the pub afterward, and then a home-cooked dinner. But is this enough? Do I have communion with this man? And how much communion can one expect?

Mrs. Hurst gave me several very good books—one the *Letters of Direction* of the Abbé de Tourville.[27] I like her. But she's no Kathleen. Oh no. She's not Kathleen. There's a whole dimension left out—

FEBRUARY 4

More and more I understand what Father Webbe means when he says we are living in eternity. Tonight, as I walked down Old Church Street

---

25. Andrew Baker had been one of the tenants at the Wests' Tregunter Road boardinghouse. The Wests had moved their "youth brothel" to 21 Old Church Street in August 1962, and Stella Anderson, Gail's friend from Chapel Hill, arrived a month later.

26. Justice Walk was a picturesque alleyway across the street from 21 Old Church Street.

27. *Letters of Direction: Thoughts on the Spiritual Life from the Letters of the Abbé de Tourville* records the nineteenth-century French cleric's letters to penitents.

at ten, I thought: How silly for me to think moving away will make me any better off than I am.

The clear night, the Embassy and Grosvenor Square, where, less than three months ago, a crowd of shocked Americans stood waiting to hear more news from a portable radio held high over one man's head. London is my city whether I leave it or not.

FEBRUARY 5

Monie[28] had a heart attack. I must try and give her something of myself. She must be told once again that I love her.

Mrs. Hurst wrote again. I think I read the last page of her letter over about fifty times. "I hope whatever happens that you will be very happy and I hope that happiness will be with our family . . ."

FEBRUARY 10

> *Do not worry about your feelings, but act as if you had those which you would like to have. This is not done by making a mental effort, nor by seeking to feel that which you do not feel, but by simply doing without the feeling you have not got and behaving exactly as if you had it. When you realize that lack of feeling does not hinder reality you will no longer put your trust in your own thoughts, but in that which our Lord makes you do. We are very slow in realizing this, but we must do so. Come now! have a little of that tranquil fearlessness which makes for good, without so much thought and scrupulousness. Behave just as naturally as if you were coming downstairs!*
> —HENRI DE TOURVILLE, *LETTERS OF DIRECTION: THOUGHTS ON THE SPIRITUAL LIFE FROM THE LETTERS OF THE ABBÉ DE TOURVILLE*

28. Gail's maternal grandmother, Edna Rogers Krahenbuhl, whom she called "Monie," had lived with Gail and Gail's mother in Asheville before Gail's mother married Frank Cole. Edith, in *The Odd Woman* (1974), is based on her.

Neurotic suffering is an unconscious fraud and has no moral merits, as has real suffering.

—C. G. JUNG, *THE DEVELOPMENT OF PERSONALITY,*

"Analytical Psychology and Education," Lecture 1

THE GAME AT Twickenham played in English spring sunshine . . . the picnic lunch eaten on the roof of the car . . . my sandwiches . . . a gradual progressing into the evening. Says Andy: "I think there's one vital thing for two people who are going to get married. They should have the same sense of humor. And we seem to have."

Andy about my marriage: "If you hadn't had that, you might have been brash or naive. I don't think of that. I just think of you as you. I'm not complaining. I'll settle for you as you are. Do I appear reluctant?"

FEBRUARY 12

Sometimes his conversation loses me. He goes on and on about things—something today about an attitude toward the Lancaster Gate Grammar School, later something about dogs in Hyde Park, sometimes about Steve and him camping. I am conscious of myself watching him and not listening . . . All these things could really go into a story. I could write some good stories about the male-female relationship. We went to the Crown. I had given up alcohol for Lent, so I had bitter lemon and a ham sandwich, and he had one beer and two sandwiches.

I learned tonight from Neil, whose brother is a solicitor, that solicitors make £1,000 a year after they are qualified. I am making almost £1,500 now.

Andy gave me hell, in his blushing, polite way, on Sunday. He said I had a habit that annoyed him. "What is it?" I asked, trembling. YOU DON'T FINISH EVERYTHING ON YOUR PLATE, he said. I actually thought he was joking for a minute. He also won't take taxis and sends aerogrammes.

FEBRUARY 14

Last night I dreamed I was rushing back to register for journalism school. I barely made it, registered, and was then told Dean Luxon had died the night before. I woke up crying.

Tonight was a ghastly affair: Robin, Jack Malone, and myself. Jack talks about himself too much. This is deadly. I came back feeling like a big nothing.

This weekend. I am invited to the country for two days of rest. Why not, then, go and savor it, as if there were not great stakes involved? Enjoy it, watch, learn what there is to be learned, listen to all of them, remember it's Steve's birthday weekend, forget completely about feelings.

FEBRUARY 17 · *Monday*

This weekend at Sandford-on-Thames in Oxfordshire. It has become a kind of ritual now. Mr. H. watching the Wasps[29] through his binoculars, presented to him by the Egyptian government; Mrs. H. and myself talking about Steve's love life, Andy's childhood, and teas and dinners, occasionally clasping each other and crying, "Oh, pass the ball down! Let Andy have a try!"

He is so intense about his game. He is comical when he runs because his chin juts out. He strides about the field like a penguin. Later in the car, he kissed me and said: "You're very long-suffering. Not many girls would be that long-suffering." We rode back to Oxford in harmony, clasping hands between gear changes. A small disharmony on the subject of extravagance vs. *la philosophie de* camping, but it was smoothed over by laughter. Steve's birthday weekend, and God sent Mrs. Hurst a lovely American girl just for the birthday tea. Jay Weed from Boston:

29. The Wasps is the name of Andy's rugby team.

fresh faced; burnished, dipped hair; American legs and clothes. Afterward, Steve and I took her back to Professor and Mrs. Blackman's, where she is living, and I had access to yet another world. Prof. B. is an expert weed-killing research man (says Jay: Here's one Weed you're not going to kill) and Mrs. B. is a sculptress who does stringy satirical figures mocking the Oxford stiffness. The house, their looks, the talk—even Mrs. B.'s matching turquoise slip—bespoke people who knew how to live, but, as I told Andy later, there was still something lacking.

FEBRUARY 19

Lucid letter from Frank about Monie's heart attack. He told me just the things I wished to know—in terms of spasms and blood clots. It is better to know.

My heart tells me to stick out this nasty job a while longer because the alternative (other than the busy occupation of shifting my home) might be far emptier.

This room is closing round me.

FEBRUARY 21

I have been reading over some of my old work. These flashes come:

1. There is too much explaining. I treat readers like unsubtle dopes. If I expect to write for subtle people, then I've got to give them the benefit of the doubt.
2. The writing goes on for a little while—smooth, sustained—then a note of whining seeps in, a navelish, melancholy note.
3. Too long.
4. I should never write when freshly under the influence of people like H. James and Lawrence. This just isn't me at all.

Before I go to sleep tonight, something has got to be settled about a project. Even if it's taking one simple story like "Bay Bridge" and going back and packing all that's possible into it. It's got great gaps at the moment. The dialogue isn't current enough. I don't let the characters let themselves go.

Oh, God. Some of the old excitement just came back. There is something about motels and open roads—stacks of books in a room on Sunday, papers, omelets, coffee, and marmalade; knowing you've been living your life all the way, that you enjoyed it in the past and will enjoy it in the future. Mother wrote today. "It is ridiculous, all this worry about middle age. I won't have a daughter of mine feeling older than I do."

Dinner party last night.

Andy. I saw how he'd be with my sleek American people. He will always be a bit rough in sleek groups. He does not look composed. His face reddens. He sits with his shoulders hunched, chin out, chunky and for all the world like a New Zealand farmer. His voice booms out when he's nervous, he screws up his face. I see his goodness, whereas, perhaps, the showy people don't. I can offset him as he offsets me—

FEBRUARY 23 · *Sunday*

Is there to be a breakthrough or not? I feel a positive turbulence of creative energy inside me but it is all dammed up and has no way to get out. I want to describe things as I see them—built up one on top of another, all the innuendoes and implications.

DINNER W. A. TONIGHT. We put the roast on, went for a walk under a clear sky, watched the trains from the bridge, and then went to the Quill—for a drink—then ate. We are finding out about each other, telling our dreams, explaining ourselves, airing discrepancies, perhaps finding out if we can live together. I saw a list he had made for a party he was planning. It had names of people. Then at the bottom it had

A.

G.

S.

Coming back in the car, I told him how I wished I had something purposeful to do after work—something to occupy my time.

"Don't I?" he asked.

"But I want to stay out of your way while you're doing your things."

"Well," he said, easy as that, "I'll think of something for you to do."

Steve had been cutting up a car with an acetylene torch all day; he had been doing his law. Something so comforting . . .

FEBRUARY 24

Spring is in the air, there were two stars in the sky, it was light at the bus stop—

I feel nauseated with lack of purpose. Just a glimpse through the window today. Dorothea wrote Doreen from America. She's going to Columbia U., working at American Express, dating congressmen, and coming in with the milkman.

There is something blocking me from writing—

FEBRUARY 25

Get thee behind me, Satan. I'm coming back to life. Something is trying to get me to despair so I'll write down anything as it comes. It is all mental, all created inside me because of some need, some desperate balancing attempt on the part of my psyche.

Last night, disgusted with myself, I did not feel I had earned the right to take my clothes off and go to sleep. So I left them on, a pink sweater and maroon skirt—this seems important—and I left the light on and I slept. This morning I woke up remembering my dreams and went to work not feeling much differently. It was only as the day progressed that I began to see. There were many dreams, most of them about the nuns at St. Genevieve's and my mother. My mother (as in the dreams of the night before) was a comrade, she was helping me, boosting me, buying me something like gold earrings. Mother Winters was admiring me. There was an exam to take. I didn't know it all, but I wasn't especially worried. Now comes the significant part. I was asked by Mother Leible (I

8

9

remember her as a strict taskmaster) to do some chalk murals on the blackboard and I thought: I'm not capable of this. But then I remembered another dream (this, in my dream) where, at her command, I began drawing pictures that just came out of my fingers with no effort from me. And I began doing it again. This dream speaks for itself.

Tonight I felt a strong urge to rewrite "Lazarus"[30] and do collages. I know also that I must get out of here in June, have two months of sun and fun and go to New York. London is over. I see this as from a hilltop, as Andy once put it. "When you're on top and can see things clearly, look down and survey the situation and register it. Then when you get down in the depths, you will have the evidence if not the vision."

FEBRUARY 26

The spiritual man is increasingly becoming aware that his essential satisfactions proceed, not from his life's being what the surface-minded call "happy" or "sad"—a material success or failure, exciting or drab, gay or tragic—but whether or not his life is constructed on the lines of a sound story. It must have a pattern—a beginning, a middle, and an end. It must, in short, have meaning—a too rare overtone only produced when, as it were, the fingers of free will move across the strings of destiny.

—GALE D. WEBBE, *THE NIGHT AND NOTHING*

This has been a crisis week, starting with Mrs. H.'s letter.

Last night when A. took me to this little Greek restaurant in Notting Hill Gate, I decided he does not have a good sense of timing. Each time he comes to get me, we have to start all over again. He's stiff. His conversation was so mundane—all about his appetite and what a good night's sleep he had the night before. He's not smooth—little subtleties

---

30. Gail began writing "The Raising of Lazarus," an unpublished story about a turning point in the life of a playboy, in 1959, and she completed a draft in 1961. An aspect of the story—Lazarus's management of a Miami hotel—contributed a little to Gail's 2006 novel *The Queen of the Underworld.*

don't play across his face. So we got back here, I fixed Ovaltine, and we came up here. He told me about his mother: "I think I've upset her." I pretended not to know anything about it. "But what did she do?"

He said she had said arch things, presumptuous things, things that would make a girl think: My God, how am I going to get out of this trap? And make a man want to go to Australia. Then he said, "And I told her all about what you'd had to put up with, about your father and about the newspaper and about your marriage." Then I said how glad I was that he didn't care and he said, "That's all history. What I care about are your LIVING qualities—your warmth and your sympathy. They're worth a thousand of anything else." Then I said it was something for us to decide ourselves, every person was different, every couple was different. They had to feel things out. "Let's just give it plenty of air," I said. He "couldn't agree more." Then he said something about "who could dare try and predict the future?" And then he said something I may have misinterpreted, but it hurt even if it was misinterpreted. He said: "A lot of people think I'm twenty-eight and should be settled; now Steve is settled, he wants to get married, but I'm not settled at all, this is one of the most unsettled periods of my life."

After he left, I read Father Webbe's chapter on "decisions," prayed in a sort of clean, lucid despair, and, after a brief trancelike state, during which I saw the ephemerality of my anguish, went to sleep.

Father Webbe is right: It isn't the "happy" or "sad" moments or even the anticipation of either that really satisfies. It is the continuum, the pattern and the meaning of a life.

How could I bear the camping trips if they are the way he describes them—savoring a damn cup of coffee, exhausted, after pitching tent. When my idea is a luxury motel, having whiskey in bed listening to music, making love, sleeping late, making love, taking a shower, and having a huge breakfast—then going on to the next town in a streamlined little car. And also plenty of sunshine, new ideas, a *New York Times* on Sunday kind of life with a steady stream of vitality. And already we have serious disagreements on how money could be spent.

And what do we really talk about?

Could we, for instance, have a conversation comparable to those between me and John Bowers, Frank Crowther, Alden, or Jim Jensen? Or James?

Is it me speaking through these journals? I feel so relieved.

MARCH 2

A Story[31]

—

That Sunday morning, the knock on Ginny's door turned out to be Richard's mother instead of Richard. Usually on these weekends in the country, Ginny would lie in bed, awake from about seven thirty on (for she was not a heavy sleeper), and attend to the ritual beginnings of the rest of the house.

Richard's mother always stirred first. She was the breakfast maker and once a month it was her job to fetch the vicar in her green Hillman and drive him to the small, square Norman church in time for eight o'clock Communion.

Richard's father, learned Egyptologist and civil engineer, then clomped downstairs perhaps a quarter of an hour later and, with his departure to the lower floor, left the upstairs free for Ginny's hopes. John, the elder son, an artist, Richard's senior by three years, then took a bath. Ginny's room, the guest room, was between the Martins' bedroom and the bathroom. As in many older English houses, there was one room for the tub and washbasin and another for the toilet, as if it wouldn't be quite proper to have both in the same room.

Oh hell, loosen up, try another tack—

---

31. Gail, struggling with tone, begins to write a story based on her Oxford situation, in which Andy's mother courts her more aggressively than does Andy.

She had not slept well the night before. Things had come to a premature crisis with her and Richard and she now felt in the position of a rejected love, although, when you got right down to it, Richard had said nothing like this. Also, every time she kept dozing off, she ran smack into the beginnings of a nightmare, of indistinct description but evil enough to make her force herself to stay awake most of the night. She had been reading the Penguin classic of *Faust, Part I*, before she went to sleep. This perhaps triggered it—or was it the ghost from upstairs? The Martins believed in their ghost, but then he stayed in the empty room upstairs.

Richard's mother rushed into the room and sat down on the bed and put her arms around Ginny. The night before, she'd left a note under Ginny's pillow: "Good night, God bless you, Ginny darling."

I am just beginning to intuit something. "I just can't lose you, I love you just like a daughter. If you go back to America, I'll have to go, too [Mrs. Hurst wrote]." This is a woman who accepts the fact her husband is eighty-four and she may have a good ten to thirty years to go it alone.

"I just can't understand it [she went on]. It's sheer <u>stupidity</u> on his part. He'll lose you and then he'll realize. When rugby season is over, he'll go crazy. There'll be the long summer and you'll be gone. He wrote to me this week. It was a lovely letter; then he added up all your qualities almost like 25 percent for this, 60 percent for that. Then he left a small reservation: as if you weren't a superwoman already! He said he'd never been in love before like this, never so near the brink, but that he needed time to see. I know he's going to fall for some fairy doll about twenty years old. Or marry one of these English society types. If he can't rise to <u>this</u> . . ."

And here is where it went, somehow, too far. It transgressed that thin line that divides well-wishers from lovers. I began wondering whether my loyalty was to her or to myself. And here is my intuition, awful as it seems. It may be false, I hope it is, but I'd be a fool not to take it into consideration. Mrs. H. realizes my value and likes me as a person but does not think she can compete with me for her son. Therefore, her shadow side is trying to exclude me and get Andy back on "safe ground" with a "fairy doll" who will not compete in the mother's chosen spheres. This is something I can't utter to anyone. Because the last person on earth to suspect anything would be Mrs. H. herself. But she admits that she lives for her sons—and this is indicative.

I felt too close to home while reading a Cheever story in an old *New Yorker* tonight. It was called "An Educated American Woman," and it chronicled an American woman who recited French when climbing into bed with her husband, and who chided him for his lack of imagination.

MARCH 3

Spent a pleasant evening talking to Melva—the thirty-eight-year-old wife of the East African gamekeeper who's staying at no. 21. She is so refreshingly herself. We talked of men—hers, mine—marriage, etc., and I didn't even wince when she said things like "It's a fifty-fifty proposition. Give and take." She was twenty-eight when she married Brian. "I was just having a good time."

What a contrast in talking to her and to Miss Elizabeth Nethery, the newest addition to our staff at USTS. Miss N. doesn't like nicknames. She doesn't like to share flats, she doesn't read too much because she doesn't want to mess up her own style of writing. She has no sense of humor, she doesn't eat lunch. She has analyzed her own handwriting and found herself excitingly neurotic. My handwriting, she said, showed a well-balanced nature (this said condescendingly). She scares me.

MARCH 4

Miss E. N. has it all figured out. She doesn't tell her age. I know it, but she doesn't think I know it. I found out something, though, through casual conversation. (Sometimes I ramble good-naturedly to people and act silly and laugh and make rash statements. Then, thinking they have less to fear, they open up—and open up some more.)

I said, "You can meet lots of men in London, you know." She got her "determined look" and said through her teeth, "Why do you think I wanted to come here?" She said: "I think Mr. Miller tends to choose the people in this office rather carefully. Everyone here seems to be intelligent and with a mind of their own." Then she explained to me how she had seen Englishmen looking at her on the Underground: "First they put their newspaper in front of them; then they hold it up and look at your bottom half; then they lower it and look at your top half." She's a small person with jet-black hair, which she wears in her own inimitable style—sort of an elongated duck cut. Her hips are extremely low slung and her ankles are sturdy. Her eyes are set close together and they are dark and small. Nice teeth and skin, no lines. I can't imagine her kissing a man really wholeheartedly.

Steve rang this morning, first coming through on Mr. Miller's line. I rang him back, thinking: He's at home sculpting and Andy's asked him to ask me to dinner tonight or something.

"Steve?"

"Oh, Gail. Actually . . ."

"How are you?"

"Well, actually, I rang on the spur of the moment. It seems Jay Weed told Mrs. Blackman that I'm pushing things and Mrs. Blackman has written my mother."

"Oh, no!"

"Yes."

"Oh, why don't they leave us alone?"

"I know. That's what Andy and I were saying last night."

"Yes. We can do fine if everyone will just stop pushing."

"Well, but wait. That's not all. You see, last night I wrote her [Jay] a letter in Old English, illustrated with cartoons and imploring her to come down next weekend."

"Did you mail it?"

"Yes, this morning. So she'll get it today. If you see her, maybe you could just tell her I have a silly sense of humor."

"But what did she tell the Blackmans for?"

"I don't know. Just because I asked her to tea and asked her if she was coming down next weekend."

"Well, what did your mother say?"

"Well, actually, I think it's a good thing in a way because it seems to have restored her sense of humor. She said one of her sons was too slow and the other was too fast and ruined things, so she's washing her hands of both of them."

Then we got on the subject of me and Andy and the interferences. The whole conversation was interrupted at various (crucial) stages by vacationers seeking advice on their trips to the U.S.A.

"I'm up in my studio cutting pieces of metal to bits."

"Well, I wish I had something to cut. Can't you send me some metal?"

"Ha, ha."

"You know, I think I'll write about this whole thing."

"Yes, I know. But nobody'd believe it. They'd say it was too improbable. You know, the best thing to do when things get like this is to put on a pair of old boots and go for a seven-mile hike. But I don't suppose girls do that."

"Oh, I'm going to a horror film tonight. Get out of it all completely."

"Listen. Tell you what. I have an evening class. I'll meet you afterward for a drink."

"Do you think that would be a good idea, Steve?"

"No, it probably wouldn't."

"There's no use making things more complicated than they already are."

"No, you're quite right."

"Oh, Steve. Let's you and Andy join a monastery and I'll join a convent."

"Well, let's leave a connecting tunnel just in case."

WHEN I GOT HOME, there was an envelope with a Putney postmark on the hall table.

It was a cartoon, drawn by Andy, entitled "Nightmare." It was a picture of Old Church Street and his minivan turned to a pumpkin.

———

I'VE SAVED THINGS to do this weekend. Pack two boxes. Work out finances. Clean out envelopes. Send in income tax. I'll give Andy the madras bedspread, the towel, the pictures, the glasses. Last night I dreamed I was wearing Andy's greyhound sweater and for some reason (he did something loveable) I said, without thinking, "I love you." Then I thought, Perhaps I shouldn't have said that. Then I said, "Why did you do it?" He replied, "Because I love you."

MARCH 5

Saw Fellini's *8½*, which was one of those pictures within a picture. The theme: Can I justify making a work of art out of important milestones, mistakes, happinesses, and disappointments in my life?

IF I CAN STAY more or less true to myself, then I'll at least be going in a direction; or is it as B. used to say: "Make sure your clipper is the smoothest and best-sailing of the lot, even though there is no direction in the sailing. Devote all your time to steering your ship with no time spared looking back at water over the dam."

MARCH 15

Back again to the notebook. Patterns, everything. A rainy Sunday. Thank God. One thing I love and hate about England is its bad weather. Listening to Bach's *St. Matthew Passion*. "Could ye not watch with me one hour?"[32] I think I'll go again this year.

The dream of Friday night / Saturday morning:

I was returning home from a journey, back to Asheville, on a bicycle. There were several roads, one leading uphill and around the mountain (very similar to the approach of 1000 Sunset Drive) and I decided to try it. The pedaling was difficult and I think, just at the crest, I got off and

---

32. In Matthew 26:40 and in Bach's *St. Matthew Passion*, Jesus addresses his sleeping disciples at the Last Supper, asking, "Could you not watch with me one hour?" He is soon to be betrayed and crucified.

started walking. Then, for some reason, I became afraid and decided not to follow that path. Then I saw a ledge jutting out from the rock.

On the underside of this ledge there were some little houses which I knew were the long-sought-for "upside-down cliff dwellings built by some ancient peoples." I had come on them by accident. Then (prompted by some voice) I knocked on the door of one of these little dwellings and a tiny man emerged and poured water into a slate container. He handed the container to me and I drank the water.

Last night the associate members of the Wasps (those who support the team but were never old Wasps themselves) gave a dance which was an utter flop—wrong lighting, no enthusiasm, middle-aged couples trying to "carry it" by twisting in outdated frocks. I admired Andy's determination to do his part in making it better. He forced me to dance—and he's no great dancer—and he stayed till the band played "God Save the Queen." He has got character.

MARCH 19 · *Thursday, 11:00 p.m.*

Tonight—and five nights out of ten—I feel simply grateful for small favors. Having an evening finally end was a favor.

The Lunn Poly travel promotion evening at the Victory Club.[33] First a deadly dinner with Elizabeth and Doreen at the English-Speaking Union. How nice to come home in a taxi with a splitting headache, take a hot bath, and get into bed.

MAILED DR. MILLENDER's data on Mittenwald today.[34] The genuine pleasure in being able to do something for someone who has done so much for you.

That day when Steve and I had been walking back to Basimore Cottage in the drizzle—Andy running on ahead toward his hot bath after

33. Lunn Poly was a major British travel agency that specialized in Caribbean cruises. Its slogan was "Get away!" It is now part of Thomson Travel Group.

34. Dr. Charles Millender was Gail's childhood physician, who made violins. Gail's half-sister Franchelle Cole later married Dr. Millender's son Charles. Mittenwald, Bavaria, is a resort town in the Alps near the border with Austria; it is the location of a violin museum.

the squash game (he had worried half the day before about how he was going to get his exercise)—and I said to Steve: "I wish I could write like D. H. Lawrence."

I WENT INTO THE new Gill's bookshop on Oxford Street. It was clean and spacious but had lost the very charm that a bit of dust and crowded shelves had given to it. And alas there were no notebooks.

GORDON LANDSBOROUGH, surrounded by four girls, telling us how he had once saved Spike Milligan's life by reading his manuscript when he was at a "low point" and sending him a telegram: "There's not a dry seat in the house." At 11:30 this morning the sun came out; Andy called and said, "How about some lunch?" He knows what he is doing, he calls the plays. "How about the Crown?" He knows what he is going to do and he remembers things. "You made your speech last night." "How did you remember?" "I always remember things that interest me." Sometimes he doesn't appreciate my sarcasm. I must stop it. It's just nervousness. I want to write over Easter. Now that this notebook is ending, I want a flourish.

FOR NOW, JUST LIVING is enough. At this period, I am concerned mainly with looking good for Andy and his rugby team and the Lancaster Gate team he's captain of on Sunday. He even asked his instructor if he could bring along "attachments." Passing a Danish restaurant whose window featured two porcelain figures making love, I said: "That's what I feel like doing now." He said: "Wouldn't you feel uncomfortable against that cold porcelain?"

MARCH 23

Saturday: rugby in the rain; Sunday: rugby in the rain. Each day had a charm of its own. Perhaps Sunday was one of our best days. Down to Guildford on the coach, intermittent rain and sun, patches of country-side, suburban towns (ugly) . . . the rustic clubhouse. The ladies' room with chintz curtains, mirrors; the Saracen captain's girlfriend, Jenny. "I'd like you to meet Jenny," he said, helping her out of the car. I saw immediately that she was pretty. She had all the best that England can put into its girls and none of the worst—poised, discreet, ladylike but warm, curious, jovial. She looked a little bit like Stuart P. and this added to the fascination. I asked her where she worked and she said, "Oh, I'm a secretary for the British gov't." Finally I found out that her working address is 10 Downing Street. She told of Kennedy last summer at [Prime Minister Harold] Macmillan's country home, coming across the lawn to her and saying: "Oh, you're the secretary. I've heard a lot about you." And the little boys in red mackintoshes lining the drive, saluting him in the rain—how he got out of the car and spoke to each of them.

Andy was a good captain, although it annoyed me the way he kept yelling, "Well done, Bill!" "Come on boys, we've got to go through! We're going through!" "Feet! Feet!" But he enjoyed it—made two tries and won the game. Afterward was a tea on long picnic-type tables and then drinking in the bar for four hours till the poor bus driver put his foot down. I sat on a beer keg and listened and was spoken to, on and off, when rugby wasn't being discussed. But I honestly didn't mind. A Welshman with blue eyes said: "Are you sure you aren't bored? Are you sure you aren't thinking, 'Ah, I've wasted a whole Sunday when I could have had Andy to myself'?" "You know women," I said. "That's the difference between public and state schools," he said. The Welsh contingent was singing, to the tune of "Onward Christian Soldiers," "Lloyd George knew my father; Father knew Lloyd George."

MUSIC: "ISN'T IT ROMANTIC" from the *Black Satin* album, popular the summer of Marty and Lakeside Inn. I have so many lives. And at a quiet time here in bed listening to airplanes, I can think, right before dropping off to sleep, about Copenhagen.

The Missing Journal

Gail Writes About the Journal for the Period

MARCH 24, 1964, TO JANUARY 30, 1965

———

This volume of *The Making of a Writer* has opened with what had been my twelfth journal book since I started my adventures as a writer. As presented here in Part 1 and Part 2, the journal book covers the period July 23, 1963, to March 23, 1964. In Part 3 my journals pick up again, covering late January to March 18, 1965, when I filled in the blank pages of that twelfth book; then in Part 4 they jump to a fourteenth journal book for the period from March 20, 1965, to February 12, 1966.

Unlike the famous missing floor in hotels, there really *was* a journal 13, but I left it behind with the Wests in a box with some clothes until I could settle into my new rented flat on Beaufort Street in Chelsea. Why did I never retrieve the box? I was within walking distance of it and often took walks after work. Beaufort Street to Oakley Gardens was less than a ten-minute stroll. The clothes must have been dispensable. But the journal covering the period from late March of 1964 to January of 1965—why was it dispensable? Looking back and guessing, some forty years later, I think I may have been less than straightforward with my journal during the months Andy and I were engaged. I suspect I omitted many troubling and rebellious thoughts and wrote what I thought I ought to be thinking. The part of me I left out was undoubtedly the part that knew all along I was not going to make that marriage.

The Wests had moved us into the Oakley Gardens house in the late spring of 1964. It was the most grand and spacious house yet. I was newly engaged to Andy Hurst. We planned to marry the following spring. There were some things to be worked out, the foremost one being the blot of my divorce, since we wanted an Anglican church wedding. Meanwhile, we basked in the prospect of a long engagement. The courtship intrigues were over and we could relax and enjoy the long summer days.

At Oakley Gardens, I was given the choice downstairs room overlooking a walled garden on the condition that I share the window with the Wests' elegant, moody Siamese cat, Enrico. Enrico was to be allowed to go in and out of the window whenever he scratched, and I was to provide door-opening services to and from my room, as well. Enrico and I coexisted through the long summer and autumn and into the early winter of 1964. We outlasted my engagement to Andy.

I would bet that if the missing journal 13 ever comes to light, the most honest and readable entries will be about the love-hate power struggle between Enrico and me.

PORTRAIT OF A WOMAN

Beaufort Street, London

JANUARY 31, 1965, TO MARCH 18, 1965

In limbo between the end of a romance and open prospects—and between an increasingly routine job and an urge to go home— Gail produces much writing in this journal part. It begins with one accomplished story ("A Dollar's Worth of Hygge") and ends with another ("The Illumined Moment, and Consequences"). The first story will eventually form part of "A Cultural Exchange" (published in Mr. Bedford and the Muses*); the latter will play a big role in Gail's career, gaining her entrance to the Iowa Writers' Workshop in 1966, and publication in the* North American Review *(under the title "An Intermediate Stop").*

A fiction-writing class at the City Literary Institute spurred Gail's productivity. It created the necessity to examine and employ a backlog of story drafts and ideas, and to try new ones.

Gail also began to develop a way of diagramming stories—not as plot outlines, but as webs of associations. Henry James's novel The Portrait of a Lady *becomes a key influence. Not only does it relate to a big theme in literature at the time—the independent woman out on her own—it displays James's way of creating an architecture of interactions, and it presents a male protagonist (Gilbert Osmond), whose absence of heart Gail wants to counter with a more redeemable character—a man whose deep secrets prevent him from acting with heartfulness.*

JANUARY 31, 1965

It seems almost like an admission of failure to begin these notebooks again. The purpose is even more odious. Then let it be another purpose.[1]

---

1. During the period of the missing journal, March 24, 1964, to late January 1965, Gail had become engaged to Andy Hurst and had broken her engagement with him. A fight with his mother at their house had precipitated the break, which came as a relief to both Gail and Andy. They laughed about it over an expensive dinner on the way back to London. Andy

—

I HAVE JUST READ a condensed novel called *Nina Upstairs*, published in *McCall's* magazine—another story of a girl in N.Y.C., only written more honestly than usual. It made me wonder, once more, what was stopping me from writing such a story: say, about girls in London—three. Perhaps the decision outlined so well by Father Webbe can be my outcome.[2] This, too, must be an honest story and not fall into any prescribed, clichéd patterns. I'll start with "Roxanne."[3] The form is what leaves me blank.

IT IS SUNDAY, the last one in January, and I have spent another weekend alone. Any ordinary stranger reading that first sentence would assume this solitude was far from intentional. The stranger would be wrong. What amazes me, and somehow compensates, is the change I have noticed in myself. I am not so compulsive anymore.

And yet I enjoy a little bit of suspense. This Swiss man who followed me from the supermarket—the novelty of his approach has worn off. I know, having seen him again, that he is one of these worldly, competent human beings without a trace of warmth or compassion. Before, I would have agonized: What was he thinking about me? What was he doing on Sunday? So, here I sit, not quite sure of what comes next.

admitted that he had made "a list of attributes he'd ideally like in a wife," Gail relates in *Heart: A Natural History of the Heart-Filled Life* (Morrow, 2001). "Then," she writes, "he ranked me on each and averaged out the sum, on a scale of one to ten." Gail got an 8 overall. "Eight's no good," Gail had told him, "especially at the *beginning*."

2. Gail had found Gale D. Webbe's book *The Night and Nothing* while plundering the philosophy and religion shelves in Hatchards Bookshop during a lunch hour. "It was a moment of pure serendipity," Gail says. Her former mentor Father Webbe's chapter "Decisions" opens: "Between our jumping out of bed in the morning and our falling back into it at night there are, especially in a high-pressure culture, literally hundreds of additional decisions we must make." Webbe advises making one's responsibilities a ritual, freeing up God's energy for one's soul's progress. The crux of this chapter, which Gail took to heart, was that one's essential satisfactions proceed from knowing one's life is being constructed on the lines of a sound story. "It must have a pattern, a beginning, a middle, and an end. It must, in short, have meaning—a too-rare overtone only produced when, as it were, the fingers of free will move across the strings of destiny."

3. "Roxanne" is Gail's unpublished short novel based on her friend Lorraine. See August 29, 1963, entry.

—

CHURCHILL'S FUNERAL yesterday[4] and I got out of a feverish bed to walk two miles in the bitter wind to look down from a second-floor window [of Andy's office] on the small coffin (it seemed too small to hold such a big man). I am sure people all over London have colds tonight as a result of queuing for hours for the lying-in-state. Why? I like Andy's answer: It was not so much that he was the greatest man of this century, [though] it was that for a start. It was that it gave people justification for trying to contact a higher life. Standing for hours in the rain so that they would pass a coffin and pay their respects was their religious experience.

STORIES OF IMPOSSIBLE LOVE:

> The Girl with Green Eyes[5]—*young, naive girl with older, married writer man.*
> Nina Upstairs—*young, intelligent working girl with older married man, his wife insane.*
> The L-Shaped Room[6]—*unmarried pregnant girl and tenants of boardinghouse.*

Why doesn't the man get hurt for a change?

SAD TALES BORDERING ON THE MAN GETTING HURT:

> *Marty—there is always something terribly sad about a father figure.*[7]

4. Winston Churchill died on Sunday, January 24, 1965, following a stroke he'd suffered fifteen days earlier. He lay in state in Westminster Abbey for a few days, the first person since William Gladstone to do so, and more than three hundred thousand people viewed his coffin.

5. *The Girl with Green Eyes*, by Edna O'Brien, included as the second novel in O'Brien's *The Country Girls Trilogy* in 1964, had originally been published in 1962 as *The Lonely Girl.* It portrays a girl who falls in love with a sophisticated, married man in Dublin, and experiences some fulfillment before the inevitable disillusionment.

6. *The L-Shaped Room*, published in 1960, was Lynn Reid Banks's debut novel. It follows a young career woman who leaves home upon becoming pregnant and does not return until her pregnancy and sense of self are resolved.

7. Marty, an older man, had been Gail's nightclub-owning friend in Miami.

Wuthering Heights—*romanticized type of man, the kind that*
really kills me.
The sea captain—Cliff.[8]

Or: As far as sex goes, it's a natural joy for him, but he's not the planned seducer. He must be able to surprise himself. He's a self-sufficient man with inner resources who takes lonely walks and has a secret—an insane wife or . . .

Look how Gilbert Osmond attracted Isabel.[9]

How about an Englishman with a little boy? An Englishman is married to an American woman who has gone back to the U.S.A., leaving him with a little boy, Marcus. He advertises for an au pair. The advertisement reads: "Wanted: educated girl, over 25, to care for young boy of 4 during the day. Some light housework, typing skills preferred."

FEBRUARY 13

Another Saturday night almost gone. All day I have been battered down by emotion and nostalgia. The thing is: Describe it, let it wash over you, understand it. One form it has taken is a massive guilt spree.

This fall when I was home, saying to Franchelle "Can't you roll your own hair?" when what she wanted was to be with me.

When Wiggles was alive, how I shut the door to my room and wouldn't let him in. I wanted everything pure, idealized, no dogs messing it up with their happiness.

Although it was not entirely my fault, the thing with Charles Cleveland.[10] But I could have sent him a Christmas card.

This Ivory Tower period. I sit up here weekend after weekend.[11] Yet it isn't bad. I have a feeling I'll be in a new stage soon.

---

8. Gail had dated Cliff when she was a reporter in Miami. The first novel she worked on upon embarking for Europe in 1961 involved his character.

9. In Henry James's *The Portrait of a Lady,* Isabel Archer is won over by the presentation of Osmond as a man of ultimate refinement and good taste, something to which she aspires.

10. Charles Cleveland is a cousin by marriage. A Miami attorney, he got Gail her divorce from Douglas Kennedy and sent a token bill to Gail's stepfather, who refused to pay it.

11. Shortly before the breakup with Andy, Gail had moved to an upstairs flat by herself on Beaufort Street.

FEBRUARY 16

I must stop crapping around, as Lorraine so elegantly puts it, and make up my mind and stay or go.[12] Now is the right time. I have to understand who I am and not wish for the achievements or attractions of others.

THE CINEMA ON Saturday night. Everybody comes expecting something. How funny it would look to an outsider—a building with colored lights and large pictures on its walls. People come out of the night to queue in its brightly lighted foyer, pay money to the girl in the stall, arm themselves with sweets, and enter with hushed expectancy.

For two hours, surrounded by the soft darkness, fitted in safely among others, lifted or let down with the music, they live with figures in a square of light. For two hours, they have purchased peace, vicarious love, and adventure. And then the lights go on, the candy wrappers are on the floor, you look your neighbor in the face and look away. Everybody scrambles toward the exits before they get caught by "God Save the Queen."[13]

THIS MORNING, a woman fell off the bus, was lying there, legs spread apart, old-fashioned shoes. The bus conductor had covered her with his coat. They waited for the ambulance. Other buses passed. Faces stared at the empty bus, the still figure on the street, covered by a conductor's coat.

FEBRUARY 21 · *Saturday*

All along, I've been storing up impressions for that time when I'd be home. I must have known all along I wouldn't stay.

---

12. Gail is thinking of returning to the United States.

13. The British national anthem was played at the end of every performance, and if you didn't get out quickly enough, you'd have to stand for the duration of the anthem.

"Yuh musta been away." Tom Wolfe suddenly intrudes.[14]

Driving along down Buckingham Road with Briggsie,[15] I see the English policeman and think: I will miss this—the calm courtesy, the clean, pressed look. But I can't stay here just for the policemen. Officer Banks, about twenty-five or twenty-six, comes into the office to get any unusual stamps. "We have to wear our topcoats until March 30. Oh, we can wear them on April 1, if it's cold, but what I mean is, if it's a hundred degrees on January third, we must wear our topcoats." On handling lunatics and schizophrenics: "You have to act interested in a disinterested way. Agree with them, while walking them to the door." He stands there in his neat blue. The tall hat with patent leather strap cutting into his firm chin. (I don't think they hire them unless they've got good chins.) He has a nice face. Direct eyes. Straight nose. Always a slight smile. "What would you look like without your hat?" I ask. "Short," he replies, good-naturedly.

FEBRUARY 22 · *Sunday night*

Fifteen minutes ago, I was in hysterics, sobbing on Andy's Harris tweed shoulder, and now I am sitting calmly in bed, toes on hot water bottle, face cleaned, hair done up for tomorrow. The storm has passed. Why did I put on that performance? It started off simply enough, he getting lecherous. Then I began on "it"[16] again. And yet, even yesterday I had made up my mind not to see him anymore. I had this thought: I was weeping for a concept of Andy.

"It was like you were two people," said Andy. Was I?

Tomorrow night: Do creative writing assignment.[17]

---

14. The quote is from Thomas Wolfe's short story "Only the Dead Know Brooklyn," a landmark work in the representation of colloquial, and at times vulgar, language. It was published in *The New Yorker* on June 15, 1935, and in the collection of Wolfe's stories *From Death to Morning* (1935). Years later, Robert Starer, Gail's life partner, set the story to music for a premiere at Brooklyn College, where he served on the faculty from 1963 to 1991.

15. "Briggsie" is Robert Briggs, assistant director of the USTS in London.

16. "It" is the polarizing subject, Gail's fight with Andy's mother.

17. Gail had begun taking a fiction-writing class at the City Literary Institute in High Holborn.

FEBRUARY 23

You cry for the fading shape of love.

LATEST CHIMERA: someone to catch all my longings and fantasies—
Officer Banks, the calm, cool, young, clean policeman, who is so very
self-contained.

Gail: "Why didn't you come in earlier today?"

"Because I had things to do."

"What?"

"Things to do."

He is his own man, he has his code, he shines by it. His code is like
a competitor's, an opponent's. All day I waited to see him stroll up Vigo
Street. [The bobbies] came singly, they came in twos—little ones, tall
ones, slumpy ones. The ones of his height had wedges of dark hair peer-
ing out behind their tall hats. His is light. Most of his face is under his
hat, but he has square white teeth, an amused look. Yet I've never seen
him laugh. I wore my glasses all day long so I could see out the window,
neglected to stuff my envelopes. It got dark, but he never passed.

IDEA FOR A story sometime.

The Photographer

—

Told by a photographer. A girl comes in, wants engagement pictures.[18] He takes photos of her naturally, in a blouse; thinks she's
lovely that way. But her fiancé and [his] family don't like them.
She's terribly apologetic to the photographer. He arranges another sitting. Tells her to have her hair done up fancy. Wear a
ball gown. He shoots some "fashion pictures," which don't look

18. Gail had gone to a well-known photographer, Lotte Meitner-Graf, on Bond Street for
her engagement pictures. The Hursts didn't like the resulting prints, but Gail bought them
anyway. For the purposes of her story, Gail makes the photographer male.

like her; he is violating his artistic principles, but can't stand to see her unhappy. She writes a note saying her fiancé was thrilled with them. Orders several. Photographer is suddenly unreasonably concerned for her, tries to put her out of his mind. Then, curiosity and "something else" make him get her number out of the file and call her. He says the prints are ready, but he is leaving town and wants to bring them around. She sounds strange but agrees. "Yes, I might as well still have them." He takes them around to her and then goes off on his holiday. (He has blown up one of the naturals of her and has it in his studio.) When he gets back, she visits him. She has broken off the engagement, just wanted to tell him he was right. She sees her photograph in his studio and is moved. Now, we've got to arrange for a meeting or a suggestion, something to show he is right for her. (He already knows she's for him.) She feels she can talk to him. Perhaps she says: "Listen . . ."

FEBRUARY 23

Peter Perry[19]: "You can't change your personality. You may change facets, but beware: Those facets may affect other facets."

Irene Slade[20] was enthusiastic and lovely and I see why I dreamed about her. I also see that I can learn from her and use her as a sounding board, but that she is not God Writer and cannot go all the way for me.

I WALK DOWN Saville Row, hoping to run into Officer Banks. The thing is: I enjoy these illusions, I enjoy agonizing over my policemen and sea captains and I accept the disillusionment before it comes. I get in. Andy calls. We have *nothing* in common. It is a trial even to make conversation.

19. Perry had become Gail's Sunday walking companion.

20. Irene Slade, a BBC culture commentator, was Gail's fiction-writing teacher at the City Literary Institute.

FEBRUARY 26

Next Tuesday's assignment for Irene Slade: "The Mask." This is a subject that attracts everyone. I think I'll write a monologue. A man, after a masked ball—the Mardi Gras—has moved to his room and decided not to leave until he discovers who he is.

MARCH 2

Miss Slade had chickenpox, so our class was taught by a high-powered individual named Geoffrey Davis who writes TV scripts. I liked his method of teaching. As Peter Perry says: It *was* a script. He treats writing more as a highly skilled *craft*, with definite approaches, with definable methods. He brings in the medium of films and TV in this approach (selection of objects in a description; vantage point; etc.). I may try to enroll for his spring term class.

Sunday. Peter Perry took me for a walk—from Fleet Street to St. Paul's to the East End docks to Bermondsey, then walking all the way back to Lyons Corner House at Charing Cross Station. Here, over eggs and sausages, he told me the story of Cyrano de Bergerac and I cried. Then we taxied to the Tate. Afterward, we walked back to Beaufort Street in the waning light. Dark blue sky. Lights of double-decker buses, the smell of the river—London, which I perhaps love better than I realize. I was expecting it to yield up too many dividends per moment, that's why.

MET OFFICER BANKS at the corner of Old Burlington and the back entrance of the police station. What astounded me was that he was much more talkative—and even cocky—than I imagined. He talks to men more easily than to women. Witness the difference between his conversation with me and with Alan Wooley, who happened to be in our office and was a former policeman himself.

Here is Officer Banks's conversation with me:

"You look cold," he says.

"I am."

"Do you have a cold?"

"Yes, I have everything." Then I add nervously: "Have you been walking around in this cold?"

"I don't mind it. Now I've got to be on traffic for the next hour at Piccadilly Circus."

"Oh, look, there's that fascinating crane driver way up there. Have you ever wanted to be a crane driver, Officer Banks?" Savoring this, calling him by name at last!

"No, I like the ground better myself."

Then he was off about the weather: "It was down to forty," etc. But what struck me was the casual, sort of swaggering way he talked. He has a sort of inoffensive cockney accent—or perhaps North or West Country. He seems pretty satisfied with himself. He has a bemused look.

Then I said what I'd planned about Elizabeth[21] and my wanting him to take us to the wharves one day. He said, "Oh, they're not so dangerous, really." But I quickly went on until he said, "We'll see what we can do," or something.

Back in the office (I went in dragging him like a prize cabbage), Alan Wooley, seeing me followed by a policeman, said: "I knew it would happen sooner or later."

And Officer Banks chatted quite amiably with everyone, took out his light brown wallet and swept my stamps in, saying, "Thank you very much . . . Gail," hesitating over the use of my name. Then he commented on various things, how lazy we were—"I come in once a week and ask them questions just to keep them in practice"—and said to me, "See you anon."

"Don't forget the wharves."

And he said, "No, I won't."

What I can't get down is his style, damn it. His walk, for instance, swinging a bit, a slight plunge forward, a bit of head motion, as if he's on his way and nothing will stop him—yet still the calm, bemused look

21. Elizabeth Nethery, Gail's colleague at the USTS.

on his face. The face itself is strong, good chin, sort of Roman or Jewish nose, blue or gray eyes, different tones in his skin, slightly sallow, not all peachy-cheeked like some.

Then he stood and talked to Alan and the level rose. I couldn't hear it all, but they were talking about "the work" and I thought he was conscious of me because I sat and watched, and several times he blushed. Some I learned from listening, the rest from Alan afterward. He's been in six years, plans to make a career of it, not CID [Criminal Investigations Department] or anything else, but go up in the Metropolitan Police Force. Says the turnover is great because so many want to get married, live in country. Therefore, we assume he doesn't plan to marry soon. Alan says he'll go places. Also there is a slight gap between his front teeth.

MARCH 3

Andy in his smart new coat—looked the real Londoner. Reminded me of Doug in Miami when he came to sign the divorce papers; he was wearing a new suit.

The snow this morning. Quiet all around. I went to Welbeck Street for my mole killings. Lying on the table, I looked at the snow, some birds, bare twigs of trees. Miss Shepherd, neat in white nurse's kerchief and uniform, attended to my face with the electric needle—platinum-tipped, 8 shillings per needle—and described her banana boat trip to the Cameroons. At 11:00, I am finished and take another taxi to the office. Elizabeth is in raptures over the snow. Also, she tells me, Officer Banks has already passed. "I think he looked in, but didn't stop." I go upstairs and comb my hair, come back, get settled behind the front desk, for once not looking out of the window. "Here he comes," says Elizabeth. I look up and there comes my policeman, cutting across the street, looking at us. I know he is coming in. He has snow on his shoulders and hat; he brushes it as he comes in and it's a long stay this time.

"Come in and melt," I say.

"That's a good idea." He stands before us, removes his gloves. On the fourth finger of his hand is a signet ring with some initials. Three. Which three? Something. Something Banks. What is his first name? I like not knowing it.

He stands by the desk and, at first, it is Elizabeth and I together, just as before. We usually ask him questions. Today he tells us he has been on duty since 5:00 a.m. The snow started sometime around 4:00. "Did you see it start?" I ask. "No." I picture him still asleep in his bed. Does he wear pajamas? Yes, in this country, only a jackass wouldn't.

Then I told him about seeing the policeman helping the stalled driver in Mayfair. A curly head bent over the hood. A tall blue hat on the top of the hood. I told it in mock dramatic eulogy. He laughed. I asked him about the police force. How old did one have to be to join? What did they have to do? Crawl under barbed wire fences? Again he laughed. He trained in Hendon, he said.

Then Dick Prescott enters and the conversation becomes more complicated. There are the four of us, then lapses of Elizabeth and Dick, me and Officer Banks. "Where are you from—London?" I ask. "I was born in Hong Kong," he says. Then Dick says, "You were born *where?*" "After that I lived in Australia. Now my parents live in Maidstone, Kent." None of this was volunteered. I squeezed him like a stubborn tube of toothpaste. Dick pipes in: "You're getting the third degree." "I know, it's always like this when I come in," says our good policeman.

Then I am saying how slowly things get done in England. "Someone asks you to dinner a week from next Thursday. You might be dead by then." Officer Banks comments on how people come back from the States and say how in a hurry everyone is. He makes some clever logical remark about "if you don't die before next Thursday week." Then Dick says to me: "When are you going to have that dinner party you promised?" Officer Banks answers for me: "Next Thursday week." I explain about my flat. "I thought I was going to leave, then decided not to," etc.

Then, somehow, it's only Officer Banks and myself again.

"Do you live in Earls Court?" he asked. "You mentioned it a while ago." (I had asked him if he ever did his beat as far as Earls Court.)

"No, Chelsea. Why, don't you like it? Your nose turned down."

"It couldn't have, it's not that long."

"Yes, I like Chelsea," I went on, "because it's a little different from the ordinary. A bit like the country. And I'm near the river."

"I would say somewhere near Sloane Square. To the left of the King's Road?"

"No, farther down."

"By the—what's the name of the hospital where the Chelsea pensioners live?"

"Royal Hospital. No, farther down, Beaufort Street. It's near Battersea Bridge."

"Ah, past the Essoldo Cinema, turn left and go toward the bridge."

"Yes. I live in an ugly block of flats, all alike so that if you've had a drink . . ."

". . . you can never find your own."

"Yes, exactly! I live on the top floor and on a clear day, and with my glasses, I can see Big Ben. To my left is the river but I have to look out the window and it's too sooty."

"You turn and do—this—and there's the river."

"Yes. Precisely. And across the street there's the Convent of St. Thomas More. The bells keep ringing every hour so the nuns can go to chapel."

"Oh—*char*ming. So you don't need an alarm clock."

"No." I am temporarily quieted by his quick patter, the good-natured but alert answers.

"Then how do you get to work?"

"The 19, 22, or 11 bus. The 19, usually."

"Oh."

I asked him why he always walked alone when most of the bobbies walked in pairs.

"I don't particularly like walking with somebody else. Sure, the time passes quickly, but you aren't aware of what's going on."

We elucidated at some length on the advantages of aloneness on a beat. I said, "I knew you were different."

"Thank you," he said, snappily, in a tone that was meant to make light of the compliment; but still he took it in.

Then the phone rang. I had to tell a woman what to wear in San Francisco. I said first [to Officer Banks], "I have a stamp for you," to keep him from leaving. While I was on the phone, Elizabeth asked him why Trafalgar Square was dark last night. When I hung up, they were talking about Nelson's birthday.

"Whose birthday?" I asked.

"Mine," said Officer Banks. "What are you going to give me?"—saying this with a meaningful stare.

"I've already given you two stamps," I said.

Then, why didn't I stop? On I went. "But today is also *my* birthday and you can take me to see the wharves as my present. Ah, please, Officer Banks. We've been giving you stamps for an entire year . . ."

"Do American women play on feelings the way Englishwomen do?" said Officer Banks to Dick.

"These two do. Watch 'em. They're clever."

Then Officer Banks addressed himself exclusively to me. "So you're tired of that Chelsea flat and you want to exchange it for a pub in the East End?" He looked me dead in the eye.

I looked back. "Yes."

"*I'll* come for a drink with you in a pub sometime and tell you about these two," said Dick Prescott.

"No!" I cried. "Then he'll never take us!"

Laughter.

Exit Officer Banks, smiling. He crosses the street. The snow covers his shoulders and hat once more. He has a brother of twelve who is mad over trains. But so is he—and stamps. ·

MARCH 8

How can you describe the sound of a taxi? Does it vibrate? Yes, a little. But it also clicks. The clicks gain speed and become a purr.

A spring day—and evening. Elizabeth, Pauline,[22] and I sit outdoors at a table at the Sands. Bond Street is our study tonight. My feet are cold,

22. Pauline McEvoy was Bob Briggs's secretary at USTS.

but it is too pleasant to think of leaving. Pauline tells about her automo-
bile accident Saturday night. Elizabeth: "But wasn't Robert *looking*
where he was going? Had you *said* something to him . . . ?"

The policeman passes, doing his steady beat-walk. Clump. Clump.
Round-toed shiny black shoes today. They all wear a new silver badge
and a headpiece on their helmets. Clump, clump. In the spring dusk of
my fourth March in London.

MARCH 12

I had a choice between company on the weekend and lying to myself; or
being alone. All I had to do was to respond to Andy.

I feel somehow if I can really master this weekend, then I won't be
so afraid.

Andy is sleeping with a secretary in his law firm. She is small, dark,
with very blue eyes, drives an MG. "Likes classical music and lives in the
country." The way Andy "confessed"—like a proud boy: "*Now* do you
think I'm so holy?"

STEVE HAS TAKEN Sylvia home for the weekend.[23]

WELL, IT'S OVER. In my card file along with "Despair."

MARCH 13 · *Saturday*

During the night I had dreamed of a first-class rejection by Officer
Banks. As a symbol, he embodies London. He is a protector of the status
quo. He gives first aid to fainting women, wears a silver badge on his tall
blue helmet. And the *real* Officer Banks offers tempting morsels for
speculation.

My dream: I am proposing an outing to Officer Banks. He is politely
declining. I press it. Finally he agrees. Then he adds: "You'd better know
I plan to be married next year." He brings his fiancée. I write to Lor-

---

23. Gail had introduced Sylvia—Robin Challis's on-and-off girlfriend—to Steve and Andy
Hurst.

raine and ask her advice. She replies: "It's very clear he does not love you. Get out now if you don't want to be hurt really badly."

I woke up feeling as if it had really happened. The sun was shining. I dressed, put on my new Portuguese handmade walking shoes, and went to town—to the bank in my slacks and sunglasses, hoping at every traffic crossing to see you-know-who. Then to USTS. Doreen is coping gallantly as usual. I offer assistance, and then leave, silently.

"Where's Gail?"

"I don't know, she was just here."

I walk out of my way through Mayfair. Three policemen stand outside the American Embassy. I am sure they are laughing at me. Then through Hyde Park, past the spot where Andy had proposed. I hurry toward a policeman. He quickly crosses the road. I am sure he is evading me. There is probably a notice about me in the station house: "Beware, female huntress, especially keen on policemen."

MARCH 14

Today was easier. Festival Hall tonight—the twenty-seven-year-old Japanese conductor, like a black elf, conducting Berlioz's *Fantastique*.[24] Then, later, I stand by the window of my flat. "Mondo Cane" on the radio. I feel joyous. I open the window and breathe London. The [Beaufort Street] traffic swishes below. It rained and the streets are wet. I reread the bishop of Woolwich's article on a god-less religion.[25] Several things become clear to me. I also read Jung's *Modern Man in Search of a Soul* and this helped. If I am a modern, not a phony, then I cannot take refuge in the old ways.

24. On March 14, 1965, Seiji Ozawa led the London Symphony Orchestra in a performance of *Symphonie Fantastique* in Royal Festival Hall. Also on the program were Beethoven's Symphony no. 1 and, with Peter Serkin, pianist, Mozart's Piano Concerto in F.

25. John A. T. Robinson, the bishop of Woolwich, had written an article in the London *Times* that related to his book *Honest to God* (1963), which Gail had read at the time of its publication. The book popularized the writings of Dietrich Bonhoeffer, Rudolph Bultmann, and Paul Tillich. With a first printing of three thousand copies, it created a furor with its unmaking of orthodoxy in the light of modern science; it went on to sell more than a million copies.

MARCH 16

Chink was in town and wanted to have lunch.[26] It was one of those color-less, harsh, glarey days that have come to characterize London for me. We went to [Edward Albee's play] *The Goat.* Laughed a lot. It takes a bit of getting used to a new conversational pattern. Whereas Andy would take a subject and follow it through, usually working it to death, Chink surprises with his rapid transitions. "I was listening to some Bach last night . . . A real afternoon ahead of me today . . . ," etc. His laugh is good, nothing compulsive or hysterical about it, just real.

I said, "Did you read the article about the bishop of Woolwich in *The Sunday Times?*" He said, as one who has waited for an opening, "No. What are you doing tonight? I'll come over and read it."

We argued about Chagall. He: "I don't like him. He doesn't move me." I got exasperated and went on about how "it's a lonely world," you couldn't communicate with anyone, etc. He saw some of what I meant, but not all: "In other words [he said], my world is the world of facts, that's what I've been trained for; yours is the world of imagination. You have to decide what you think and then fight for it. But you're not sure."

He seems to be an honorable person with a code. He doesn't tell things. For instance, he said it was interesting the way he met his boss and the way he went to work for him. I said: "Tell me." He said: "Not yet. When I know you better, maybe."

TONIGHT-CLASS. I read my place description. My endings are weak. But on [Miss Slade's] written criticism was one sentence which will keep me in England: "If you can follow criticism like this, you will do well as a writer."

After class, the psychiatrist approached me.[27] It turns out he lives across the street from me! I asked him and his girl around for coffee

26. "Chink" was a young man whom Gail had just met. He sold bellows.

27. The psychiatrist was Dr. Ian Marshall, an Englishman who was taking Irene Slade's class along with Gail.

Sunday. He pushed it. I don't know if they are engaged or what. It doesn't matter. At last we'll have some good conversation in this flat. Maybe Peter Perry will come, too—

MARCH 18

I am learning what it is to create something meaningful out of my own experiences. Interesting how far I've come with the writing. Learning to make every word count.

Heavy head. I wrote a fifteen-hundred-word story tonight.[28]

28. The story was "The Illumined Moment, and Consequences," about an English vicar who sees God in the mist, writes a book about it, and almost loses his soul on a book tour. It was the story that got Godwin into the Iowa Writers' Workshop in 1966, and was the first story of hers accepted for publication. It appeared in the *North American Review* under the title "An Intermediate Stop" and was republished in *Dream Children* under that title. Gail now feels that her original title was the true one.

Part four

ACCOMMODATING
LUCIFER

Beaufort Street, London

MARCH 20, 1965, TO FEBRUARY 12, 1966

Approaching her third year at the London office of the U.S. Travel Service, Gail sat at her familiar desk, poised behind a window that allowed her to view the city's men-on-the-move, and them, her. Many of her female colleagues had made the transition to other stations in life: marriage, mostly; marriage and divorce, in one case.

Yet Gail continued to follow her course: holding on to a secure job while pursuing her calling as a writer. Security, she knew, could also be gained through a good husband. If a match was right, a married woman could attain more independence than an unmarried one. Among the men-on-the-move, there was a class that appeared reliably at home in their environment: policemen.

MARCH 20, 1965

As I sit in the fishbowl in front of a multicolored map (for which duty I get paid $50 every two weeks), another day begins. Like others, it is dominated and colored by men. Some pass the window and look in. Others come in and ask for travel advice.

There is one who does not pass by. This is the one I look for.

Every five or ten minutes, a policeman walks past—going from the police station to Regent Street, or back. Many walk in twos. The more interesting ones walk alone.

For the last month, I have begun policeman watching as a result of an imaginary affair with one of the policemen who walk alone. He comes in every other week to see if I have any interesting stamps for him. It gives me added interest in this tedious, well-paid job: watching the window for Officer Banks to pass.

I have to wear my glasses for this purpose because I am nearsighted.

When I am wearing them, distant things become smaller and farther away, but much keener. Today, a rainy March day, I feel he is not going to pass. There is the sharp-featured one, the best-looking of all those on the W1 beat. Then, the older one with the ginger mustache. Then, two young peach-cheeked ones. But no Officer Banks.

Jack T. Malone, the hobo, comes in, gesturing as he approaches the desk, keeping one eye peeled for my boss, the police, and all those authorities he fears and hates.

Jack never asks for money. All he wants is a few words' exchange. Jack has been coming in for two and a half years. He makes his living appearing on radio programs and telling what it's like to be a hobo. He is only forty-two but has heavy lines on his face. He has slept in boxcars and outside in freezing weather for about twenty years. He is fighting the system. Whenever I suggest he get a job, he always has a good excuse. Nobody will hire him. They don't like his face. He does have an up-to-no-good face. He asks me if I listened to him on the BBC Light Programme last Saturday. I did. Then Jack leaves, asking first, "Do you want anything?" In the past, he used to bring me coffee. Sometimes he would refuse to be paid for it. The day continues.

Fred Cedarberg, a tall, forty-year-old Canadian, bursts in. He has just sold his book, "Mushrooms and Men," to Michael Joseph![1] He is highly nervous and keeps pacing the office, patting his short gray crew cut, saying, "Jesus Christ! Wait'll all these bastards back home hear!" He said he knew it would be all right this morning because he woke in his fifth-floor hotel room to the tune of "I'm Looking Over a Four-Leaf Clover," played by the Happy Wanderers street musicians [a formally dressed group that featured an accordionist]. Standing in the open window in his shorts, he had thrown 5 shillings into the street below. Then Fred leaves. I go back to policeman watching.

Around the corner wheels Sandy, a Pan Am PRO [public relations officer] from down the street. He sports a bunch of colors, tan from his holiday in Rio, a madras tie, and varicolored shirt, suit, and coat. Some-

---

1. Michael Joseph was a British publisher of scholarly books, including, in 1966, the first bound reproductions of Audubon prints in color. "Mushrooms and Men" was never published.

thing about his pace appeals to me as he hustles by. I greet him through the window with outstretched arms. I know he will come in now. He does, carrying a bundle of tear sheets about Miss Disneyland.[2] He stands by the desk. I talk shop with him, but the electricity has already started. "Wait till I run an errand and I'll take you for a drink."

He comes back twenty minutes later and we wait for Doreen to come and relieve me in my fishbowl. She does not watch for policemen, but she is nice to everyone who comes in. I tell Sandy about Fred Cedarberg, knowing he, too, is a writer. Sandy looks agonized. Finally Doreen comes. Meanwhile, I have helped two customers and enjoyed Sandy's obvious observing of me. He is sizing me up. We leave the office and he keeps looking around at me as we go up the street. I do not know whether to take his arm, so keep my hands in my pockets.

We pass the Burlington Arcade. I notice Sandy is a funny man, a boy with shoulder-length red hair. At the zebra crossing, I say, "You've still got your suntan, damn it, everyone looks so awful here—including me."

"You look all right." He takes my arm, and the zebra crossing at Bond Street is our turning point. As we walk down Bond Street toward Bruton Street, speaking of President Johnson's speech about Negro rights, there is a strong undercurrent of arm pressing. He keeps looking, appreciating, pressing. At the bank, we meet a friend of his from his Reuters days in Fleet Street. We agree to lunch together at the Guinea pub.

When we left the Guinea, it was still raining. He held my arm, then changed his mind as we walked, and put his left arm around my shoulder. He'd drawn me to him, and it was hard to walk. I had put my arm around his waist. We'd walked back to my office under his umbrella.

THE GUINEA IS an "in" pub in a mews behind Bruton Place. I have been taken here several times by people who were trying to impress me; also by Bob Briggs because it is near his bank. We come in out of the harsh rainy noon into the red-and-brown dimness. "I've got to go to the ladies' for a minute," I say.

2. Disneyland opened in Anaheim, California, in 1955. For its tenth anniversary, Walt Disney held a beauty pageant to crown a "Miss Disneyland Tencentennial."

"I'm not sure where it is," Sandy says, looking around.

"It's upstairs," I say.

"Oh. I'm not boring you by bringing you to some place you've been before?"

"No. It's just that it's near the office."

"It's good to see you again." He looks down at me. He's always sleepy-looking. He also slurs his words slightly.

He is still looking, he is always looking. "I thought you and Bob . . ."

"I know you did. But we aren't."

"There's nothing wrong with it. I mean, I know Bob's an unhappy man."

"No, he's not. He's just up and down and shows it. Most people wear a mask . . ."

"And he does."

"No, he doesn't. He is just all his moods. He lets people see them all and doesn't conceal the bad ones."

"No, you're wrong. He does wear a mask."

"All right," I say. "He does."

He picks up my hand and turns it over and over, as if he is deciding something. Then he brings it to his mouth and kisses it. Then he looks at me.

"Nice eyes. Let's see. What other assets do you have? Nice smile." He looks at other things but does not enumerate them verbally. "I'd like to touch you."

"Well, you can't in the Guinea, old chap."

"What?"

I put my mouth to his ear. His hair is longer than most American men allow it to grow. It smells of rain, feels lank and silky. "I said—you can't in the Guinea, old chap."

"I never thought I'd like a girl from North Carolina. You're quite a . . . I was very impressed with your flat, your books."

"I rent the flat. The furniture's not mine. But the books are."

"I know."

It is time to go back.

"I don't want to go back," I say.

"I don't either."

We step out into the rain and begin our walk out of the mews. He takes my arm, then changes his mind and puts an arm around my shoulder. He is much taller. I look up at him. He is thirty-seven and looks as if he's lived two years for every one. He has good skin, though; blue eyes. Deep lines and pouches under the eyes. Several gold inlays, but his teeth are good. His chin is not his strong point. I try to put my arm around his waist, but he is too tall and I keep reaching up, up. It is now impossible to walk with all those arms. I look up. He looks down. It starts to be a peck-type of kiss, but turns into the kind people usually do not exchange at lunch hour in Mayfair outside a pub. It is a warm exchange. I know from it that this time there will be no games.

"That was a surprise," he said.

eanwhile, Gail had another world in which she moved, that of her City Literary Institute class. It involved her with an interesting cast of characters, including Dr. Ian Marshall, a psychiatrist, who introduced Gail to Scientology and would soon propose marriage. At the first meeting, Ian had been with his friend Audrey, a Scientology auditor. Gail invited both of them to her Beaufort Street flat.

MARCH 21

"We're interested in the workings of the human mind," they had explained.

So am I.

WHY IS IT, if anyone asked me "What are you most interested in?" I would not answer the truth. What is the truth? What most interests me in the world is my reactions to other people and their reactions to me.

And what is it I *should* answer? Rather, what is it that would be acceptable to answer?

"Oh the situation in Vietnam . . . other people . . . just life going on around me."

Lies, all lies.

I think most people are interested in themselves. Then, as you get into the more introspective classes of people, they begin to study reactions.

Tonight, for instance. I took on a handful when I asked those two around. Both of them are in my writing class. I don't know exactly what their relationship is. I think there may be some alliance other than professional. They practice something called auditing, which is part of something called Scientology. They get together with another couple and audit one another when they are not auditing clients. He is a medical doctor but gave up his practice to explore this kind of work. He got out of Oxford in 1950. She also went to Oxford and then went into secretarial work. She met him at a party, and he introduced her to auditing. She is writing a novel, said it was terribly close to her. Miss Slade thought it rambled. So she gave up for a while.

There were a few awkward moments. I shouldn't even be wondering whether they were bored.

We ended up talking about the barriers people put up. He said he wished there were more people who knew what he was talking about. It was a terribly lonely world. I said, "But you have a way about you that puts people on their guard." She agreed. "Yes, Ian. You're always focusing just *beyond* them."

I had resorted to a low trick and had felt his pulse. He was mystified. I diagnosed a superiority complex. All this for the purpose of touching him.

I don't know. It provided entertainment for the evening. But they were so *cerebral.* I kept thinking of the sleepy eyes of Sandy.

"I have nothing to hide," said Ian. "I have nothing I wouldn't want you to know."

Oh brother, I thought, *I* have—all my subterfuges, ploys, and ruses. And it is so awful to be caught in one. Like the time I had caught Peter Perry. The only reason I caught him was that he was doing the exact thing I myself had done many times: feigning sympathy for someone in order to get physically closer to that person. But if I go on hiding behind barriers, then I can only associate with people who can't possibly see beyond those barriers. But how does one rid oneself of subterfuges?

ANDY CALLED. I got through my first big no to him. But I think it was mutual. He is just proper enough to think he should take an ex-fiancée out every now and again.

Dr. Ian Marshall's method: He says he listens to what people say. But does not try to draw conclusions, to connect or intuit. He simply observes and remarks to himself, "X paused before mentioning his father. Is something not quite defined, then, toward his father? Or, X got visibly angry when he mentioned his job. Why?" These subjects become work points. He observed the accompanying symptoms as the man told his story. He watched how certain subjects affected the man.

MY LACK OF PERCEPTION stems from being overintuitive. I am ahead of every person's story, usually fictionalizing. Perhaps this can be used in writing. In personal relationships, it is a destroying thing, however. I am always deciding what X "really meant" when he acted such-and-such a way to me. If only I could stop this cerebration and substitute observation. For instance, Tommy G.'s blush as he spoke to his secretary on the phone, all done as a preliminary to asking me out. But there you go, intuiting again, you say. How did you know that was why he was blushing?

Blushes. Nervous habits. Touching one's face. Picking nonexistent lint off one's clothes. Looking at the ceiling, down at the floor, away from the eyes of another person. Licking one's lips. A stiffening about the lips as one talks. (Doreen, when she is nervous, gets a certain "rapt look" on her face. This look wouldn't apply to anyone else. But it lets me know when Doreen is nervous.)

Some people talk more when they are nervous. Some people pretend to listen. Or keep asking others questions so that nobody will question them. Take people in my immediate circle. Some people who control facial expressions, hands, etc., are still caught by the blush: Dr. Marshall, Officer Banks! Mr. Miller becomes jovial and fast-talking. Pauline smiles. Elizabeth gets pink splotches on her neck. I touch my face, look at the

floor or away, have a bad time with my mouth. Peter Perry puts on a dis-
play of overconfidence. Shelley Burman used to start pointing up other
peoples' weaknesses: "Your feet are so ugly." Andy gets tongue-tied. Many
people act overly casual: "Not that it matters anyway . . ." But it does.

MARCH 22

I hope I can remember how one gradually becomes a writer. Gradually
the blur that has eluded you comes into focus. All those wishful after-
noons when you sat on the grass looking at Tom Wolfe's mountains,
wanting to write like he did, right off the bat. You had ideas. The story
of Paul, slightly fictionalized; the story of your affair with A. Oh, you
would change *names*, but you had not yet learned to concede reality to
art. So your faithful mimickings of reality seemed more unreal than
ever when you set them down on paper. And another thing you noticed:
There were parts of stories that bored you to write them. ("I'll just
make myself finish this description.") It didn't occur to you that if it
bored you, how much more it would bore the uninvolved reader.

WHAT ARE THE most valuable lessons so far?

1. There is a secret to successful emotional scenes. Chekhov sim-
    ply reports what he sees, hears; and he lets the reader supply
    the emotion.
2. You must try and cut out those details that may mean a lot to
    you personally, but only tend to separate the reader from you.

For now: Concentrate on taking a small subject (a relationship, an
incident) and expanding it until you feel you've captured it right down
to its tiniest detail, that you've seen into it as completely as possible.

HOW TO RESURRECT "Mourning," for instance: Anna's father commits
suicide. She has never lived with him. She does not cry, but wants to feel
something. (She tells her logic teacher, "Yes, he killed himself.")
    This much should be compressed.

She goes to see a priest, Father Flynn. Then she finds Jack Krazowski in the delicatessen. She "uses" her father's death to elicit sympathy, and finally cries because of the picture Jack has presented of his father.

When Anna's father committed suicide during her last semester at State University, she felt no pain. Nothing at all. She went over all the things about him that might make her cry, but none of them did. She had never lived with him (her parents were divorced), but he had signed the checks that had provided her with nineteen years' worth of good food, clothing, and education.[3]

He had visited her at school the semester before (his visits were rare) on his way back from the sanitarium where he had been taking the cure. A rather vague person, tending toward sarcasm, he had taken an empty match-cover from his pocket. "I've jotted it down on this," he told her. "What the doctor said I was." Lip curling scornfully, a flat expression in his eyes, he read from the match-cover.

"Psychoneurotic with compulsion to drink."

Anna laughed, which pleased him. He and Anna had been sitting in a campus coffee bar. Then they left the coffee shop, walked back to her dorm, and he pressed a $20 bill into her palm and departed. She felt more at ease as soon as he was gone. That was the last time she ever saw him.

Now, six weeks had passed since the funeral. It was a weekend. Anna's roommate had gone home and she had no date for Saturday night. Aimlessly, she drove, shuddering with doubts about her father's soul.[4] She had inherited his two-year-old Cadillac, but the novelty of driving it around campus, looking appropriately sad, had worn off. Besides, the thing ate up gasoline and drank oil. It was like a dangerous animal that had to be fed.

It was the weekend.

3. This is a fictional embellishment. Gail's father, who had committed suicide, had never sent money.

4. See *The Making of a Writer: Journals, 1961–1963*, Part 8, "My Father's Soul."

—

JUST TRY TO EXCITE emotion without becoming sad yourself. Jack Kra-zowski is the only human, feeling element in the story, and thus is able to make Anna feel, too.

> *"There, there, kitten," said Jack, the last man on earth, passing her his handkerchief and looking approvingly at the real tears. "You're not such a goddam beatnik, after all."*

There was a chapter in *The Prophet* that I loved at eighteen. "Speak to us of love," it began. That is just what I propose to speak of now. But with a few qualifications to my eighteen-year-old viewpoint, which has lasted far past eighteen, I am sorry to say.

DAUGHTER: What do men want most?

MOTHER: Sex and tenderness, without emotionalism or silent re-proaches.

DAUGHTER: But, Mother, then he won't marry me—if he has it all before.

MOTHER: That is not the point. Can't you see? That is not the point.

DAUGHTER: You don't talk like a mother, Mother.

MOTHER: I am talking like a human being, which is what I hope you'll grow up to be. Don't you see? If you are maintaining a relation-ship for the sole purpose of getting something out of it—i.e., marriage, security, guaranteed affection (can such a thing exist?)—then you've missed the boat. You're still in the dark ages of the mid-twentieth cen-tury before people learned that the only real duty was to love. Some-times I think you are very old-fashioned. Even if you *are* my daughter.

MARCH 23

I didn't have to kill Tuesday. Late in the afternoon, Sandy, the Compli-cated American, passed. He had been to a travel film with Briggs and Miller.

They pass through the office. He glides by the window, comes back; I blow him a kiss. He disappears. Then in a moment reappears, smiling to himself. Comes around the corner of the fishbowl and into the office. Says, "Can you get away for a coffee?" As soon as we are on the pavement, we resume last Friday's thing. In the coffeehouse, we kiss. It doesn't matter about the stuffy English; and the Italians understand.

"I missed you," he said. "What are you doing after your class tonight? I don't want to wait until tomorrow."

He is full of pickings from the human situation. I tell him about the two psychiatrists. He says how a friend of his, twice married, was just about to do it for the third time because his analyst told him it was time to form a lasting relationship.

"But you . . . or I . . . We can make up our own minds," he continued. "We haven't even begun yet, and who knows where it will end?"

MARCH 28

It is seven o'clock Sunday evening. The week that I was in such a hurry to get rid of has now ended. The sun is still shining, reflected in a window across the street. Gulls flash past against the still very blue sky. There is some schmaltzy music on the radio. Whatever the word is— malaise, despair, or an acute awareness of what being alive involves— I've got it, and it hurts.

My most natural impulse is to sit here and do nothing and let it carry me away. Suddenly I think of a similar sun reflected in the window of the Wasps rugby club. What home truths am I now going to pen with a sense of shame for not being more artistic about it?

In a minute I am going to start another love story.

LAST SUNDAY I sat wondering if Wednesday would ever come, and it came on Tuesday. I attended my creative writing class in a fever. Earlier in the evening, I had stood in the barely-dark at Piccadilly Circus and watched the lights, feeling exalted and tensed to high pitch. I came home after class (Mr. Mayhue gave me a ride) and began preparing for what I kept telling myself would not be permitted to happen. At ten o'clock, the phone rang and Sandy's lazy voice said: "Can I come see you?" In twenty minutes, he was there, looking Uriah Heepish with his funny face, slightly hooked nose, receding chin, and floppy red hair. In his buttonhole was a wilted yellow carnation, and in his hand he held a bunch of similar ones. The anticipation of that moment when I would open the door and let him take me into his arms was more intense than the actual doing of it.

TODAY, HE TELLS ME he writes straight from his unconscious. Whereas I am afraid I am going to find tedious old craftsmanship the only way out.

"I think I'm a lucky man," he says. "I have three outlets: writing, sex, and jazz." At 2:00 p.m. [at his place], he sat down at the old upright piano with the sun coming through the window onto his already burnished hair—everything about him is *orange* to me, both in color and feeling—and played himself away. First the tune, then the foot-tapping counterpoint to the notes. He sang, too. A kind of hoarse grunt, then a lazy sigh and spewing out of words. No Jungian analysis on this man.

His little daughter and I were dispatched to wash the dishes. Until that time, there had been a feminine wall between us. Even at four, she had sense enough to know I might claim a chip of her father's affection.

ME (effort at being friendly): Oh, look, you have electricity in your hair.

CHILD: I do not.

DADDY (trying to pacify us both): Everyone has it, honey. Look.

So I got her a chair—as she commanded—and stood her up in the chair at the sink and left her slipping into the too-large black rubber gloves. Then I went into the bathroom and took my time putting on lipstick. When I came back, she was standing in the chair, looking terrified. Her face was very still. She had broken a glass.

"Oh," I said, picking up the pieces and dropping them in the wastebasket.

"I'm very sorry," she said to me. "I really am. I didn't mean to do it."

This was too much. I took her in my arms. "Of course you didn't, darling. Of course not."

MOZART FILLS MY coffee-cup-and-Sunday-paper-littered room. I do not want to be a hard woman living alone in my ivory tower. I want to touch my own little girls instead of borrowing other people's for the afternoon.

We went to Kensington Gardens and lay on his old tattered sexy tweed coat near the round pond. There was a Russian father with his son flying a red kite. Sandy sat there with his floppy red hair, unconscious of his dissipated face, reading the *Telegraph*. He reads about a million periodicals. Whatever I ask about—"Did you see where . . . ?"—he has seen.

She, with her matching red hair—she is truly beautiful and feminine—put on my pearl bracelet and sunglasses, and I gave her my mirror and she admired herself. "Oh, I look funny."

Little coquette. She knows that "funny" is not the word. From time to time, I am shocked at the way he makes no allowance for her small, innocent mind. He discusses lesbianism on the police force and in the WACs as a hefty woman police officer strides by. The sun is hot. I feel acutely the difference between my age and the child's downy cheek.

I keep remembering the absent mother. I cannot help but think she is a threat. But she is not. But what is she doing, then, this afternoon? Does she miss her warm, feminine child? Does she think of the moment of her conception? But then, that is "a naive statement," as he would say, as he did last night as he set about disillusioning me on the Tube [subway] coming back from the East India Docks.

We hadn't been able to get a table at the New Friends restaurant because Ken Tynan had written the place up. It was filled with Knightsbridge debs. He [Sandy] was annoyed. The phone box wouldn't work. He cursed.

Coming home on the Tube, he told me of his infidelities, what a bastard he'd been, "not the marrying type," how he'd brought women home flagrantly toward the end, how he'd gotten tired of the same woman, wanted something new and different. It wears off. This talk horrifies me. But I don't completely believe it. My woman's mind searches for an explanation.

But it is probably true, what he is saying. If I choose to distort it, to read a message of hope into his clear warning, then I can have the solace of reading that over later and saying, "You knew, but chose to hide it from yourself." Later he adumbrated: "It sounds awful. But I don't find many people who *wear* well. I like new ones."

TODAY—LEAVING KENSINGTON GARDENS. I am holding her pig-puppet. He looks at me, all appreciation, then says: "It was nice having your company. Something new and different."

MARCH 29

Seventy-two degrees in London. Lying in Green Park during the lunch hour, rereading my old manuscript.[5] Decided to do it over with what I know now. I am tired of all these exercises and no results. I will do most of it over Easter and let Miss Slade read it. I have a built-in opportunity with her. After all, she is an editor at Hutchinson.[6]

I know the area of Miami. I know the story. What will enrich it is to dispense with Al and put in the Englishman—the unknown quantity. He represents all the qualities Bentley isn't used to. Evan has got to be more of a Bob B. and a little of Bob L. when I didn't like him. You've got to feel he's an American possibility—rough diamond, etc.

> *Gull Key is an island on which middle-class American couples live their lives. Bentley lives there. Why did she marry a man like Evan? Because she was scared. It was an escape from the unknown. And that is her tragic flaw. She can only exude freedom and rebelliousness in an atmosphere of total security. Faced with the real thing, she runs for the nearest prop. In the end, she stays with Evan because the Englishman rejects her. But he says, "If I said come back to London with me, you'd be scared to death."*

5. "Gull Key." See January 24, 1964, note.

6. Hutchinson & Company published works of history, science, and literature—usually of a scholarly nature—but also some popular fiction. For instance, in 1965 it published *Love Holds the Cards* by Barbara Cartland and *The Gladiators* by Arthur Koestler.

Man to wife in bed, after trying unsuccessfully for an hour: "What's the matter? Can't you think of anybody either?" Bunny[7] tells this at the beach.

Chink returns from his Wales trip. We go out to the river and drink beer. It is a lovely night, but there is no joy. His edges are blunt compared with—compared with—that is the trouble. When you are secure in your preference for one, the others flock to you. But you have lost your taste for them.

There is not enough time in my life to waste whole evenings with people who give me nothing in the way of conversation or help to continue the search. If I'm going to get anything done, let's not be so bloody concerned about pleasing everything in pants.

I am deeply impressed by Sandy, but the fatal thing would be to live for his attentions. If I myself demand other minds to be constant in springing novelties on me, how much more, then, should he? Don't overestimate him. Just because he's the first intelligent man you've known in a year (and whose fault is that?), remember: He might be the devil to live with. ("I disgusted my wife.")

APRIL 1

I return to myself and find it not at all unpleasant, though too much life has come crowding in. The run on men continues. Chink; Tommy, mustached Tommy, full of a lifetime's accumulated defenses; Jurg—yes, when it no longer mattered, I bumped into him on the street.[8]

Sandy is cynical, unpredictable, supercritical, and perceptive. He steals the show. He slouches back, chinless; long red-gold hair sweeping the cushion behind him; he pokes his nonexistent belly out, stretches his long legs, talks and talks in his supersleepy voice. He is the only person

7. Bunny and his wife, Thelma—Bentley's neighbors in "Gull Key"—had moved to Gull Key from Tahiti after Bunny had failed at writing a novel and Thelma had become pregnant. Bunny became an insurance salesman, and Thelma broke out of the housewife mold by taking art classes.

8. Jurg was a Swiss banker whom Gail had been seeing occasionally.

I know who can talk without moving his mouth. He talks about himself, about literary critics, about his daydreams and night dreams. "I want to be reviewed favorably by Cyril Connolly[9]—I want to be in there with the big-league intellectuals, I don't want to grow up—I need women— there's nothing worse for me in the world than not having a woman. I can't do without them—ah, women are wonderful! Sometimes, I, too, feel made unreal by all the others. That's why I (very gallantly and a bit embarrassed) am very glad to have . . . ah . . . met you. Ah, women are so transparent. They give themselves away. Come here . . . you'll probably tire of it after a while . . . Who can say?"

Yet, for a cynic, he is happy. Or content with his lot. He is free, feels his health running in him. He shares a house with the foreign editor of *The Spectator*, a young man of twenty-five, one of the intellectual elite, of whom he speaks.

He has the love of his daughter, but not the day-to-day annoyances. He is free to screw as many women, lovely women, as he can get into his schedule. He has a job that allows enough leeway for him to nip home and write. He would like more money and to have a well-reviewed novel out. He likes women, needs new and different women, needs their closeness, their sex, their approval, *both* their ears ("Sometimes I feel like just snapping my fingers to get their attention"). But so cynical. I must not let it wear off on me.

HENRY JAMES AGAIN—he gets me reverberating. What unresolved aspects of ourselves are we seeking when we seek lovers?

"GULL KEY"—at last I have a definite goal. Bentley sees the Englishman on the beach, doesn't know him. He looks foreign, from another time and place. She dreams about him. This is the opening of the book.

TODAY, MY CUSHY JOB involved going to Charing Cross with Bob Briggs to look for prints for Lynn Beaumont in D.C. Out-of-the-side-of-mouth-

---

9. Cyril Connolly was the most influential literary voice in England; he had cofounded the epochal literary magazine *Horizon* and edited it from 1939 to 1950, and then served as a book critic for the London *Sunday Times*.

talking Sandy joined us for a drink. We headed up Shaftesbury Avenue in the pale spring sun. We got to the Western Bar. ("Let's go in here. I've always wondered what it's like.")

Sandy has two books in his tattered coat: *Better Dead than Red,* a novel about Communist witch hunts, and a book about spies. He asks Bob what he did for the CIA.

"Can't tell you that, Buddy," says Briggs, putting on his sunglasses. He goes for refills.

"Have you been behaving yourself?" Sandy asks. We argue over the Negroes in Selma. I say, "People have archetypal fragments in their makeup." Sandy says, "That's nothing but Jungian mythmaking."

We move on from the Western Bar, back into the sunshine. We part at the crossroads of Charing Cross Road. I look over the top of the National Gallery and see the top of [the statue of] Nelson, a misty outline of the great warrior against the haze. "I like that. Look," I say.

Sandy looks. "I like that, too." Then he says, "Nice seeing you both." He goes off to the right, toward Nelson; we hasten up Charing Cross to buy our prints, full of purpose.

"Jesus, this goddamn traffic," says Mr. Briggs, shifting painlessly from the threesome to the twosome. I answer with some wisecrack, seeing in my imagination the floppy red hair, the threadbare coat, the lanky man with the books in his pocket going down to the Strand, away from us.

BOB BRIGGS HAS this dream about children on a bridge. They are hellish. They say "here's what we do to cowards" and pummel his head open with a swinging stone attached to a piece of wire that runs through the boy's hand—like stigmata. The boy's hand is bleeding. Bob's head cracks open. He wakes up, takes two aspirin, reads. Then decides to try and sleep again. He closes his eyes. He sleeps. He dreams. Once more the children are coming toward him on the bridge. This time he pushes them away, like insects. "Just as they're going over the rails, into the abyss, they look at me and I see my children's faces . . ."

HENRY JAMES, "The Private Life." How does he manage it?

MISS SLADE: You're an American. What do you think of him as a fellow American?

GAIL: He became English at the end of his life . . .

MISS S.: Are you trying to disown him?

G.: He's one of my favorite authors. I think he's great.

MISS S.: Why? Oh, good. Tell us why.

G.: Well, because he always manages never to quite go over the line, but he makes us go over. Do you know what I mean?

MISS S.: Yes! Yes. Yes, I do.

Well, then, my dear friend, if Clare Vawdrey is double (and I'm bound to say I think that the more of him the better), his lordship there has the opposite complaint: he isn't even whole . . . I have a fancy that if there are two of Mr. Vawdrey, there isn't so much as one, all told, of Lord Mellifont.
—HENRY JAMES, "The Private Life"

APRIL 4

It was always there, waiting—after her various attempts to dispel it, which included being with people as often as possible. But sooner or later, when others departed to take up the threads of their lives, she was back—alone with it. After years of forced company with this nameless presence, she came to look forward to seeing it again. She found, in spite of what she said, or wrote, or thought, her allegiance was to this nameless spirit alone. As time went on, her loyalty grew. She began to shorten the periods of alleviation in order to get back to the reality.

SANDY CAME OVER, and is now gone. I am first of all relieved. It is good to be with my quiet spirit, the sound of traffic through an open window, the BBC, cool air, the smell of lemon cologne, and the remains of breakfast for two. He has that redhead look of always running a fever. At times, I watch him and marvel at his hedonistic calm. I simply doubt that he has any moral equipment in that cynical cauliflower of his. What I mean is, his goals seem to be immediate pleasure, whether in the form of writing (so that he can read it over and laugh) or in sex, or in smoking pot. He is loving and affectionate, but somehow I instinctively don't feel any human love exchange in our exchanges. Perhaps that is why I can't give myself up to him.

"I have something new and different," he says. It turns out to be little squares of a chocolate substance. He slices it with a razor blade over the eye of a model on *Vogue*.

"Would you mind not doing it on the eye?" I ask, getting nervous. Satanic, I called him. He wasn't especially pleased. Then he bundles the little flakes up in tinfoil and sets a match to them. They emerge all crumbly. Then he rolls them into a cigarette paper and takes a deep puff. I do the same. Nothing happens. I puff until tears roll down my cheeks. The stuff burns my throat and nostrils.

He feels it almost immediately. I keep saying, "When am I going to?" Meanwhile I get a pillow and lie down on the floor because I feel I might fly out of my chair. I am completely aware of every object around me. But time has slowed down and sometimes there are unexplainable "lapses" when I "disappear" for a minute, then come back, lucid as ever, and wonder if the whole thing was my imagination. I am acting sensual, yet my body is doing it. I am not willing it to do anything of my own accord. I feel like the great earth mother.

He tries to make me talk about it: "Tell me what you see. How do you feel?" Finally he says: "Well, baby, you've been down a new road."

A polarity in me wants to bestow a blessing on him, but also to want wholeness, direction, God. It has nothing to do with convent-bred guilt. It is something built into my system, and I am responsible for replenishing it and keeping it intact.

DID TWO THOUSAND WORDS from seven to ten, taking a break for oyster stew. I will rewrite this book. I am finding a difference already. First, the sustained underlying sense of humor. The slight detachment. And the characters are going to be deeper than those others.

Evan is going to be a certain brand of "the best America has to offer." Not the eastern school brand. The Midwest transplant who makes good.

Bentley is inclined to frequent "flights," distracted, still at that stage where she hasn't completely become herself and therefore needs constant aids: daydreams, soul searching, etc. She has a desire to fulfill some role, but isn't sure which. She's always after something new.

But where does the island fit in? The inhabitants?

The coming of the Englishman makes her see these people and her environment from a new outsider's view. The irony is, she eventually sees Evan for his real worth—but loses him. If he insists on a divorce for her one offense, he would be narrow.

We have to see why Evan chose her, as well as why she chose him.

Now, the Englishman. An unknown quantity. It is her first contact with the European mind: refined, reflective, cynical.

It isn't just an exercise. It's a story of innocence craving experience; and then, experienced, seeking—too late—a return to innocence. Gull Key: Garden of Eden.

What kind of man is Geoffrey Sykes [the Englishman]? This is one of the keys. He's a complainer, a cynic, a malcontent; a brilliant, charming Old World type. The difference between the moral view and the aesthetic. You reach a point where you crave to return to the moral.

APRIL 17–18, EASTER WEEKEND • *Beaufort Street*

It is time I moved out of this flat. It has stopped being a clean-limned ivory tower and has become a haven where two distraught Americans can put things off for a little longer.

Sandy needs his solitude, too. He must go home for five hours and read, and make his model airplanes. In Battersea Park yesterday, surrounded by high-powered New Yorkers—Gillett and his little hat and camera;[10] the Queen of the 1965 New York World's Fair ("I'm so upset. I broke my favorite fingernail.")—Sandy was a slow orange blur of retarded action. No incentive. But he did finish his book. He has no ulterior motives, plays no games. He isn't deviously trying to get something. He's just riding along. My tiny good voice says: "Is this what you've come to? Have you no will? Can you not hold out for someone with

10. Charles Gillett was the president of the New York Convention and Visitors Bureau and the president of the National Association of Travel Organizations.

will?" Then the other voice answers: "Like who? Everything has its penalties. To be the type of man he is—'I'm always touching you, if not physically, then mentally'—he had to forfeit some of those other qualities."

AFTER EASTER

Of course, I am once again verging on being homeless—but Barbara Frey's[11] voice comforted me: "Oh, I *say!*" She is going to let me know. Six months. Good God, what a godsend. But let's not even hope.

THE GHOST OF SANDY roams this flat. On the sofa, reading. Eating an apple or making coffee. His model airplane is here. He made himself at home, always cleared the table, washed dishes, turned off heaters.

"It's nice having you here."

"Well, I like it, too, honey. So that's fine."

Speech rhythm a bit like Uncle William's.

APRIL 22

This evening, standing in the door of the launderette, waiting for my sheets to dry, I watched spring come back for the second time this year. Imperceptibly, the vapors and temperatures shifted. Suddenly one finds oneself in the wrong clothes. London weather teaches people stoicism.

I have a list of things half said. What salvation can I offer the world?

The first way to universalize love experience is to be minutely specific about voice tones. I read a book today where the lover spoke like anyone. You could not determine what sort of man he was by his actions or words. The authoress told you in long philosophical paragraphs.

SANDY, HE'S MAKING a model airplane, which he carries to the Baker Street Classic Cinema in a paper bag. It is Monday, the last afternoon of

11. Barbara Frey was the owner of the Beaufort Street flat that Gail was renting.

the holiday, blustery. We are going to see a Frank Sinatra movie [the romantic comedy *Marriage on the Rocks*]. Afterward, the rain. The long Tube rides, the buses. "Have you brought a book?" He puts his stamp on all of London for me, and when he leaves, he takes London with him.

"What did you have for lunch?" I asked him.

"Oh, I have the same thing over and over again. I've just gotten in the habit. Toasted ham and cheese and some tomato soup. I like it."

I used to say: Just let me get this man in the bag, then I'll write. It doesn't work that way.

APRIL 29

I suppose it is good to read other people's unpublished stuff. It teaches a good lesson— namely, that putting down personal experiences, meaningful as they are to us, doesn't mean a damn to anyone else until they are transformed into something that produces a universal emotion.

> *The major novelists . . . count . . . in the sense that they not only change the possibilities of the art for practitioners and readers, but that they are significant in terms of the human awareness they promote; awareness of the possibilities of life.*
>
> —F. R. LEAVIS, *THE GREAT TRADITION:*
> *GEORGE ELIOT, HENRY JAMES, JOSEPH CONRAD*

I have the seeds of destruction in me. Ambrose had them.[12] I am attracted to people who have them. The pleasant lugubriousness of sitting in a pub with a fellow failure and discussing how much your failures have in common. As much as it hurts, the truth is this: Succeeding is evident only from what has been done—not from what is shown, thought, sensed, or dreamed, but *done*.

The story: a man and a woman and his little daughter. The point is, it is Ginny on Sunday. Sundays are for Ginny. "Ginny on Sunday."

---

12. Ambrose is the father who commits suicide in Gail's story "Mourning."

It was London's first lovely spring day of the year. [As it was] a Sunday as well, families, couples, dog owners, and lone walkers filled the gardens. Near to the Round Pond, there was a man, a woman, and a little girl of about four. All three were sharing the man's mackintosh, which was spread on the grass.

How the woman has dreaded Sunday mornings, when he says: "Got to be up early to pick up Ginny." She tries to be understanding. After all, was she not the daughter of divorced parents? Was she not a Sunday child? But the fact that she is makes it impossible for her to accept this threesome—precisely because she remembers triumphing over her father's women. She reads herself into Ginny, and it is fatal.

APRIL 30

Asking questions and not listening for an answer form the keynote of this day's gloom. "Hush," said Sandy. "You asked me once and I said I didn't want to talk about it." He was sharp for the first time (about his book). I had the good sense to shut up.

THE PSYCHIATRIST [Ian] has written a story called "Sampson." It is good. It comes pouring out. And this is what is sad. He writes better than Sandy. He has more to say.

MAY 5

I'm having a date with Andy on Sunday and the old thrill is back. He asked me proper. It will be good to be with Andy, on the side of order rather than chaos, for a change.

A NUMINOUS CONVERSATION with the psychiatrist on Monday night.[13] Next morning, he takes me on the back of his motor scooter to Battersea for breakfast in a truckers' café.

13. In Jungian terminology, "numinous" refers to heightened or altered consciousness.

—

SITTING IN THE WRITING class on Tuesday night, I look at the back of the psychiatrist's head. How I used to fear his ridicule. Now I know I have achieved him. "Diary of a Seducer."[14] Andy? Sandy? Once B. said, "You want a carbon copy of yourself." I found one in Sandy. Which side am I not being true to? Writing—Andy—Sandy—Ian.

MAY 7

Almost flying apart at the seams—

Moving day tomorrow.[15]

Just when the old ghosts become friends, we must accustom ourselves to new ones. Gordon called to ask travel advice. He's married to Barbara. All that agonizing for nothing. I could have been doing something else.

I've thrown out a lot of my writing. I know what's good now. How tight it's got to be. My big enemies are anger, proneness to depression, and laziness. These notebooks are a waste of time. I have to produce now. No more anger.

In July, Gail married Dr. Ian Marshall at the Chelsea Registry Office and moved to his flat on Beaufort Street. Gail wrote little between May and September; she was almost always together with Ian, talking or studying. "In the first months of the marriage," she later recalled, "I actually sat on the sofa and took notes while Ian talked!"

14. "Diary of a Seducer" is a part of Søren Kierkegaard's *Either/Or.* In it, Kierkegaard imagines an aesthete who, with calculation and charm, enjoys a woman by making her yield herself to him completely, and then moves on. Gail had been reading it at the start of her European sojourn—in October 1961—and had commented, "It should be required reading for all girls before they reach their eighteenth year."

15. Gail was moving to a riverfront flat on Cheyne Walk in Chelsea. She stayed only two months.

SEPTEMBER 20

Four years ago tonight, I was in Asheville and fed up with my family.[16] What was the matter that time? It seems I am always fighting with somebody. I could not stay with Monie. (She was pressing in on me with too much love. Dear Monie. I wouldn't spurn it now.) And I was having some battle with Kathleen and Frank. So the result was, I tore off in my little car and went and sat in the lower part of Pack Square, in the autumn darkness, glowering, feeling alienated and unable to get along with anybody. I sat in my dark car and gradually became coolly and intensely satisfied, watching the familiar scene from a place from which I'd never watched it before: seeing the policemen changing shifts, the hodgepodge of small town architectural pretensions; listening to the billiard balls; feeling slightly scared (bad part of town, dark); feeling sad, misunderstood, betrayed; and wanting B.—feeling that this new travel adventure of mine would entitle me to his sympathy.

Now it is four years later. I have been places I lusted to be in. I have had the job I wanted, the independence, the money to spend, the glamour, the change, the complete freedom to be as selfish as I like. I look slightly less young, more drawn in the face, but better groomed. I have read a lot more books much more thoroughly. I have still not become a great writer. I am wishing tonight to be in the embrace of my family, to be kind to Frank, to let Monie pay me all the attention she desires.

Self of four years ago, let me fill you in as you sit in your little white car in the bosom of your town, in the crisp, clean fall night. Let me tell you the news—what happens to people like you.

I am married again—to a man of thirty-four (today is his thirty-fourth birthday). He is a dark, turbulent individual who is a little bit too much of himself to fit in anywhere or to make me comfortable. In his absence I can cope with him. But his reality, his presence, fills me with

16. On September 21, 1961, Gail sat in Pack Square in Asheville, two weeks before her departure for Europe, reflecting that she was "choosing between leaving [her] family and losing [her] sanity."

awe, confusion, and revulsion all at once. He is brilliant, he is the most intelligent man I've ever met. It bothers me that he has loved me too much. He watches me with soulful brown eyes from behind his glasses (chipped in the right lens from a somersault he turned on Hampstead Heath two years ago). The brown eyes dart, taking me in. Without his glasses, the brown eyes blur with joy—he was too joyous, too naked when he loved me. Now I have alienated him, he has drawn himself in. From his wounds he will manufacture new independence. He is estranged and hurt. He has locked himself against me and cannot open if he tried. I have split his male's pride and must now wait until he repairs it, as an animal tends its wounds.

Meanwhile, I have got to do a little growing, be honest with myself, and decide what is to happen next. I don't know how far I'll get.

Why did I marry him?

— I wanted to marry, I was getting worried that I would grow old alone, that nobody wanted me.

— His mind fascinated me. He gave me new ideas, set my mind soaring.

— His quick falling-in-love impressed me. This is the way I liked things to be done—quick, clean, dangerous.

— I liked the fact he was a doctor and I could tell my friends I was married to a psychiatrist. But the fact is, he does not practice medicine now, he does not take patients at the moment, he is tied up with Scientology—a noncreditable organization, even though the ideas are good. He has no persona—he is not the kindly psychiatrist in the pressed suit who is capable of disinterested love. He is a jittery brown-eyed lad who is uncertain, moody, and unfulfilled—and I am making it worse.

Hiatus

Gail Looks Back on a Period of Journal-Writing Silence

AUTUMN 1965

———

In October of 1965, after three months of marriage, I took Ian to Asheville to meet my mother and stepfather and young brothers and sister. It was a confusing, unreal visit.

There was a big photo in the Asheville paper of me hand-in-hand with my new husband, with the notice, "Dr. and Mrs. Ian Marshall; Dr. Marshall is a practicing psychiatrist in London." We looked like the svelte, ideal couple. A girlfriend's mother phoned me to say I had "done well." She only wished her daughter had been a little more choosy for her second husband.

Mother baited Ian and he did not show up at his best. He seemed out of his element with her. The children were afraid of him; he held seven-year-old Rebel upside down to make him be quiet—the only thing Rebel remembers about Gail's strange husband from England.

Ian liked Frank Cole best. He thought Frank was a man whose potential and keen intelligence had been thwarted and blocked by the circumstances of his life. During our two weeks with the Coles, we went on outings as an extended family—to the Blue Ridge Parkway; to the beach in Charleston, South Carolina. Ian and I rode in the back of the station wagon with the children.

When Frank hit his twelve-year-old daughter for sassing him, Ian and my grandmother covered their eyes and moaned. I felt right back in the old family trap with no grown man to protect me.

Ian and I went for walks, on Frank's land, and I berated him for getting caught up in Scientology. I wanted him to go back to being a conventional MD psychiatrist.

The sunny day we left Asheville for our return trip to London, I felt like Persephone returning to the Underworld with Hades. When we were aboard the Asheville–New York plane, waiting for it to take off, I had a sobbing fit. Then I looked across the aisle and there, of all people, sat Voit Gilmore, head of the USTS, smiling his perpetual smile. I had to get myself under control and introduce him to Ian.

DECEMBER 9

Why have I pursued the courses I have pursued? Was it me devising the action—did my decisions come from within, or without? Could it be that someone other than the center me pursued the courses, studied, read to reach some conclusion? If so, then the person who gets saved isn't going to be me at all. I will simply have dedicated my time, body, and emotional energy toward saving a false self—and the barren real me will remain at the starting gate.

Now I am married. The world cannot touch me. I go shopping by myself. I see no friends other than Pauline. I see her because I need an audience at least once a week. I like Mary ("I love your clothes—what an exciting drawing—what excellent taste!").[17] These things matter to me! I think of the friends I have in the world—Lorraine O'Grady Freeman (she did it!) is the nearest kin. How few people there are whom I admire.

DECEMBER 12

Rainy Sunday—sore throat—cleaning out Ian's filthy kitchen for Mr. Maten to paint tomorrow—old pastry mixes—dusty cereal boxes—jars full of half-dissolved things. I had a scene with Michael in the kitchen. Michael the Mess lies in bed all day, leaves cigarette ashes on the carpet, and leaves used razor blades on the bathroom edges for little fingers to

17. Ian rented out a room in his flat to a photographer named Michael and his girlfriend, Mary.

cut themselves on. Michael says he needs a place to put his photo equipment. Can he have a cupboard shelf? Ian says yes, if you'll keep it there and not on top of the refrigerator. Michael says, "You're going all Daddy-ish." I can see Ian's been strained. I started chanting "Pompous ass, pompous ass" to allay some of the tension, to balance Ian's roughness. Then everybody disappears, Mary to crunch her apple, Michael to sulk and feel trod upon. Ian goes, too. I keep chanting. Then Ian returns with his scraggly lip-out look I hate so much. The dark, puffy look—puffed up with childish stubbornness—"Did you really mean I was a pompous ass?" No, of course not. I explain. He wants to discuss it, "work through" it, "mend the A-R-C break."[18] I want to clean the kitchen so that he can put away his emotions long enough to help me. Split——rupture—now I am locked in this nasty little bedroom where I have spent so many horrible hours dreaming bad dreams, worrying that I had cancer, imagining and cataloging all the possible catastrophes that might happen to me. It is 3:10 on a rainy Sunday—nothing in the papers, Alan [Ian's three-year-old son, who spent weekends with us] filthy from being scrubbed back and forth across the carpet to show him we love him. Emotions drag you down.

DECEMBER 15

Now it is beginning to make patterns as I wanted.

FRUITLESS YEARS SEARCHING in philosophy books for answers to my practical problem—trying to solve physical problems, communication problems, bad mechanical problems with the archetypes. Now I am seeing the variety of tools; which tool to use for what. Several gold mines, lately, have led to new vistas: Arthur C. Clarke's *Childhood's End*, with its maxims, and Virginia Woolf's *The Waves*.[19]

---

18. An "ARC break" is a Scientology term for a sudden break in "affinity, reality, and communication" with someone.

19. *The Waves* was a radical fictional experiment by Woolf, as she had six characters interact and progress as if they were part of a single organism, while the story is told in a succession of short monologues.

Accept the fact that there may be other frameworks, universes of thought where none of your old premises will work. Only an open mind can be ready for a revision of known laws.

"We believe—it is only a theory—that the Overmind is trying to grow, to extend its powers and its awareness of the universe. By now it must be the sum of many races, and long ago it left the tyranny of matter behind. It is conscious of intelligence, everywhere. When it knew that you were almost ready, it sent us here to do its bidding, to prepare you for the transformation that is now at hand."

—The Overlords' message to humans in
CHILDHOOD'S END, by ARTHUR C. CLARKE

It was a tribute to the Overlords' psychology, and to their careful years of preparation, that only a few people fainted. Yet there could have been fewer still, anywhere in the world, who did not feel the ancient terror brush for one awful instant against their minds before reason banished it forever. There was no mistake. The leathery wings, the little horns, the barbed tail—all were there. The most terrible of all legends had come to life, out of the unknown past. Yet now it stood smiling, in ebon majesty, with the sunlight gleaming upon its tremendous body, and with a human child resting trustfully on either arm.

—ARTHUR C. CLARKE, *CHILDHOOD'S END*

Lucifer's "I will not serve" may be comparable to the assertion of the Ego.

Jung's idea: The Trinity is really four, the Devil being the fourth side. The way to salvation might be: Get free from the total unconscious, develop Lucifer (in the sense of the intellect, not in the sense of sinning), then, with Lucifer's help, go back and incorporate the Great Unknown, fit the pattern together.

DECEMBER 16 · *Midnight*

Ian: I just realized what you've been up to. You've been dramatizing Lucifer all your life.

TO BE DONE: Work out the myth the way I want. Don't try and make any decisions about what to do with this knowledge. Remember Jung's danger of identification with any of the archetypes (some people dramatize their father, mother, etc.). I simply picked the devil.

DECEMBER 29

Things have been happening so fast (inside me) that today I don't know whether I'm nearer madness than ever, or nearer serenity. Underlying my dreams for the past two weeks has been a commentary from some new awareness.

One night I dreamed of going mad and saw and felt what it would be like. In the dream, Ian said: You are now near to finding out what it is that you really worship. That something was my evil. Then this "something" began attacking my sanity. My face became numb and I started sinking down and becoming unconscious. I screamed—"Get me to a psychiatrist"—then woke, woke Ian, and talked to him for some time.

I am now aware of dramatizations I perform almost daily in my life:

the *"cruel" valence*
the *"unmoved" valence*
the *"tearful" valence*
the *"angry" valence*[20]

Today, walking home from a checkup at the hospital, I carried on a half-dozen arguments with various people who were "attacking me."

20. A "valence" in the terminology of Scientology is a borrowed personality, a substitute for one's true self, which one uses to act out prescribed dramas.

However, I also (for the first time in my life) sat back and observed my-self, smiling calmly like the Buddha.

JANUARY 1, 1966

No two characters can be alike, but there are "types."

Example, last night: Ian and I trying to describe or to name some-one who would have certain characteristics—a person who would be bell-like, clear, joyous, with so much energy to spare that he/she could function effortlessly. We tried to think of examples in life, in litera-ture.

I can think of plenty of the dark types—they, too, are fascinating. Heathcliff, Rochester, Birkin (though he saw how it should be, as did Lawrence himself), Nietzsche. But where do we find those rare, golden individuals—JFK was probably near enough. Do I know any-one? No, this kind of clarity gets muddied up even as early as early childhood.

OH, THE PERILS of being oneself. I see why so many decide for a nice comfortable persona—but wait a minute. Don't I change like a chameleon when the situation demands it? Yes, but this is my style.

For me to be straightforward would be the biggest lie of all. My way is weaving cunningly through mazes, not chopping down the mazes with a razor-straight, unyielding disposition (like Ian). That is why so many of my battles have been with people who trumpeted honesty above all other virtues.

I think it is right (for me, anyway) to put out empathy waves to an-other person, even if it means camouflaging my own opinions for a while—something that Ian won't do. This is why he comes to an ab-solute standstill in some of his relationships. He won't let up on his in-tegrity long enough for the other person to be comfortable—but that is *his* style.

WEAVING THROUGH THE MAZES—getting "killed" once for each mistake before going a different route next time—like Al Barker in *Rogue*

Moon. He was the first man to get successfully through all the traps of the Great Unknown.[21]

That is the way for me—

What little knowledge we have, really. It would be so easy to cotton to Hubbard or Jung or Ian, and say, *yes*, life can be explained by eight dynamics or seven levels or six archetypes—all this is true, yet there is always more, always an extra piece that doesn't fit in.

What kills me is to hear profound music all around me and know that I am not (yet?) equal to profundity—I can't ride Ian piggyback into heaven. I've got to work out my own categories, find my own salvation. My temptation is to take his sweat after it is fashioned into ready-mades and try to wear it as my own. No wonder it sometimes doesn't fit, as close as our ideas may be.

Dear God, don't let me be another MWG,[22] babbling great nothings after a few drinks, running off to Florida (or its equivalent) every time responsibility raises its disagreeable head. If I could only avoid that fate—being a dreamer, a half-fashioner of poetry who somehow floats away into dreamy sunsets and evaporates with the fumes of alcohol.

SO IAN'S MOTHER rides off all parceled and be-diamonded in her minicab, and I of all the people in this universe know what she thinks. I can't tell Ian, because he would feel—no matter how hard he tried not to— "How dare you understand my own mother better than me?" But I do. She let down her sticky prickles and showed me how it was with her. I would not like to have been Ian's mother—and one day Alan will show Ian just how it feels.

I MUST DO SOMETHING with that old manuscript ["Mourning"]—if I could only understand MW's failure to live, to *become*, then I could use his drops of blood as stepping stones to the life he couldn't reach.

---

21. *Rogue Moon* by Algis Budrys was a finalist for the Hugo Award for best science fiction novel in 1961. In it, scientists are able to create duplicates of characters that then negotiate a deadly maze. Whenever a duplicate dies in a trap, the original person, maintained in state of suspended animation, goes a little more insane. The hero, Al Barker, finds a way to traverse the hero's psychological purgatory.

22. Mose Winston Godwin, Gail's father.

JANUARY 5

Ian and I had another fight—as of old, a really bad one. I always start hating him and wanting to twist the knife: What can I say that can hurt him? This is senseless.

BACK AT "THE PLACE"—USTS.[23] Those people have nothing to do with me. I have nausea and a headache that runs all the way up my back and branches out all over my head.

In two hours, Ian will be home. I'll cook a late supper and try to be alert. I must at least try. At the moment, it's impossible to tell him everything I feel because it would only make him worse.

How I wish he wouldn't use those Scientology words. They sound sillier than ever. I'm afraid my curiosity about it—taking the course—has got him all gung-ho again. He clings to things like that as if he were a drowning man. Doesn't he see that he's outgrown their solutions?

Hubbard's trick, it seems to me, is to keep waving the promised land in front of his pupils until they become addicts. I don't think Hubbard is malicious. I just think he's played God too long to remain fair (e.g., his vague answer to Ian regarding Power Processing).[24] Hubbard has a lot of the circus about him. He loves circus people, he'll say himself.

How I wish Ian would be able to *sustain his efforts*. At first I kept excusing him, thinking it was my bitchiness that may have depressed him, but the pattern was there long before I was.

If anything keeps him from being a great man, it will be just this "Let me see, how do I feel today?" But if that's the best he can do, I must shut up and not make it worse.

23. Mr. Miller had asked Gail to come back as a contract worker and write a travel handbook for the U.S. Travel Service.

24. Ian and Gail were involved with Scientology's founder L. Ron Hubbard at the onset of his major educational project in psychic healing at Saint Hill Manor in East Grinstead, Sussex. The overall goal was to "clear the planet" by clearing individuals of irrational impulses. Though the center had been established in 1959, it wasn't until 1966 that Hubbard instituted Power Processing, a profitable method of "auditing" and training people in achieving a state of Clear.

What a headache. God, I hurt in so many ways. I am really alone now.

JANUARY 16

Dreams of machinery and evil cannibalistic men; marriage with gray-haired successes; wading through strange cabbage country, forsaking Ian for various animus figures—seeing hints everywhere, pointers labeled "Meaningful!"

But meaningful of what?

A grand plot for a grand novel fades before my eyes. Inchoate thoughts bubble up and overwhelm my good sense. I want to protest to everybody, and as I rant, I see the glint in their eyes that reads: "What is she going on about? What 'by-passed charge' has she?[25] What cause is she championing? Really!"

JUST READ A BOOK by the occult-woman, Dion Fortune.[26] A lot of it disgusted me—as a certain type of ecstatic ranting does—but she, too, speaks of opposites being parts of the same thing, the dynamic impetus of woman and the receptive in man both being as important as the passive woman and the positive man. The sex suggestion made me remember feeling passion in certain conditions. The night on Old Church Street, in the narrow bedroom overlooking the garden—was it Gordon himself or something I felt "about" him? And at age fifteen, reading the rituals in *Quo Vadis.*

IT JUST CAME to me that Jung's sexual side remained underdeveloped; he cut loose from the earth too soon and spent his life in myths and the Great Unknown.

---

25. "By-passed charge" is the Scientology term for mental energy that has gone awry.

26. Dion Fortune was the founder of the Society of the Inner Light and the author of many books, including *The Mystical Qabalah* (1935) and *The Cosmic Doctrine* (1949).

JANUARY 19

Who am I *not* fighting?

MY MARRIAGE IS one of the biggest unrealities in my life. Gail *Marshall*, who is she? I've had so many names. Perhaps that's part of the trouble.

Who is this husband of mine, this man who puts me on my guard the minute he comes anywhere near me? I've taken him at his word that he was in good condition, but is he? He can't manage ordinary situations, can't walk into a room with grace or confidence—always the twitchy little smile hovers about his face, like an uncertain sun going in and out of clouds. The only way he seems to be able to sustain any effort is for somebody to shame him into it. And his girlfriends abide with us now and forevermore. He has no new friends, so has to cling to the old ones.

How can I feel married to a man whose style is so totally alien to mine?

He's a wonderful pilgrim to have with me on the journey, but I can't feel proud of him. He comes into the USTS office wearing a smelly old coat. He has that uncertain look.

Like tonight in HASI [Hubbard Association of Scientologists, International]—I waited to see him before class. Anne came up the stairs, her huge teeth leading the way, and sure enough he followed. He'd had dinner with her and some other Scientologists in a restaurant. He came in and saw me and said "Oh, hello" and some other formalities with the usual number of stops and uncertainties—like I was someone whose name he couldn't remember. I said, "Who did you have dinner with?" and he got all defensive and said, "Oh . . . some people," and then gradually let it out. I said jokingly, "You philander the minute I let you out of my sight." Even old phony-baloney Voit Gilmore could have handled that one. So then I said, "Have you written anything today that I can read?" He said, "Yes, but not that you can read." Then I said, "Did you know Michael called me a bitch this morning?" He said, "Oh?" I said, "Did he say anything to you about it?" He said, "Not that I can repeat."

I ask you, is that a husband? He sounds more like a very nervous U.S. State Department official talking to a Russian newspaper reporter.

But somewhere in the records, it's written in ink that I am his legal wife.

FEBRUARY 6

When I'm getting along well, like a patient who has been cured, I forget the dark side, which may be in need of a boost sometime. I was typing Ian's book when I thought: I must record the experiences I've been having.

There are higher states which one can achieve, having gotten lower problems out of the way first. I just listened to Beethoven's *Pastoral* and for the first time really heard music. I was so clean of my usual ruminations that I could concentrate completely on the music.

All this clarity I'm having, I want to preserve it. Short stories shorn of vanity might be the answer. Try "The Confession at St. Mary's"[27] for a start—

> *Daffodils—their wet, springy, turfy look—so tight, so fresh, a*
>   *student flower.*
> *Wet turf. Library smelling of newsprint.*
> *The way to fast—St. Thomas Aquinas.*
> *Priest—an athlete by proportion and stance (he can't die).*
> *So real—St. Patrick all in green and athletic; St. John, "the*
>   *favorite," pale and delicate.*

What sins had I to put down?

Children at eleven or twelve are so clear. They have just about solved the problems of childhood and are not yet into the muck of adolescence.

---

27. See "Possible Sins," in the Ballantine Reader's Circle edition of *Evenings at Five: A Novel and Five New Stories.* Gail wrote this story of her first confession many years after, but this 1966 journal entry was the first impetus for it.

FEBRUARY 6

Ian off in the woods by himself.

Listening to *A Sea Symphony* (by Ralph Vaughan Williams), I decide to go for a walk over old territory [the Chelsea embankment]—the river high, the sky showing signs of life. Somehow, I do not enjoy this walk as I should. The other times, when I'd taken the walk, I'd always come back the same way—and I am doing it all over again.

So I crossed over and ambled silently down Sunday streets with no traffic—up Flood Street and by the Chelsea Town Hall; met James Montgomerie for the first time in three years.[28] Any spark of creativity or mischief or spontaneity that flickered in him when I knew him is now dead. Even Ian and all his therapy could not save him. He even tried the old cocktail party armor on *me*. I just stood there and talked to him and looked at him, and he didn't show one fraction of anything but guardedness. What was he afraid of? That I would try to hoist him off to a coffee shop, love him for hours? Finally, we parted with relief after speaking for a decent interval.

He'd asked all the proper questions, hadn't volunteered much. "Why, Gail, this is your old haunt." Yes, and I felt haunted by all my old Sunday depressions. They accumulated on the walk until the air was thick with them.

FEBRUARY 11

Dreamed of Aunt Sophie giving a party—and I had no good clothes— threw together something mismatched, but passable—met Frank's aunt Lona, on the way; she'd been to the party and was going back—she looked terrible in a country getup that wouldn't have passed anywhere— Woolworth jewelry and a flour-sack skirt and sleeveless blouse. She said, "They're all so *dressed* in there, do I look all right?"

28. In April 1962, Gail had become attached to James Montgomerie, an attentive, never-married, thirty-eight-year-old lawyer employed by the Rank Organization (a media business machine, and hotel conglomerate). He had been so dissatisfied with his bureaucratic job, he was thinking of leaving the company—partly to focus on his writing.

"Yes," I said "You've got a sleeveless frock and jewelry, that's what they wear."

She seemed reassured. "I didn't want to get thrown out," she said.

So I went down to the cloakroom, hoping to fix myself up before Aunt Sophie saw me—but there she was, having her hair combed by a slavish attendant. I noticed Aunt Sophie's unsightly feet—her face was still powerful but her neck was wrinkled as a rooster's and she wore a plain print dress.

"I've been wondering why you hadn't come," she said. "Oh, what a nice tennis skirt you have on. Margaret is here, she's holding up well under the circumstances."

"What circumstances?" I asked, feeling chilled for my uncle Johnny.

"Didn't you hear," she cried, "about the tube coffin?"

"No. Mother didn't tell me."

"Well, Johnny got caught in a tube at the plant and was spun round and round for hours, until he died . . ."

This dream was strong enough to stay with me all morning. I was back in the year 1954, visiting my rich relatives in Alabama and resuffering all the humiliation of being the poor cousin "who made good grades." I worked up an anger at all of them for not recognizing *my* things, the games I excelled at. I was uncertain of my right to be different and tried playing life in their style. No wonder I floundered in a halfway mode and was not anything.

AND MY ANGER has extended to HASI. How dare they accept Hubbard's word as gospel without doing a little searching on their own? How dare they not *want* to know about other viewpoints?

It seems to me that one can write anything meaningfully if one has a viewpoint. George Eliot, Henry James, Jane Austen, all had their framework. Secure in their moral certainty, they spent their time creating characters and situations to dramatize and point up their structures.

In any story I write, a viewpoint is needed. A viewpoint gives to a selection of incidents (and characters involved) a meaning all its own.

OH, GOD, HOW LONG, how *long*?

FEBRUARY 12

Depressed all day, apathetic. But this evening I worked out more things
about writing. I want my characters to solve their life problems in a new
and more effective way. There are several forms for the combinations I
want.

    I.   THE DILEMMA. What is the moral thing for the individ-
ual to do? (Lydgate or Bulstrode in *Middlemarch*; Isabel Archer
in *Portrait of a Lady*.) The tragedy is when he knows what he
must do and can't do it. Is it moral to reduce one's awareness?
How detached can one be and still remain human?

    II.   WHAT WOULD HAPPEN IF? An imaginary situation is
conceived, and then characters react to that situation. There's
the datum, and then the variables.

    III.   SLICE OF LIFE. Social realism. The way it is without of-
fering any solution or suggestion. A key phase, as in *Portrait of
the Artist*. Heightened awareness, as in *The Waves*.

    IV.   DIDACTIC. Philosophy in novel form: Ayn Rand, Sartre,
de Sade, Lawrence.

Story idea: "Movers"[29]

—

"Merrymount."

"Hmph," said Rachel. "It sounds like a girls' riding academy. I
should think Olympus Hall would've been more apt."

---

29. Gail was beginning a story about her proposed visit to Saint Hill Manor, the headquar-
ters for advanced studies in Scientology.

Part five

THE OUTSIDER

1 Argyll Mansions, London, and
Saint Hill, East Grinstead, Sussex

MARCH 21, 1966, TO MAY 22, 1966

In the mid-1960s, Gail's contemporaries sought to confront a deep-seated social malaise by probing their subconscious depths. Caught up in the human-improvement phenomenon, Gail assembled around her key texts related to such topics as the essential self, freedom from prejudice, and heightened experience. One of the books was The Outsider, *Colin Wilson's 1956 survey of writers and artists who sought heartfulness (to use a term featured in Gail's 2001 book* Heart*). She referred to these books while exploring the cloistered world of Scientology, into which she had been drawn through discussions with her husband, Ian Marshall.*

[UNDATED, 1966]

I am married to Ian Marshall.

> *"I simply sat and watched him with the queerest, deepest, sweetest sense in the world—the sense of an ache that had stopped...I myself at least was somehow off the ground. He was already where I had been."*
> *"And where were you?" the Brother amusedly asked.*
> *"Just on the sofa always, leaning back on the cushion and feeling a delicious ease. He was already me."*
> *"And who were you?" the Brother continued.*
> *"Nobody. That was the fun."*
> ——HENRY JAMES, "The Great Good Place"

By March 1966, Ian Marshall had become wholly committed to Scientology, and had involved Gail. They'd enrolled in all-day courses at the Hubbard Association of Scientologists, International (HASI) in London; it was a place that demanded submission to a group and a process.

Although she was fascinated by some of the tenets of Scientology, Gail was also making an effort to save her marriage by sampling her husband's passionate interest. She tried salvaging from Scientology theories that might excite her imagination. She took a stab at that process with a story idea, "The Woman Who Killed Plants," and explicated it with Scientology terminology.

The Woman Who Killed Plants

—

A woman sets up a flat—she's married—and, of course, buys a plant, or is given a plant. It dies. She gets another, thinking nothing of it. It also dies. This goes on for a while until she gets angry that these plants keep dying on her. She consults people about it. They advise various things. She does them—but to no avail. If the plants don't die, they grow in weird ways—it's the absence of this woman's life-giving force (she has no YIN).

"You have to have a yen for growing plants." (Fifth dynamic, Tone 40 on an object.)[1]

"Tone" is any level of survival—or state of being—on the tone scale of the L. Ron Hubbard Chart of Human Evaluation. "Tone 40" means intention without reservation or limit. Have her sit down and talk to it (a plant)—the fifth dynamic. One day, her little stepson overhears, comes

1. The Scientology term "dynamic" means the urge toward life. There are eight dynamics and various corresponding tones that lead from apathy through knowledge to unobstructed experience of self and world. The fifth dynamic is the urge toward survival through animals and plants.

in and helps. She's always had too much logos, or dignity, to talk to a plant before. They do this every day for a while. What is happening is that she is warming up to life by contacting it—she gets into empathy with it. Her little stepson, who has always been dutiful but slightly suspicious, warms up to her. Before, he had only given her the outward signs of a filial affection with the adherence of someone who has signed a contract and is determined to stick by it graciously. All his witty, childish originalities, and all his outbursts of joy or rage, were saved for his father.

OTHER STORY IDEAS:

Someone who dramatizes all the time—strip the dramatizations away and you have a person who is "just himself."[2] He does not go around having to create an effect on people—he may be rather quiet—but he is effective. He is totally freed from the need to be admired or noticed by others.

The Know-to-Mystery Scale also has possibilities.[3]

"Why mother!" said Lou [the heroine] impatiently, "I think one gets so tired of your men with mind, as you call it. There are so many of that sort of clever men . . . It seems to me there's something else besides mind and cleverness, or niceness or cleanness. Perhaps it is the animal. Just think of St. Mawr! . . . He seems a far greater mystery to me than a clever man. He's a horse. Why can't one say in the same way, of a man: He's a man?"

—D. H. LAWRENCE, "St. Mawr"

2. "Dramatizing" in Scientology means acting out a "valence" (powerful force) in an "engram" (traumatic experience). One example that Hubbard gives is the experience of an abused child, who dramatizes the valence of the abuser in reenacting the engram of the abuse experience.

3. The ultimate state of being in the Know-to-Mystery Scale is the "native state." It is ranked above belief in deities, and above knowledge. It involves experiencing self and world simultaneously, without losing the will to act.

MARCH 21

How to avoid fanaticism in Scientology: Don't be intellectually isolated; don't stop reading good books; don't stop caring about aesthetic growth. Remember H. James, Colin Wilson, D. H. Lawrence, etc.

> The [great good] place represents no less than the still center of one's own being, access to which is generally obstructed by innumerable irrelevancies... The whole dream in this case becomes a verbalized representation of that trance-like state, the SAMADHI of Indian tradition, in which man is face to face with his Self and which opens his eyes to the heart of things.
> —KRISHNA BALDEV VAID,
> TECHNIQUE IN THE TALES OF HENRY JAMES

Have friends who are intellectually stimulated by interests outside Sci y. Remember, the compulsion to know can get you into trouble. Do not <u>need</u> help from any one source. Do not look on HASI as a place to relax, be accepted, run back to. Keep up other standards which HASI neglects.

HOW DO PEOPLE respond to a cult?

> *Repression—I don't want to think about it, it's dangerous.*
> *Suppression—Keep it down! Wipe it out!*
> *Dramatization—It's all! I'm saved! It's the way.*
> *Understanding—I'm not stuck in a viewpoint. I can create new viewpoints at will.*

Movers
—

A newspaper reporter sent to investigate a cult doesn't come back. "The seeds of fanaticism were always in him," said Sullivan, "I just wasn't being observant."

Of course! Isn't it logical that anyone who could hate a subject with the intensity he could, might also suddenly go into reverse with equal intensity? Look at St. Paul, for instance. Cases are strung out all through history.

"I just wasn't looking."

Fanaticism is getting stuck in a viewpoint, losing the ability to see from a distance. You become a viewpoint, lose all your space.

Sullivan sends a second reporter to investigate. This reporter is known for his extreme, academic care in being as objective as possible. He seems to have a built-in proboscis for ferreting out reality from unreal situations.

Note the myths and fairy tales in which the hero has to search for something precious in a dangerous place. There is always the fear of being sucked in, of flying too close to the sun.

"Voyage to Arcturus"[4]—What is true, what is false? Sometimes one masquerades as the other.

THE THREE HINDU fundamental states of the human spirit: Sattva: loftiness, goodness; Rajas: manifestation, struggle, and dynamism; Tamas: obscurity and brute instinct.

> *Sattva attaches man to happiness, rajas to action, and tamas,*
> *shrouding knowledge, attaches him to heedlessness. Sattva*
> *prevails, O Bharata, having overcome rajas and tamas; rajas,*
> *when it has overpowered sattva and tamas; likewise tamas*
> *reigns when sattva and rajas are crushed.*
>
> —*THE BHAGAVAD GITA*, translated by Mahadev Desai

---

4. Colin Wilson called David Lindsay's *A Voyage to Arcturus* (1920) "the greatest novel of the twentieth century," apparently for its imaginative metaphysics rather than its literary merits. The novel's hero, Maskull, travels to the planet Tormance (which orbits Arcturus) and encounters various races and belief systems before climbing a tower of revelations. With that perspective, he learns that the instinct for pleasure corrupts, and that pain is a truer instrument of evolution.

Read Professor George A. Kelly, Ohio State University, about Personal Construct Theory.[5]

> *Let us consider the case of the person who is construed by his neighbors in such a way that he is expected to do certain things. Whenever he fails to perform according to their expectations he finds them acting as if he had threatened them. He has. Now he may start to fancy himself as an unpredictable person... In order to maintain his pose he may have to construe himself as a "shocking" person. Thus, even though he rejects the expectancies of his neighbors as being invalid, he has had to construe himself in relation to those expectations.*
> —GEORGE A. KELLY, *A THEORY OF PERSONALITY:*
> *THE PSYCHOLOGY OF PERSONAL CONSTRUCTS*

In a half-dream this morning, I started "writing" a story and realized it was about a mile off the ground, high-flown and pretentious. Not touching the ground at any point.

APRIL 8 · *Good Friday*

I thought of that other Good Friday, in 1951:

A spring day with an earthy smell, everything fresh, the daffodils coming up all around St. Mary's Church, and a very few of us at the afternoon service. Father Webbe was in black cassock. He went through the Stations of the Cross, all around the church and then, just before three, when Christ died, he knelt down, a humble athlete, and his body looked truly sorrowful. Good Friday was never the same after that one. For one thing, I have lost my religious fervor. But it was beautiful while it lasted.

---

5. George Kelly analyzed the ways in which people see and believe what they expect to see and believe, and how, when they're confounded, they adjust their beliefs as painlessly as possible. Readers of Kelly hoped that people would develop an awareness of their self-deluding processes for their own good. Gail applied her reading of Kelly to her HASI experience.

—

LATELY, I HAVE BEEN dreaming on a new plane. Whether it's Sci y's influence, or all the science fiction and Colin Wilson, I don't know. But in the dreams, I and others are learning how to evolve into a better species.

If one could truly rid himself of his aberrations and projections, then he could recognize when he picks up other people's emotions. He would be able to distinguish them from his own. Thus, the gradual growth of ESP.

ELLEN A., A HASI classmate, said: "I didn't want the baby. I'd finished that cycle of action. He was an overrun.[6] I knew it was wrong to have him. I was going against my own reality to have him."

IN THE TAXI COMING HOME, I realized that no therapy, including Power Processing, could solve my problem if one intention belonged to me and the counterintention belonged to someone else. Only with problems where both the intention and counterintention belong to a single person can the pressure be relieved.

For instance, I think I can do something about my writing because the opposition lies within, but about other things—liking sex with Ian; feeling motherly and loving his son—these may not be for me to solve. In fact, if only Ian didn't mind, I would feel perfectly happy accepting what is.

About the problem with Alan. The only children I could love and tolerate were my kin, because I felt they were tied up with me somehow. I could never love Alan the way I do Rebel[7]—even though I haven't seen Rebel often. I understand how he operates. Alan is a silent, morose little person. I haven't the slightest idea what he's thinking, and I consider him mainly as a threat to my freedom.

Yes, this is the way it is: I feel totally outside everybody's group.

6. "Overrun" is a Scientology term for a behavior that belongs to an earlier period of development.

7. Rebel Cole, the younger of Gail's two brothers, by her mother and Frank, was seven at the time.

I can't "go back" to N.C. (in spirit, or as a way of living). The past is dead. I can't agree with their way—it isn't wide enough. On the other hand, I will never merge into a partnership with Ian as he wants it; he is alien to me, too. I never have felt totally at home here.

ELIA GOLLER AT the Mensa conference I went to with Ian, after I had been telling him how I'd like to live in Arizona, and describing the end of Lawrence's story "St. Mawr": "I know what's wrong with you. You just don't like your fellow humans."

But I'm not unhappy all alone out here, the only nonmember of Mensa. If only people would not protest. Couldn't Ian and I come to some arrangement where we could live together but not merge?

> "So I have told him. I said this evening, when no one was about: 'Rico dear, listen to me seriously. I can't stand these people. If you ask me to endure another week of them, I shall either become ill, or insult them... I tell you, I shall just make a break, like St. Mawr, if I don't get out... Won't you come with me to America, to the South-west?' "

> "I don't hate men because they're men... I dislike them because they're not men enough: babies, and playboys, and poor things showing off all the time, even to themselves. I don't say I'm any better. I only wish, with all my soul, that some men were bigger and stronger and deeper than I am... There's something else for me... It's here, in this landscape."
>
> —LOU WITT, heroine of "St. Mawr," by D. H. Lawrence

Next week: Power Processing—keep notes.[8]

---

8. Ian had booked Gail and himself for Power Processing at Saint Hill Manor, the English mecca of Scientology, a Gothic-looking estate formerly belonging to the Maharajah of Jaipur.

APRIL 12–13 · *At Saint Hill, East Grinstead*

First impression: big tree in the front of the manor. I feel resentful that Hubbard should have such a tree. Waiting. Waiting. Cold and damp. "Suppressive" bandied in the atmosphere. College days have been overrun. Let me out of here.

APRIL 15

What have you done? What was that a solution to? What have you not said? What was that a solution to? Masturbation—what kind of release do you feel that was? What is a nonsource? Did you notice perceptics[9] were clearer?

What is a source? Water, fire, mother, the snake Uroborus. But what are mine? Is there nothing I can go back to, that I lived out of?

Many things now return—a ballroom on a summer's night full of Russian counts, all long ago.

My source is the imagination.

THE CENTER OF ONE'S own being is capable of illimitable energy—colors, pictures, patterns, answers.

APRIL 19

In the mechanism of Saint Hill is the seed of a totalitarian government. I am getting a taste of the outrage an individual feels, the muffled protest against a looter of the spirit.

Mrs. Marshall and Ian in the dining room of the Regent Palace fight over the bill in a way my family never could—each with the confident aggression that he/she means to pay.

9. "Perceptics" is Scientology's term for the fifty-seven senses, which include balance and awareness of awareness.

—

WHAT IF THE "DOORS of perception" were cleansed? Have they ever been? Is there a way? Has Hubbard found it?

APRIL 27

"Tell me an existing condition. Tell me how you have handled it."

YOU HAVE BEEN connected to: Freudian psychotherapy, analytical psychology, Ayn Rand's Objectivism, existentialism, the Methodist church, the Presbyterian, Catholic, Episcopal, tranquilizers, smoking marijuana.

I AM GETTING rid of my mechanisms by becoming aware of them. Today in the session, it was as if I looked around the room and saw all my "existing conditions" sitting in the chairs, wearing hats. All my aberrations—Mr. Lying, Mr. Exaggeration, Mr. Procrastination, Mr. Protest, Mr. In-a-Hurry, etc. I laughed and laughed and then wanted to cry.

And yet there is something still to come. I saw it (during Hanna's excellent management—she handles me like an experienced horse trainer handles an unruly horse) in the image of a hole, and at the bottom of the hole, dark water. Only when you get to the water, you find it is not dark blue at all, like you thought. That is the shadow—the shadow I make—from looking down the hole. The water itself is clear.

HANNA'S A COOL ANGEL with absolutely no dramatizations that I can see.

THIS WEEK I STARTED auditing. Got a tough one, Mrs. Wenda P., thirty-seven. Hatchet face. Bitch "Bank."[10] Valence: "I am a tough one. Nobody can help me." The first night it was like being pushed down a ski slope, unsure of my skis.

The second night: locked up in a cage with a tiger, knowing nothing about tigers.

10. "Bank" is Scientology's colloquial name for the reactive mind, which stores the irrational responses of a "preclear."

Tonight, a vast improvement. She did the CCH 2 as a young woman, holding herself proudly.[11] She had had her hair done. She was helpful, looked at me after a supreme effort (embarrassment), and wept to relief on the question "If you could talk to a child, what would you talk about?"

"Look at that wall... Thank you."
"Walk over to that wall... Thank you."
"With your right hand, touch that wall... Thank you."
"Turn around... Thank you."

Wenda is a dominant woman, yet she accepts force and control. She has had two stillborn babies. She has a mentally deficient daughter. She is tied up emotionally with images of freedom—running through the grass in the sunshine. She, too, is having the "busy" dreams. I had them when I began the Sci y. The unconscious is getting ready for housecleaning.

MAY 5

I am auditing a young man named Guy H., who is part Indian. He is worried about being acceptable to people, can't go in Tubes alone or into restaurants, is still haunted by an early homosexual experience he had as a child: "Did I enjoy it? Am I enough of a man? Yet I am good at sports, and have a wife and son." What miserable messes we all are.

Lunch in the Chelsea Potter with Michael, who is Chelsea personified. Then driving around in his battered car to kinky dress shops owned by friends of his. Rain. The sweet flowers in Blake's. Michael gives me a good perspective on Ian. He has known him longer than I have.

Ian is strange to me. He does not live completely in the world of mammals. He is part fish or bird or rare creature who is not really at

11. The CCH 2 is the second of four control-communication-havingness techniques by which an auditor has his "preclear" establish control of his body, improve his communication, and gain a grasp of present-moment reality. The preclear strives to clear himself of things that have taken control of his "thetan," or essential self. In practice, CCH techniques are repeated to the point of hysteria or hypnosis, so that the preclear begins to break down and communicate secrets.

home with people or dogs. The way he carefully made friends with Michelle's poodle the other night.

MAY 9

Ambrose [in a new story, "The Possibilitarian"] reading, reading, yet never really understanding. The feeling, the music, and the twilights and sunsets are absorbed without needing to know the words.

ANNE, IAN's Scientology colleague and former girlfriend, is here for the weekend. Her form of courage: All her life she has made herself do the very thing of which she was most afraid. "It's like being in a very fast car, going round steep curves. I can do nothing about the speed—it is constant—but I have learned very good control of the curves. Now, after all these years, it is paying dividends. I am beset by my demon, but, in comparison, the things most people fear are nothing for me to confront." Her two examples:

Fifteen years old—vacationing in Ireland—rode a wild horse on a beach. He threw her. Her mother came down to the beach and made a racket. "I thought of that horse for a whole year. I knew I had to ride him. The next year we came back. I rode him every day. I loved that horse. I'll never forget him. I was always just a little bit afraid of him. I used to pick blackberries for him.

"Between my junior and senior year at university, I stayed with a French couple. When I went back to Oxford, I thought of that man for the entire year. The day I graduated, I packed my bags, bought a ticket to Paris. When I arrived in Paris, I picked up the telephone and called him. I said, 'I want to see you!' This went on for three years. I went back and forth between England and Paris, staying in little hotels, with all my belongings in two suitcases. Of course, I could not live at home."

WRITE A SHORT NOVEL about Vertical Lives, and how the Horizontal livers miss the point.[12]

---

12. Gail began working on the short novel "The Ruptured Link," renamed "The Possibilitarian," involving a visionary but failed father named Ambrose.

—

RIDING IN THE BACK of the van with Ian and Anne and friends in front, on the way to dinner in Earls Court, a gloom suddenly materialized. It was as if the little dark spirits were all around me, buzz, buzz, there in the back of the van. I breathed their sweet poison and surrendered all my resistance. I was naked, powerless, gloomy, and without hope. It was comforting, in a way.

MAY 14

"Tell me an existing condition."

I am floating down the river on a barge that knows where it is going. It is nighttime and warm. On the banks of the river stand people, places, and ideas that have dogged me all my life—all my wrong concepts, all my dramatizations, all my favorite things—they are all personified and wearing strange hats and dumpy clothes. They wave to me as I go by.

Ambrose:

> *"In this mammalian world I have moved tentatively, not quite sure of the games the mammals were able to play to such a sophisticated degree. I was much more at home being a kind of bird-cum-fish— sometimes sliding through oceanic caverns, at home in watery dream worlds; other times soaring with a bird's-eye view. No, I never felt at home with the mammals, though I loved them and envied them."*

I don't dare to breathe. The insight is coming of itself.

> *"I have attained my visions through bonded bourbon. However, I can see another way: through a kind of supersonic alertness. One could concentrate, focus, make his consciousness a precision instrument. It is too late for me. My tips are too blunted for any change. But for another, however... ah!"*

Once again it is time for Rachel's summer visit. Ambrose, her father, in the beach cottage he has rented for the two of them, slips smartly into his white linen suit, slaps his cheeks with aftershave, and prepares to meet the train.

Or:

Once again it is time for Rachel's summer visit. Ambrose, her father, newly settled in with suitcase and fishing gear in the beach cottage he has rented for the two of them, slips smartly into his cream linen suit and prepares to meet the evening train. He is nervous and as alert as a boy on his first date. This is partly because his daughter's style fascinates him, partly because he has not had one drink since lunch. This summer, things are going to be different.

There are six stages of consciousness one goes through with LSD. The stages always follow in the same order, although not all people reach stage 6: (1) things get brighter, cleaner; (2) the physical universe is seen in a new way; (3) ideas combine in new ways; (4) one reexperiences past lives; (5) you perceive GPMs;[13] (6) you achieve whiteness, mystical attainment.

IAN HAS MADE the mathematical discovery of the century.

MICHAEL: "I think men are saved because they can get enthusiastic about odd little hobbies, metalwork or electricity; also, I think they can hear the fairies sing. I can be on a bus or walking down the street when, bringgg! I hear the celestial music and am wafted right out of the intensity-ridden world."

Ambrose has heard the fairies sing.

---

13. GPM is the Goals Problem Mass, the tightly bound complex of hidden goals underlying people's aberrations. It is possible to undo the mass through auditing, Scientology proposes.

As Gail approaches the end of her HASI involvement, she re-works her character Ambrose, the benighted father figure in "The Ruptured Link." Some of the material would eventually be used in Gail's first published novel, The Perfectionists. Psychotherapist John Empson, the featured husband in that book, tells his wife, Dane, "I am pretty sure I have found the basic pattern of human thought." He shows how a hundred values and their opposites are arranged in a snowflake pattern, representing a spiritual progression that is laid with despair-inducing traps.

MAY 22

What is a word that would describe the state of mind when you visual-ize how something might have been, accompanied by nostalgia, resig-nation, and a quiet acceptance. Not "regret," because that implies sadness. Just: "That is how it is."

AMBROSE AS A DIARY of the gulf between action and thought. He can vi-sualize but can't convert his visions into actual energies. Some ball bear-ing or spring seems to be left out of his makeup.

Drank too much at our party. Spent the day lying in bed looking out at a blazing green bush (if fire were green, Ian said), and then watching the patterns of the shadows of its leaves on the wall inside. I seemed to withdraw into my world of images and abandon any idea of sharing them with anybody.

IAN: "I COULD PLAY chess in my head, only couldn't see the board. But I could feel where the pieces were, like they were moving on my chest."

WRITE DOWN THE basic ideas about what you think a "cult," an applied philosophy, can do to people in different stages of knowing about a sub-ject. Describe these different states.

—

SECRETS OF AUDITING: Get two poles into the situation so that preclear can be one mass viewing another mass. Ask questions that turn generalities into specifics. Cut down randomity.[14] Get preclear to identify things in his bank, compartmentalize them, get outside of them, and increase his ability to put in his own itsa line.[15]

FINAL AIM OF PROCESSING—no further need to itsa.

14. "Randomity" is a Scientology term referring to the misalignment of an organism's efforts caused by the efforts of other entities.

15. "Itsa," short for "it is a," refers to a preclear's clear identification of something in response to an auditor's question. An itsa line is the line of communication between a preclear and his/her own "bank."

Hiatus

Gail Fills in a Significant Gap Undocumented by Journals

MAY 23, 1966, TO MARCH 4, 1968

————

Now we come to a critical block of time and there is no record of it. How did that happen? Well, after May 22, 1966, due to lack of privacy, first in London and then back in the U.S.A., I stopped keeping the journals. As soon as I arrived in Iowa City, Iowa, in January 1967, and had a place of my own, I began again. But alas, those first Iowa notebooks[16] were discovered in early 1968 by a jealous poet, who threw them into the Iowa River. He said it was his symbolic way of destroying my past. Luckily for my other journals, they were still back in London with Ian.

So the day-to-day chronicling of those months is gone. Unlike my letters, which were written to project various personas (the adventuresome traveler, the needy daughter, etc.), the journals stayed grounded, for the most part, in a desperate honesty. If I couldn't confide in *them*, I risked losing track of myself. And therein lies their value for me today. It is impossible to gloss over or misremember what is recorded in your own handwriting of forty years before.

However, if you have followed me this far, I owe you some fill-in for what has been lost.

---

16. Some of the highlights of the lost diaries are preserved in "Becoming a Writer," in *The Writer on Her Work*, vol. 1, ed. Janet Sternberg (Norton, 1981) and "Waltzing with the Black Crayon," in *Evenings at Five: A Novel and Five New Stories* (Ballantine, 2004). This was the period when Gail studied with Kurt Vonnegut and José Donoso, and made friends with Jane Barnes, John Casey, David Plimpton, and John Irving. She also decided to stay on at the University of Iowa and do graduate work in literature. She earned a PhD in English in 1970.

—

AFTER I GOT "Power Processed" at East Grinstead in May 1966, I became an apprentice "auditor" (under supervision) at HASI in London. Soon after that, we took a two-week vacation to Cala D'or in Majorca. At first it was to be Ian, myself, and Ian's three-year-old son, Alan. The vacation was to be Alan's transition between leaving his foster home and coming to live with us. Then Ian invited Pauline, a secretary at USTS, and Penrose, a young woman we had met at a recent Mensa conference. Ian paid their expenses and in return they were supposed to help out with the little boy. If it had been a math problem, it might have worked out, but we were five human beings. The child stuck to me or to Ian and shrieked bloody murder if we tried to leave him with either of the "P.s." It was a ghastly vacation. Out of it, as a pearl comes out of an oyster's pain, came the story "The Beautiful French Family" (in our hotel, there was such a family, whose graceful, sensual actuality served as our daily reproach), which later became the novel *The Perfectionists*.

When we returned to London, the marriage was pretty much done for. Likewise, I realized I was not fit to raise this child, perhaps not any child. In those early summer weeks back in London, I was very morose. I did not resume my auditing duties at HASI. I had stopped keeping a journal ever since the morning when I returned to our Chelsea quarters unexpectedly and found Ian all set up at the dining table with a mug of coffee and my stack of journals. (As I remember it—or misremember it—I expressed moral outrage and he calmly replied that they were interesting to read and revealed things about me it was important for him to know.)

My moroseness grew into full-blown depression until, one summer day in our garden under an ancient mulberry tree, hoping to root out my source of unhappiness, Ian tried a Scientology technique on me in which the auditor asks the client the same question over and over again until he or she answers the truth. This was measured by an "e-meter," Scientology's version of a lie detector, devised from two V8 juice cans stripped of their labels and wired to a galvanometer. When the client clutching the cans finally speaks the truth, the needle on the meter stops jiggling around and floats. The client is supposed to feel a floating sense of relief as well. We weren't using the apparatus—Ian said he could read me as accurately as the V8 juice cans—but he kept repeating the question "Why can't you be a writer?" until I finally answered, "Because I'm afraid I might fail." At which point I felt a wonderful sense of release and we agreed the experiment had been a success.

Soon after, I felt an urgent desire to visit my family in North Carolina. Ian bought the round-trip ticket, and I set off with little more than a change of clothes and a bathing suit. I was never to return but apparently couldn't let myself know this yet: I had to make my getaway in stages, in one small, conscious increment after another.

(A later story, "A Sorrowful Woman," came out of my futile attempts at mothering in the spring of 1966. One raw afternoon when Ian and I and the child were walking glumly in the country, I started fantasizing about a wife and mother who simply retreated. Went into her room and wouldn't come out. Every night her husband, a doctor, gave her a sleeping potion so she could speed away to dreamland. At the time, Ian was doling out nightly potions to me—a brown liquid that was so fast you could feel yourself losing consciousness. A pleasant rehearsal for death. I think it was chloral hydrate. It was the same recipe as the one that Dr. Brown doles out to his sleepless wife, the ex-madam, in *Queen of the Underworld*.)

I SPENT THE SUMMER back in the Cole compound—they had yet another new house in a wooded enclave called Huckleberry Cove, outside Asheville. (My stepfather, a contractor, liked to "build up"; of their frequent moves, Mother would joke, "He knows how I hate to clean house, so he keeps building me new ones.") Weeks turned into a month. I saw old friends, enjoyed my little half-siblings, shared a room with my fifteen-year-old sister, whom I found both fey and avidly curious about every aspect of my life. She asked me to describe our London flat, and as I was describing the sofa (an unpleasant chartreuse) I knew I never wanted to sit on it again. I regaled my mother with tales of the Scientology experience. When I got to the crucial part in Power Processing where my auditor had led me through a "disconnection" with my main "suppressive person" (in my case, it turned out to be God), Mother uttered a savage snort and said, "Well, if I were you, I'd go off by myself right now and *re*connect with Him."

(A final word about my brush with Scientology. All these years later, I am still struck by its vitality of language and occasional bursts of wisdom: an "overrun" to describe a behavior that you have grown beyond; or Hubbard's Buddhist-like "native state," the ultimate level of his Eight Dynamics, which is being able to experience self and world simultaneously without losing the will to act.)

IN LATE AUGUST, still reluctant to return to England, I went to Manhattan, at the age of twenty-nine, and looked for a "temporary job," the kind of job suited to someone of twenty-one. (Francesca in *Glass People* and Violet in *Violet Clay* endured some of my humiliations, but they were younger.) At last I got a job in a roomful of proofreaders at McKinsey & Company, the management-consulting firm on Park Avenue. As long as you worked, the company fed you—anything available through take-out menus. I stayed late many evenings and dined sumptuously. You worked in tandem with another proofreader, reading consultants' reports aloud to each other. It was a comfortable room with great views of Lower Manhattan. I was living in a residence hotel on East Fifty-first Street, the Pickwick Arms. My room, with shared bathroom, was $35 a week. Then someone at McKinsey suggested I take a test. I did well on it, and the personnel director told me I could go into management training. She was totally nonplussed when I left to take a job as fact-checker at *The Saturday Evening Post* for less money. In my windowless cubicle at the *Post*, I typed furtively in my spare time on a story about a newly married couple's wretched vacation in Majorca with the doctor-husband's three-year-old illegitimate son. At night I read library books chosen to keep up my courage and verve (all of Henry Miller, Ralph Ellison's *Invisible Man*, and fiction by a caustic fabulist of the current state of planet Earth named Kurt Vonnegut Jr.).

Then I received an unexpected legacy of $5,000 from an uncle in Alabama. It simply arrived in an envelope from a lawyer. My old friend from Copenhagen, Lorraine O'Grady, was then at the Iowa Writers' Workshop with her new husband, Chap Freeman, a filmmaker, and she

wrote urging me to apply to the Workshop. The story that got me in—
by the skin of my teeth, reported candid Lorraine: "She has some
kinks," the admissions committee said, "but we'll work them out of
her"—was the one about the vicar, written in Miss Slade's class in London.

AS FOR THE 1961–1966 journals left behind in London, Ian returned
them to me after our final judgment of divorce in the General County
Court of Buncombe County in Asheville on April 17, 1968. Ian was not required to be present, but the judge had a letter from him. Harry DuMont
was my attorney, and the plaintiff was "hereby permitted to resume her
maiden name of Gail Godwin." In a moment of symbolic synchronicity,
my old boyfriend and mentor B., an attorney, happened to be in the court-
house at the time, and he "sat in" on my divorce. "Ah me, the halcyon
days," was his comment when the two of us spoke briefly afterward.

WRITER AT WORK:
"THE POSSIBILITARIAN"

The Gail Godwin Papers, held in the Southern Historical Collection in the Wilson Library at UNC Chapel Hill, includes typed manuscripts of Gail's unpublished short novel "The Possibilitarian," also called "The Ruptured Link," and an earlier, handwritten manuscript, "The Gift of Insight," with notes. The manuscripts, when combined with Gail's journals, provide valuable insights into the making of a writer.

The journals show us that the origin of "The Possibilitarian" was not the desire to rework the stories she had previously designed around the subject of her father. Instead, the germ was philosophical.

On May 9, 1966, she'd written: "Write a short novel about Vertical Lives"—that is, lives driven by enlightenment rather than purpose. This becomes a rallying cry for Ambrose Bradshaw, the protagonist of "The Possibilitarian," whose diary entries record the week during which he hoped to impart the gift of his vision to his visiting sixteen-year-old daughter.

"I will give her the vertical perspective her mother can't," he writes. "I will explain myself to her so that she, too, will see those arrow-like consistencies which make a frivolous life take on meaning."

Five days later in her journal, Gail comes up with the central plot line: a daughter spends a week with her father at his rented beach house. "Once again it is time for Rachel's summer visit," she jots down. Soon afterward, Gail settles on the idea of writing Ambrose's story as his diary "of the gulf between action and thought."

A perusal of Gail's notes for new works reveals how, starting with a few oppositions, she generates a host of associations that lead to a story design. For example, her reading of D. H. Lawrence's "St. Mawr," noted a few times in the journals from 1966, attaches itself to Ambrose's mind-set and provides a refrain about his search for animal-like living-in-the-moment.

Scientology, which was much on Gail's mind at the time, also became fodder for her fiction. She made use of some of its precepts.

*In her handwritten story draft, "The Gift of Insight," Gail wrote her story on the right-hand pages of her notebook, and various reflections and references on the left. Page 12 features the scene in which Ambrose floats off in a sea of thought as well as water and forgets about Rachel, who has disappeared to join a group of admiring surfers. The facing page is philosophy—ideas drawn from William James (*The Principles of Psychology*) and L. Ron Hubbard.*

Gail was interested in James's examination of the gap between wishing something and willing to do something. James writes that in order for an act to proceed, there can't be any conflicting notion in the doer's mind. That's where Hubbard and Scientology come in. "The whole secret of auditing," Gail notes, is "removing mental conflict."

In Hubbard's scheme, people react to traumas by reenacting the dramas that trouble them. This both clouds their perception and distracts their attention. Once he or she is freed, what can a person achieve? That's Ambrose's question, for he's dissatisfied with the "two-dimensional" world of success-oriented people, yet unable to achieve success as a dreamer.

"The Gift of Insight" ends, after 66 pages, with Ambrose continuing to dwell on his daughter, whom he idolizes. Thinking of her makes him want to be a winner. She is the Coppertone girl, and yet she is half-him, and therefore perhaps his link to normalcy.

"The Possibilitarian," 141 pages long, resolves Ambrose's conflict in a different way than "The Gift of Insight." Ambrose is no longer latching on to his vision of Rachel to save himself. Instead, he's getting drunk; writing a letter to his sister, whose quest for independence has led to loneliness; and writing a story about a fictionalized Rachel who gets her own ride to the bus station when she finds her father too hungover to drive.

You might say that "The Possibilitarian" didn't make it to full term because the ending was too short on hope. Gail, at this time, is very clear in her wish to create a literature that provides enlightenment.

Regarding the use of her own life for fiction, Gail has already taken a stand. In a note following the "The Gift of Insight" in her notebook, she instructs herself:

"The person who cherishes and values his ideals above reality can only grow or create to a certain level. After that, he gets 'hung up' because his ideas and creations no longer evolve from the source. Reality is three-dimensioned and has endless interpretations. Any one interpretation is only two-dimensional. A genius or real creative person creates and interprets from reality—the source—and thus gets some of it in his vision."

Because of Gail's method, any one episode or relationship in her life can result in multiple versions, all very different in content and theme. Ambrose Bradshaw in the short story "Mourning" (begun on the fifth anniversary of Gail's father's suicide) appears in the daughter's flashbacks after his funeral. One flashback is to their time together on a beach.

"Mourning" was never published, but the theme of a daughter trying to understand the mind of a father figure who has committed suicide is victoriously taken up in Gail's novel Violet Clay. Ambrose, the heroine's uncle, is greatly fleshed out and transformed into a largely successful man before his decline and suicide, and the heroine, Violet, finds an empowering set of answers for herself.

The short story "Old Lovegood Girls" (published in the Ballantine paperback edition of Evenings at Five) has the benighted, semi-alcoholic father visiting his daughter, Christina, during her first year of college. The focus is on Christina, and how she fulfills the father's hopes that she will have the strength to battle the world.

Ambrose in "The Possibilitarian" had begun, as already noted, with a philosophical dilemma, and the character grew out of Gail's time at a Scientology retreat. Gail's notes and story reveal that she consulted a large number of books to build the novel's framework.

The Brothers Karamazov provided a clue regarding Ambrose's attraction to his own dreams. The Night and Nothing by Father Gale D. Webbe of Asheville gave substance to the notion of three-dimensional living. The eighth-century Chinese poet Li Po provided a portrait of a poet awakening from drunkenness. L. Ron Hubbard's science fiction—about spirits from outer space who, having inhabited human bodies long ago, forget who they are—worked well for her within the context of human psychology. Existentialist novelists Jean-Paul Sartre and Albert Camus inspired the creation of one of the most intriguing characters in "The Possibilitarian": the fugitive murderer, Lamar Wilkinson.

Ambrose, running a used car lot, and expecting to find clues to his quest even there, feels he has found one when Wilkinson arrives to sell his car. Ambrose talks about the experience at a high society party, which he attends with Rachel, who's dating the host's grandson. The scene is described in the following excerpt from the novel, told in Ambrose's voice.

✑

Excerpt from
"The Possibilitarian,"
Unpublished Manuscript,
1966

—

A middle-aged woman, bearing a heavily lacquered beehive hairstyle over her tired face, approaches us. She has gone adrift in the crowd and alights upon us gratefully. "What do you think about that awful murder business in Knoxville?"

"What happened?" I ask, feeling sorry for her. Adrift, with no vitality of her own, she must offer a sensation as an entrée into conversation.

"You mean you haven't been following it in the papers?" she asks, incredulous, her voice high, but grateful.

"Miz Roe, this is Mr. Bradshaw," says Liza. "He and his daughter are vacationing at Ocean City, too."

"Oh, I see!" cries Mrs. Roe, eager to be told what to see.

To me, Liza explains, "Secretary of Commerce and Mrs. Roe are down from Washington."

"So I understand," I say, smiling at the lady. She relaxes a little with this identification as if now she remembers who she is.

"What about the murder?" I persist. The bourbon has long since gone to work, dampening down any stubborn dry growth of inhibition that happens to be around. I want to hear something sensational and shocking. I want to be shocked out of this somnolent, slow conversation.

"Well, it's just terrible, really, Mr. Bradshaw," Mrs. Roe, touching my arm, confides. "This perfectly normal wife and mother of five gets up one morning and shoots her whole family dead. They think the baby might live, but it will never be normal. She just wakes up one morning, puts on a pair of shorts and a shirt, smokes a cigarette, goes and gets her husband's pistol, and goes around to every room, shooting. The papers say there was blood everywhere. It looked like a butcher shop."

"She was mental, of course," murmurs Liza, lighting herself a cigarette.

"Well, of course," says Mrs. Roe, "she must have been. But what puzzles me is, what was she thinking about? How could she do it? How could you want to kill your own family? I just can't picture the feeling, don't you know."

"Why would you want to?" says Liza, frowning. She does not like this conversation. It has the possibility of leading into those regions that attract and repel her.

"I think I can tell you," I say, my voice syrupy-soft with good drink. "It has something to do with reaching a threshold where ordinary rules suddenly lose their reality. The person sees a vision, no matter how diabolic, and must carry it through. Afterwards, he may go back to being as normal as he was before. The action of murder seems to have taken place on a different plane altogether. His own action may seem unreal to him. It exists outside, separately living its own life, accruing its own consequence. I once met a man who had murdered a girl only that morning. He sold his car to me that afternoon. Said he had run into debt in Virginia and was on his way to Miami where he would get some seasonal work. He had all his papers and was a very sensible customer. He was an ex-Marine. Fought at Iwo Jima. I noticed that the back of his shirt was pressed into three sections, military style. I remember he had very clear, calm, slate-gray eyes. He really looked at you, without any tricks. I remember thinking, now here is a man you could really talk to, if only there was time. A couple of hours later, the State Police came. They told me that this man had strangled a girl with a nylon stocking in Newport News that morning. They thought he was on his way to Miami and from there would try to get to Cuba."

"My heavens!" exclaims Mrs. Roe. "You must have been terrified when you found out. Doing business with a murderer right there on the same day."

"No," I say, "he was not a murderer when we did business. He was a man selling his car, in order to get away. The murder was somewhere else. It existed in a realm all its own."

"You mean you don't believe in capital punishment, then?" Liza plays nervously with her overloaded silver charm bracelet, smoking intermittently, looking pointedly over us at the dancers, while she listens.

Then, miraculously, I am suddenly and completely in present time: one of the accomplishments of drinking. It disconnects the living moment from all the dross of past and future, with the bonus of eliminating any problems, as well. Here is the pleasant, damp cool of a lawn near the sea, upon which choice meat roasts and pretty women dance. There is the noise of the combo and soft, controlled laughter, and the crickets when they can get through. Above, the stars move, according to a plan of their own. And here is this sullen girl beside me, who might still be reached, and this tired Washington wife whose fascination for newspaper violence may mirror some healthy trace of it lying dormant beneath her poor, heavy flesh. I see glimpses of larger patterns that will save us all from going back on ourselves and bear us forward to a new and vital awareness. "Of course," I tell these listening ladies, "the trouble, or at least part of it is, this: We're all trapped in the stories we tell ourselves. We spend all our energy living up to agreements we have not made but that have been made for us. We have stepped into stories, to 'play' them awhile, and then forgot they were stories and think we have to live them. We are like a bunch of people locking themselves up in a cell to play a game called 'jail' and then losing the key. After a while, nobody can remember NOT living in jail and they all start believing they've always lived there. Do you see what I mean?"

"My goodness, Mr. Bradshaw, what a philosopher we are," says Liza, duly blowing a stream of blue smoke skywards and watching me through its screen. Mrs. Roe is silent, worried, fiddling with the damp napkin around the bottom of her glass.

Then, a space in the night is gone, I sip my drink and dizzily know I was just about onto something big, but missed it. Mrs. Roe is looking at me oddly, all traces of gratitude gone, looking around warily, as if expecting somebody. Liza is making no bones about staring at me, as if she is going to catch me out, at last.

"Anyway," I say, compelled to follow whatever it was to its end, "I'm sure it is a thing to be considered. However, it is a bit hard to deshcribe ... describe, really."

Part six

GETTING PUBLISHED

Iowa City, Iowa

MARCH 5, 1968, TO NOVEMBER 3, 1968

In the Company of Writers

Gail Fills in Some Material from the Destroyed Iowa City Journals

———

In early January of 1967, I flew from New York to Iowa in a snowstorm. Ozark Airlines lost my luggage (briefly). Lorraine and her husband, Chap Freeman, sheltered me in their commodious lodgings on North Dubuque Street until we found an apartment for me, the top floor of a house, 415 South Capitol, in walking distance to the University, and across the street from the city jail. Lorraine, ensconced in the Workshop, had just finished translating José Donoso's novel *Este domingo* from Spanish into English. Chap was getting an MFA in filmmaking.

Kurt Vonnegut was teaching his last semester in the Workshop and already had one foot out the door. He would shortly learn that he had won a Guggenheim Fellowship and would be on his way to Germany to refresh his memory for his novel in progress, *Slaughterhouse-Five*. I was devastated when I learned that his Workshop section was overfilled and closed. But others must have been devastated, too, because he agreed to take on a second section. The sections, about fifteen to twenty people, met once a week to critique one another's mimeographed stories or parts of novels. Jane Barnes submitted a devilish social satire, "Coming of Age in Washington, D.C." She wore big swooping hats and was engaged to another Vonnegut student, John Casey, who actually had *a novel under option* by a major publisher. Several years after leaving Iowa, Jane would publish her novel about Lenin's wife, *I, Krupskaya*. And then there was David Plimpton, who would be the first of us to have a story appear in a national magazine, and John Irving, already married, with a small son. At his twenty-fifth birthday party, Irving played us a tape of the music (from *Carmina Burana*) he had chosen for the film score of his first novel, *Setting Free the Bears*. He hadn't finished the novel, no publisher or film person had laid eyes on it, but "I often picked out my music ahead of time," he explained to me years later. "Call it my mayhem confidence."

My story about the English vicar was received by my peers with interest and enthusiasm. Meanwhile, the forty-five-year-old Vonnegut and I had a conference about my long story "The Beautiful French Family." "I'm thinking of turning it into a novel," I told him. "Oh, it's fine as it is," he said, his gangly length tilted back in its swivel chair, desert boots on the desk, cigarettes and ashtray never far away. In these one-on-one sessions he was as loose and playful as a Zen master. In our next conference I told him I had decided to turn it into a novel anyway. "Great idea!" he said.

("All I did in those conferences with you guys," Vonnegut told me thirty years later, "was to say 'Trust me. I'm going to reach in—being very careful not to bruise your epiglottis—and catch hold of this little tape inside you, and gently pull it out of you. It's your tape and it's the only tape like that in the world.' " But I think Vonnegut also consulted his "enthusiasm meter" during those individual conferences. When he sensed you were burning to do something, he affably fanned your flame.)

By the end of that first semester in Iowa, I had a draft of my novel. Stimulated by proximity to other hungry writers like myself, encouraged by Vonnegut, bolstered by solitude, and having a place of my own and enough money to last me several years if I was very careful, I felt charged with the elated focus of my early twenties when I sailed to Copenhagen.

By March 5, 1968, when this new journal begins, I had fled from 415 South Capitol to a less convenient temporary apartment to escape the jealous poet who had destroyed my Iowa journals. The first draft of the novel then titled "The Beautiful French Family" had got me an agent, Lynn Nesbit, who said she thought she could sell it if I rewrote it. I had spent the summer of 1967 back in Asheville, North Carolina, doing just this, but Lynn liked the second draft much less, saying I had made it too oblique and she couldn't place it. So I returned to the Workshop in the fall of 1967, agentless, Vonnegut-less, now almost thirty-one years old, but still hell-bent on becoming a published writer.

Part 6 we have called "Getting Published," but it could just as easily have been called "Dark Night of the Soul."

MARCH 5, 1968

Begin again!

The flabby fifties. The ossified Eisenhower era. Can I overcome being a child of such a time? Yes, but I'll have to work harder.

My journals spread all over the world. The Wests will dig one out of their basement. Ian will be able to enjoy about twenty of them over coffee.[1] Two drowned in the Iowa River, or so he claims, by Othello.[2] I clutch what's left of my secrets desperately to myself. No one shall take them—whoever tries will be wiped out of my consciousness. I will continue to grow my mad sick flowers in hidden pots.

MARCH 23

Frustration. So many good ideas for stories and I have to read other people's in order to get a degree. But this summer: maybe a breakthrough. *NAR*[3] is interested if I rewrite the poor vicar.[4] "He doesn't have enough character." Maybe do more with the *Time* magazine bit to show Lewis looking at himself. And put gestures everywhere, flourishes; and cut down a few pages.

Lewis: thirty; angular, awkward, blushes easily; losing his hair; walks on his toes; played rugby at college. Very much of the little boy

1. A month and a half later, Ian sent Gail's journals to her.

2. The "jealous poet," who didn't want her past to compete with his claim on her.

3. Here Gail refers to the *New American Review*, a literary journal that had started in 1967. The editor had praised Gail's work to Robert Coover, one of Gail's instructors.

4. Gail's vicar story, "The Illumined Moment, and Consequences," later titled "An Intermediate Stop," went through many revisions before it was published in the *North American Review*.

about him. Not a woman-hater, he's just a late bloomer. There were things he wanted to know first. Have I known a vicar? Yes, the Putney one Andy and I consulted about our marriage. But he was too elusive, sophisticated. Very un-simple. This man's priesthood is a metaphor for artisthood. He became a priest in order to continue the search, as an artist becomes an artist in order to find things out—out of wonder. Wonder → Vision → Stasis and Sterility → New Wonder. Modernize some of Ellen Glasgow's plots.[5]

During the subsequent three-month gap in the journals, Gail takes and teaches courses, and does a lot of reading. She is able to retreat to an "air-conditioned, locked office in the modern new English building," to which, she wrote her mother on June 7, "I have moved my books, typewriter, and personal effects such as a bank book, letters, etc. So there is that relief. I am here now, alone, at sundown, having filed my papers, rejection slips, and other bits and pieces from past dealings."

Several stories—new ones and ones reworked from two-year-old drafts—issue from her to be submitted to instructors and editors. Her instructors praise her, but the editors withhold their approbation. A number of the stories explore an intense desire to get beyond conventional life and to find an ideal one, which she senses exists. It may exist in fantasy, and be an intellectual achievement; or it may be just the opposite, a shedding of intellect.

In "The Legacy of the Motes," a scholar discovers a debilitating yet ultimately revelatory mote in his eye. In "The Man on the Sofa," a bored couple discovers an enigmatic little man on their living room sofa. In Gail's vicar story, eventually published as "An Intermediate Stop," she imagines a religious man who loses his grasp of a powerful vision the more he tries to name and share it.

---

5. Ellen Glasgow (1873–1945) documented her Richmond, Virginia, society through a series of novels that portrayed unconventional women and overcompensating men caught up by changing traditions and moral drift. In Gail's 1974 novel *The Odd Woman*, Jane Clifford's fellow professor Sonia Marks comments, "Ellen Glasgow makes her men seem such fools. Now *there's* a challenge. *Barren Ground* ... It's the book which tests the mettle of the sincerest militant. Most women can identify with heroines who learn to live without marriage; but not so many want to live without love of any kind."

Gail's relationship with the jealous poet she calls Othello is over, give or take a few threats to serve him with restraining orders. But recalling their time together underscores the feelings she has about her defeating need for such relationships. Unpublished at age thirty-one, she feels despair. Her stories are products of her unease; and of her mother's advice to be bravely honest in her writing and to think a little more about plot; and of the predilection for short, imaginative stories her instructor Robert Coover admires and encourages. Coover had just published The Origin of the Brunists *to critical acclaim and declared his intention to "change the shape of American fiction." He wrote high praise for Gail in her files but warned her against letting realism and her attraction to the novel of manners turn her into "another Updike."*

Yet during this period Gail begins a careful reworking of "The Beautiful French Family," begun in spring 1967 under the tutelage of Kurt Vonnegut and rejected in its second draft by the agent Lynn Nesbit. "I think I am going to go back to that story of the woman and the French family. It's too good to pass up," she writes her mother on May 26, 1968. She will get another literary agent, John Hawkins, of Paul R. Reynolds, Inc., the oldest literary agency in America, on the basis of forty-eight pages of a third rewrite. Hawkins will sell those pages to David Segal at Harper & Row in December 1968, and the novel, titled The Perfectionists, *will be published in 1970. It will feature several fully realized characters, including a husband whose metaphysical brilliance suffers from the same reductionist mania as Scientology.*

PORTION OF LETTER FROM GAIL TO
KATHLEEN COLE, JUNE 7, 1968

Dear Mother,

At the moment, things are rather black, I'll explain why. Late this afternoon I came to the English building. Nobody was around. I went up to the Workshop shelf, where letters for Workshop people are just lying naked on the shelf. I saw two manila envelopes ad-

dressed to Coover. They were from the man he sent off stories to, from the best students in the Workshop. I had to know if I'd gotten anything accepted.

As the place was deserted, I took the envelopes into the bathroom, locked myself in a stall, and looked inside to see what had been returned. There was a letter on top of the stories to Coover. [The editor] said he was taking two stories: one from Charles Aukema,[6] who's had three stories bought this spring, and one from a Philippine boy who has sold his novel to Random House. The editor said: "None of the other people interested us much. Their work seemed either too vague or the writers seemed too immersed in themselves." He went on to say he felt Aukema had used his form magnificently. Then, at the bottom, he did add: The only story we didn't take that interested us at all was "Liza's Leaf Tower" (mine).

I put the manila envelope, refastened and licked down, upon the shelf, and came down here to my office, shaking like a leaf. The jealousy over Aukema is past now. But what remains is this: The fear that the man was right. That I am behind where I should be at my age. That I have far to go. That I won't hold out. I'm only just learning to use words, as you can see from the latest story. My biggest problem in writing is also a big problem in life. That is, a certain vagueness of resolution, a certain moral vagueness, if you like. I am "onto something" but my vision is too muddy to get there.

This is probably because I am muddy and have been for a long time. That's why I get into situations like the Othello one, that's why I marry people I don't love, why I've wasted years fleeing from one alternative to the other, because I had never sat down and faced myself and what I really wanted. I put writing first now.

---

6. Charles Aukema later became a professor of English at Coe College in Cedar Rapids, Iowa. He taught creative writing as well as computer applications in writing, including hypertext fiction.

JUNE 22

Summer evening. Age thirty-one. Alone and theoretically liking it. A larger and larger pond of might-have-been-me's to fish in whenever I please. Others circling their own suns. I sometimes wonder what sun I think I circle, and perhaps if that old vision I used to see of myself—old and alone—when I went walking down Old Church Street after work might still come true. I've had so many chances to avoid it, the last one being the wife-of-Dr.-Marshall role. Seems possible now.

Will I, one day, wake up and recognize my central impetus in life to be a Great Neurosis? I think I had better write all night until I get myself some answers. Summer evenings are heartbreakers. Today's was infinitesimally shorter. How did I manage to waste my winter energies on a pudgy paranoid whose values negate every real one of mine? "You fat slob," I said walking along beside him on the street this early afternoon. "You're no beauty yourself," he said. Beside the nuclear physics research building, across the street from St. Mary's Catholic Church, I hit him hard on his clammy perspiring neck. "I'm an old woman!" I said. He hit me back, wildly, on the forearm. I ran from him. He caught up with me in town. I said foolishly at a crossing in front of others, "Don't come near me; don't go in my apartment, or I'll see you arrested." I escaped again. Into Kresge's. I had tuna fish in a tomato and a hot fudge sundae with chocolate ice cream. Saw Othello again striding perturbed through the hot sun: "Did you swear out a peace warrant?" "Yes," I said. Peace for the moment. Good old lies.

Still unsettled from my yesterday's resurrection of Sandy.[7] I hadn't been able to write in my sun-filled office. Took my novel outside by the river, lay on the bank with my dress too high. A red-haired boy-man, a workman of some sort, walked below me to the edge of the river. He turned and looked up my dress, and then walked past me, close, up the bank. We spoke. He went back to his plant. I went in. Came out again with Virginia Woolf's writer's diary. Went back in. Came out. Five

7. See Part 4 of this volume for Gail's relationship with the red-haired Pan Am public relations officer in London.

o'clock whistle. He never came back. Wrote two thousand words, not very good Sandy and London data. Walked home.

JUNE 23 · *Sunday*

Lay around shamelessly all day and finished *Bleak House*. Dickens's genius I can only stand in awe of—and let as much as I can absorb be an example for my impatient hit-or-miss. Had as hard a time as a dog settling for a snooze in finding a place to read my Montaigne. Giggly, pipe-smoking girls in library; my office too lonesome. I wanted strangers passing, life.

To the Union. Finished "Of Presumption." Thunderstorm. Started "On Repenting."[8] I might wish for him to be more of a hero, but perhaps that's his whole point. Lights all went out. I was calm and strangely pleased at first, then annoyed, as I would have to get home somehow.

Candle-bearers running to and fro in the spooky Union, lightning cracking outside. Finally I wandered out, stood under the shelter. The shrieky teens departed. I noted a blond man noting me in my short smock dress, brown legs, sandals, dark glasses, old maid hairdo. He circled in for the landing. "Think it'll rain long?"

I helped him, asked if he was here with a conference (noting his name tag). Yes, computer science. Oh. Did I have a ride? No. Did I want one? Why, how nice, if it's not too much trouble. Oh, no. New-smelling Mustang. He discreetly fires the questions. We're at Davenport Street. "Are you married?"

"Just got unmarried."

"Oh." A little familiar now. "Not much to do in Iowa City in the summer."

8. "It is no small pleasure," Montaigne writes in this essay, "for one to feele himselfe preserved from the contagion of an age so infected as ours" (John Florio translation; Modern Library, 1933). Montaigne advocated a clean conscience; a life separate from society, if necessary; and natural joy. Regarding repentance: it does not resolve the beautiful and destructive aspects of vice. Leonard Strickland, the admirable father in Gail's 1982 novel *A Mother and Two Daughters,* consults Montaigne "about learning to do for conscience's sake what we now do for glory." Montaigne's skepticism about human reason, morality, and constancy was summed up by his motto *Que sais-je?*—"What do I know?"

I say, "Perhaps it's just as well."

He gentlemanly turns the car around so it can be as close as possible to my door. I break the bad news: I have to read Montaigne tonight. But there's hope. Office 68, my name, curiously alliterative of his, Dale Goddard. Now to Montaigne.

POOR, POOR Lady Dedlock.[9] I liked her so much.

IAN WROTE LORRAINE and Chap. Lorraine called last night. She's being very secretive about her "project." I went back to my office and called Ian. He was really quite impossible. I still hope for perfection in a man. It's a pastime now, no longer a vocation.

JUNE 25

Twenty meager pages done on the novel.[10] At least I'm giving some idea of the woman's character. I started writing at 3:00—finished at 5:30. Two and a half hours. First I type up a rough draft on two foolscap sheets, then I write extensively on four pages of Corrasable Bond.

The summer flies by, dragging me behind. I am better off a PhD candidate in Iowa at thirty-one than I was as a glorified receptionist in London at twenty-six. Holding the pleasure principle in abeyance a bit better.

Called Lorraine. She has two new spotted cats: "I haven't been able to have an emotional reaction to them or even name them. They're rather mystical."

Tomorrow build the Pauline scene. Pauline serves as a link with Sarah's secular and monastic (Adriatic) life. Pauline is the healthy, un-literary alter ego. She is nearer the earth. She also sees Sarah as Sarah wants to see herself, yet has a control over her in that she refuses to ac-

---

9. In *Bleak House,* Lady Dedlock is the virtuous woman whose long-ago unmarried pregnancy is discovered by an antagonist, who threatens to tell her husband. She is found dead at the grave of her lover by the daughter she thought had died in childbirth.

10. Gail begins a rewrite of "The Beautiful French Family"—later published as *The Perfectionists*—which she had first completed for Kurt Vonnegut the previous year. With changed character names—Pauline and Sarah instead of Polly and Dane—she is also playing with a satire of her own story, which she will title "Sarah's Gothic Marriage."

cept ruses or intellectualizing about emotions. She will also follow the marriage—they will "play" to her. We will care about her and she'll end up having the gratifying but sad affair with Karl.[11]

JUNE 27

Has this month been wasted, or not? It has certainly been the most unpleasant of my life. First I'll write about it. See what can be saved from the mess, then drink coffee and do my Old English.

Jane Barnes Casey whets my resentment, although I try to hide it. I wonder: Would she have associated with me if she had grown up in Asheville? She tells of her mother making a room in their "Maine house" with a huge bay window glow red with an exquisite arrangement of curtains. She tells of a sister my age of incredible brain energy, who sizzles with electricity, has wild, fuzzy hair and green eyes that have levels of awareness, eyes whose pupils contract or expand depending on whether or not she likes the person she's with. Sitting by the pool, the sister runs her fingers through her child's hair. She channels all her energy, paints every morning, cooks lunch for the children, prepares essays on subjects in her mind. Hated Vassar, wrote brilliant literary papers at NYU. The reason these conversations hurt me is due to my own small faith in myself. I feel: If only I'd had the advantages of such an upbringing, of such an education.

But I had a good education. I was simply too crippled to use it. Look at Ian's education and money. It was not until he was thirty-four that he was able to function.

This month I have: gotten rid of Othello, written twenty pages of a novel, learned a little Old English, and read four or five philosophical essays and several novels, including *Bleak House.* I am going to have to accept my limits: I am not a great powerhouse of energy. I can write two to three pages a day. I will probably never be financially comfortable. I will probably never have a child.

11. In the finished novel, Gail creates a third woman character, who has the affair with Karl, while Pauline/Polly acts as Karl's wife, and the protagonist (Sarah/Dane) remains conflicted and unsatisfied.

What I need most now to do is produce some achievement I can be proud of. But somehow one cannot try too hard. John Casey, regarding his aborted book, was told by his editor that he was working too hard.

Now, let us have some pride. Do OE tonight simply to prove you still have mastery over your will. Get up early, make yourself breakfast. Prepare a lunch to eat in the office. Write all afternoon. Go to the Dixons' party and look pretty.

You have your book—and can make of it what you want. Montaigne invented a form to suit himself. Why not suit yourself?

JUNE 29

Great wracking thunder early this morning. Went back to Ian in my dream. It was frighteningly realistic. He was ready for me. Said he planned to get me pregnant at once. He promised a new flat. He was in the old one till September. I remember thinking: He'll never let me go to my parents' again. I was just beginning to contemplate re-running away.

Awful depression. I'm feeling bereft.

I did have an interesting dream-thought recently. The artist contains his future blossoming. But he must go through a series of stages to reach it. Only by painting bad paintings does he get good.

I'VE JUST LOCATED why I'm not doing more. I'm using three-quarters of my energy being neurotic, feeling bad, indulging in memories, envying other people. Today I envied my cousin Sophie Marie. Yet, unless I were S-M, I would go stark raving mad with that husband, that dull docile life, chauffeuring Mother from Tuscaloosa to Birmingham, picking up the children, etc. What does she do for herself? Look beautiful. Fix up her house. Shop.

Since I have to live with my neuroses, let's see how not to waste time. Keep up with OE one hour every morning; take lunch; write from twelve to three; have a break; write till six; have another break; then spend my evenings reading. That should do it.

—

REWRITE "THE LEGACY OF THE MOTES," remembering Casey's[12] criticism and the Black Monk[13]—and the actual phenomenon of what happened when I got my own eye motes [muscae volitantes] in London.

Excerpt from May 26, 1968,
Draft of "The Legacy of the Motes"

—

The park into which he [Eliott] wandered was of dimensions that Van Buren [the librarian who recommended the park] might walk an eternity of lunches to never find. Elegant white giraffes lolloped soundlessly over its thick sward whose stellate dandelions were the size of dinner plates.

Corresponding Excerpt from
"The Legacy of the Motes,"
Published in The Iowa Review *(Summer 1972)*
and Dream Children *(Knopf, 1976)*

—

At the end of this mews was a vast green park that seemed to stretch to the frontiers of the evening. He walked soundlessly over its sward. The air hummed around him. He suddenly wanted more than anything to lie down, and did . . . Eliott woke the wings [the winglike motes in his eyes] and sent their soft specters up, over the ground, the trees, to see what they would find. They hovered above a pale spot burgeoning out of the dusk.

---

12. John Casey, National Book Award winner in 1989 for his novel *Spartina*, received his MFA from the Iowa program in 1968.

13. "The Black Monk" by Anton Chekhov chronicles the life of a man—Andrei Kovrin—who is blessed by an encounter with a millennial apparition, but who, because of doubts about his sanity, and loss of faith in his genius, destroys himself and his loved ones. Through his descriptions, Chekhov leaves the question of Kovrin's true mental state open.

It came closer, sprouting legs, an undulating tower of a neck, lolloping soundlessly toward him. It was an elegant white giraffe.[14]

JUNE 30 • *Sunday*

Six p.m. I can certainly claim to having felt better in my life. The consolation of a friend is not to be underestimated. (Why all these ass-backward sentences?)

I am either in a trough and will have to climb out, or I'm going through the great darkness that precedes enlightenment. I did five pages of the rewrite today. I began thirteen days ago. I have thirty pages of the third draft.

Called Lorraine. They[15] are moving to a rent-controlled apartment in Chicago for $40 a month.

I must go on. The wheel turns, bringing me an MA with Distinction, rejecting my stories, bringing consolation dreams one night and nightmares the next.

JULY 5

I want to write a new story about what it feels like to be a cyclone—"The Life of a Cyclone"[16]—coming to rest overnight at the Caseys. Will start on it soon. Went to see Dr. Whelan at Student Health. He gave me some sedatives. Did my OE.

---

14. Gail thoroughly reworked the story, and her final draft does not contain many passages from the early one. In her rewrite, she made Eliott the agent of his visions, thus strengthening the psychological interpretation of events. The endings of the drafts differ greatly. In the early version, the "wings" vanish from Eliott's eyes just as he becomes too old to achieve great success, and he dies dreaming of parks. The published story concludes with Eliott in midcareer. He is not a failure and has gained wisdom, if not fame, for there had been precedents for his visions. His motes had disappeared when he'd discovered his giraffe in a Bosch painting. He cries when he finds his exalted condition explicated in George Herbert's poem "Easter Wings."

15. Lorraine and her husband, Chap Freeman.

16. This story eventually became part of "Some Side Effects of Time Travel," published in *Paris Review*, and was republished in *Dream Children*.

PORTION OF LETTER FROM KATHLEEN COLE
TO GAIL, JULY 5, 1968

Your letter was in the mail today, and you are in the depths. Wish I could help but it is difficult for anyone to do so when you are in such a state. All right. You're displeased with yourself. But no one is ever expected to do more than she can do. If that is all, then it is all. First get some perspective. There's really only one thing wrong—a tremendous thing to you—nothing published. But it will come—only you've got to try another tack, it seems. Yet all the utterly worthless stuff I keep reading or trying to read in books and magazines!

You've got to say something you truly believe. You need, in my opinion, for what it is worth, some more work on plotting. I told you, the story you sent me about the man with the wings in his vision was excellent halfway through, and then you just finished it off any old way. Build a story to the very end. You know all these things, who am I to tell you?

JULY 6

I feel like a vegetable. Brutal dreams. I am either hurting the ones I love, or they are hurting me. I need a car. Can't afford one. I really hate myself—and loathe the world.

JULY 8

July 5–8. Awful, awful. I couldn't move or think or read.

The dream: being a man who makes up a mystery. He leaves clues about trains, subways, and ferries all over Europe. Then the ruse is up; there's nothing on the sheet of paper he gives for the daily chase. He is exposed. Shoots himself. There was the urgency of the dream, and then the letdown afterward.

JULY 10

Went to Student Health yesterday, got some sleeping pills. Had leisurely dreams. Even in my dreams I was calm; I spoke of how I used to be "uptight," and a picture of my adolescent self was flashed on the screen. I saw how pale, anxious, and generally unattractive I was.

Went to see McGalliard[17] today. Felt the need of doing something casual. I'm still not casual, I found out. Can I hold out for a PhD?

Eight pages written on a new story. I've decided to write what I like since nobody will publish me anyway.

New Yorker. Mademoiselle, Epoch.

PORTION OF LETTER FROM GAIL TO
KATHLEEN COLE, JULY 10, 1968

Dear Kathleen:

Your letter helped. Actually, when I wrote that black missive, I was about to come down with something, which I still have a little bit of. From 4 July to today, a fever, just a degree. Unable to follow the print in a book, got nauseated whenever I tried to retain an idea. Even sleeping was impossible. Went to the hospital. Doctor said it was probably a combination of a virus and overwork. He said, "You should have at least taken a week off after an MA with Distinction."

As it was, I took the MA exams, studied for finals, ran away to Lorraine in Chicago, came back, broke up with Othello, moved out, took seven credits for summer school, and wrote four to five hours a day. Then I wondered why I was depressed.

---

17. John C. McGalliard was a professor of medieval studies at the University of Iowa. He taught Old English. McGalliard is fictionalized as Dr. MacFarlane in Gail's story "Some Side Effects of Time Travel."

I'd also lost a lot of weight, so the doctor said, force myself to eat three times a day, and he gave me some mild sleeping tablets. Last night, I had my first night's rest. Previously, I'd been dreaming, actually dreaming mysteries that I wrote and acted the lead in.

I went and paid a leisurely visit to Mr. McGalliard, the medieval scholar here who teaches Old English. One day in class, he said the mountain people in his area still said "hit" for "it," as in Old English. I noted the familiar accent and I called out, "Where you from?" And he said, "Burke County.[18] *Where you from?" "Buncombe." Much to the amusement of the class. His family lived in a little town called Connelly Springs. It was mostly McGalliards. There were fourteen children. When they started getting old enough to educate, the family moved to Chapel Hill.*

Well, I'm tired again. Here endeth my leisurely letter. Pray that I regain my energy. I'll never complain about getting old or getting published if I can just regain my health.

JULY 16

I hope I can look back someday and say, "What a lot I learned, the summer of '68," because that is all that can be said for it. I certainly couldn't go on like this the rest of my life.

Went to the State Park[19] and swam in the lake with the Hammers.[20] Got all hot about getting a car, felt suddenly American again ("How can I live without a new car?"), went back to EPB[21] that evening and all of Saturday and Sunday and rewrote "The Man on a Sofa"[22] with a happy

18. Burke County is two counties east of Buncombe in the mountains of North Carolina. In fact, Buncombe had been carved from Burke once settlers had pushed farther west in large numbers.

19. Lake McBride State Park.

20. Gael Hammer, a theater arts professor, and his wife Katherine ("Kay") had befriended Gail.

21. The English-Philosophy Building.

22. The manuscript of "The Man on the Sofa," held in the Southern Historical Collection at UNC Chapel Hill, bears the notation "Encl. 22 Feb. 1968." In it, a married woman narrates the story of her boring marriage, and the appearance of a strange little man on the sofa

ending. Today wrote three-quarters of a story about a woman science fiction writer who gets a telephone call from God.

JULY 20

A new one. Shy. But secretly sure. The scary combination took me out of town to a real bar, with a fountain, tables, love music. Metaphysical conversation. I think he's been places I haven't. He kept on about the mountains. Hope to God they're not like Ian's Spanish tree. He takes his PhD comps in October, will be here all next year. I want him all now.

We climbed out the window of his top-floor flat and looked at the stars. Sexy hand-holding and kissing. The trouble is, I'd rather do it than write about it.

JULY 22

Of all my journals since 1961, I have only this one in hand. Lorraine said my task was to document myself.

Perhaps I should lower my self-demands, and see how I can cope with the paucity of my existence. Let me start with this: Failing catastrophe, I can hide in a university till sixty-five and maybe then have the courage to kill myself. I will try to keep sane. I will do a little bit each day, I will cultivate my garden. I will not go to pieces in public like AR.

I suffer from envy of other people and their achievements. I start at the top with Virginia Woolf and proceed to Iris Murdoch and Jane Casey. The only thing that strikes me at the moment, to be fair, is this: These were/are all, to the best of their abilities, creative. But they were/are lucky enough to have husbands to sustain them. I do not believe I can do without a man. I'm not sure I would want to achieve the dubious state of blissful independence.

The trouble is, I see now how loathsome it would be to accept some-

___
in her and her husband's apartment. The police are called. Without being able to determine motive or method, they take the man away. The husband clumsily tries to make an emotional connection based on the excitement, but the woman is dead tired, and goes to bed.

one with whom I didn't feel this sensibility, the sensuality springing from a want to be closer to that other.

So, what now? The only thing for it, according to the *I Ching* this evening, is innocence. To be in a state of innocence about what I am today, what I have made of myself. About the events of the past, I can do nothing. I can do something about how I see them, and how I present them to others. I don't want to trick anyone or throw them off the track of me; but neither do I need to choose for myself the most unflattering spotlight. As a becoming-artist, I should recognize the importance of presentation.

NOW ABOUT THE new one, let's call him "Byron." I don't want to undercut what we have by analyzing it. I am only going to mention the worst possibilities.

We were happy, began tentative explorations, spoke of poetry, held hands. We began accruing little memory specimens—e.g., statues that dramatize "Keep your cool." We have each been hesitant about revealing our pasts; neither of us has asked the other.

He did ask me why I changed my name. He volunteered that he was once engaged.

All I know for certain is that it warms and excites me to be near him. I've found no faults. I am not looking for them. I know we have differences. He seems at peace with himself (after what struggles?). He is in no hurry to publish; he is not creative on a daily basis, but does write private poems. He comes across as a gentle, rather shy man; but underneath, he's certain of who he is. He calls himself a confirmed mystic, and wants "to try marriage someday."

Gail's interest in how personalities combine in romantic relationships helps drive some of her early fiction, especially "The Beautiful French Family," the novel that she had begun working on upon her arrival at the Iowa Writers' Workshop. The resulting manuscript, published as The Perfectionists *by Harper & Row in 1970, involved a massive reworking of material. Up through May 1969, when she completed the final draft under contract, Gail thinks about and works on* The Perfectionists.

For example, she rewrote a conversation that the novel's heroine, Dane Empson, has with Polly Heykoop, a friend Dane makes on a family vacation in Majorca. Polly is a free-speaking mother of twin girls, and is dealing with a marriage that has good sex but faulty companionship. Dane has arrived with her psychoanalytical husband, John; Robin, her imperious little stepson, who's being passed off as her son; and John's troubled golden-girl patient, Penelope.

In the early draft, Polly thinks that Robin is Dane's biological son. In the final draft, Polly reveals that she has learned the truth. Gail increases the tension by making Polly hungrier for friendship, and smarter. Dane is made more circumspect. In the early draft, Dane remarks that her marriage is "of the future." The final draft reveals more animus. Dane arms herself with her husband's arguments, and she enjoys triumphing over Polly's wish to get a confession from her.

Excerpt from 1967 Draft of
"The Beautiful French Family"

—

"I don't know whether to laugh or cry," Dane said.

"Why, what do you mean? Just tell me, what is it, objectively, that you don't have? Don't think me rude for what I'm going to say. But I think you want to be unhappy."

"You are possibly right," said Dane, edging away. For, sometime, during the space of the last moment, she had decided that this was the better, the prouder, admission.

"Yes, I know," said Polly. "So, it seems to me, all you have to do is to get a new perspective on things. Then you can start enjoying all you have. Another thing I think: Robin is being affected by your unhappiness. I will never forget that child's face. It frightened me. Has he always been like that, since birth?"

"A bit," said Dane, building once again upon a lie. Sometimes her whole life seemed to her like a city built over a swamp. But to start over became more and more impossible, as new structures were added to the city, and wings and partitions were added to the structures already there. "He's a very unusual child," she went on, adding a new wing. "Recently, John had him tested. He has this fabulously high I.Q. We will have to face it. He will never be like other children, the psychologist said."

"Golly, what did John say?"

"Oh, he—agreed. John was a child prodigy, too, you know. He placed in professional chess championships at age twelve; he entered Oxford at sixteen. Naturally, he is not easy to live with," she went on, feeling yet another edifice rising slowly from the mire. "He is so complicated, he takes so much energy. He needs more than most men. We have such a unique relationship, you see. Not like most married couples. It's like—well, rather like a marriage of the future—"

Excerpt from a Later, Undated Draft, Titled "The Perfectionists"

—

"I sensed this forthrightness about you, at the first, when you were standing there in the road. I thought: With such a friend I could complete myself."

"Can't you complete yourself with your husband?" Dane said, a bit of the tiger herself. "John is my friend," she added, rather triumphantly. "He's all the friend I need."

"I don't think you can do it with a husband. If you do, the other suffers. There are certain places where husbands and wives shouldn't travel together—certain areas—or the whole thing goes blah."

"Where?" said Dane. "What places?"

"In—in that area of analysis about relationships. At least, the relationship you have with each other. As soon as you start analyzing it, you—each of you—lose some of your otherness, the part of the male or female that the other keeps straining for. The unknowable part. I don't want to know all of Karl. When he comes to me, I sometimes feel he's a wonderful alien, someone I'll never interpret, another species altogether. It's only when we make love that we're really together. And we're something else then. We're something other than either of us. I would never sit around with Karl and say, 'What is this otherness, dear, that makes you so attractive? Let's analyze it—A, B, C—and give it a name.' But the analyzing has to come because I'm a Western woman and because I never know what I think or believe until I've thought it aloud to someone else. That somebody shouldn't be my husband but *should* be my equal. Maybe even *more* than me. Has got to understand and contribute and, perhaps, even go beyond. I think *you* could go beyond the usual limits."

"I think your ideas are beautifully antique, Polly. But I can't agree about this otherness thing. If you are limitless—and all complex people are—then you'll never touch bottom, you'll never give yourself away and lose all your mystery—or otherness, as you put it." This was John's argument, not her own! But with it, she'd got the other off her back; old Polly had lost the scent, wandering past John's words in search of a friend.

JULY 23

It's going to be a hard road, says the *I Ching.* Today was a bungle.

Byron came to his office, walked around outside my door talking loudly, knocking at Winifred's door. I finally went up to the third floor because I thought he'd gone to the Union with some people and wanted to look out the window and see who. I came around the corner from the elevator, and he was standing in front of the mailboxes talking to people. I foolishly wheeled and went away, back down the elevator to my office.

Gael Hammer came to get me and we went to their house. I behaved like AR. "What do you think he'll do? What do you think it means?"

Kay took it well. Gael, who acts like a brother, and I love him for it, called from the theater twice to report that Byron was at the theater for the second time this week (last night he went to see *The Miser*), and was alone. He had greeted Gael sullenly at first, whereas last night it was a cheerful "Enjoyed your party!" Then Gael talked to him at intermission (I write these notebooks to keep my sanity, and make no attempts at literary works of art) and he said he'd thought he'd go see *Misalliance* Thursday.

I must do Old English, get an A, my one achievement of the summer. Then go home, write.

Now I must perform black magic—or rather stick pins in my idol in case the worst happens, one of those neurotic snubs. I refuse to kid myself. Yes, I like Byron and hope something will develop. But, as Lorraine says, "There's something wrong with everybody, including you." Alas, here go the pins:

Gael: "I couldn't believe it when you brought him in. I'd expected something different. I've seen this character creeping around for three years in that Pendleton jacket—there's something prissy about him. I don't mean homosexual. He's got thin lips."

I find he reminds me of several previous men. Ian, Gordon W.[23] Peter W.[24] Also a bit of Rupert Birkin, though the D. H. Lawrence beard helps, and the little speeches about the mountains.

If he is like Peter W., I can expect a letter: "I do this so that you can live . . ." The thing he said that gave me the shudders at the time, and is very Peter W.–ish, is his answer to my drunken "You know, you're terribly nice." "Careful," he said. And I felt: That was presumptuous and not charming.

23. Gail met Gordon W. in April 1963. See the journal entry for July 23, 1963, the first entry in this volume.

24. Peter W. was a D. H. Lawrence apostle with whom Gail had had a short relationship in late fall 1962. He modeled himself after Rupert Birkin, a protagonist in *Women in Love* who idealized natural animal mentality. He impressed Gail until it became clear that his pose was a form of self-absorption by which he tried to control others.

I don't know much about him. Home life: very middle class. The remark about his twice-married brother "getting married all the time." He's taking five years preparing for the comps, has so far said nothing brilliant, only the usual fairly sensitive literary talk of graduate students. He has asked no questions about my past (which, I must say, I am glad of), but he has not shown any interest in my writing.

Like Gordon, he does what I call Boy Scout activities and seems to find completion in them. Maybe this is common among men, but it annoys me.

Tomorrow, if he comes in, you can expect one of these things to be happening:

1. Cat and mouse: He is playing a cat-and-mouse game because he wants to get me to care, and he feels insecure.
2. Fear and withdrawal: He can't cope with me. I'm too experienced, complex, sophisticated, full of hang-ups. He's backing off.
3. Sadistic impulse: He pursues a girl until she falls, then loses interest.

Gael said, as we passed his house, and I craned around, looking for his car: "Oh, Gail! Don't look."

JULY 24 · *Morning*

This might come in handy for a story. Signs of unrequited love: dry mouth, loss of appetite, hard to swallow, diarrhea, tight feeling in stomach. It's '63 all over again. Not only this, but I feel and know that I'm in the thick of an incident that makes me highly neurotic and partial to fantasy.

Poor Byron is being my father + all the men in the past who I feel have turned me down. He is not as much himself, whoever that is, as he is a composite of all my disappointments. I think I better write a bit today to tone all this down.

Evening, 5:40

A kind of nausea pervades the whole summer.

Months of being secure in the attentions of Othello, even though I didn't love him or like him. Then it was the first year I taught several courses—then the strain of studying for the master's—and the divorce, which psychologically threw me out of the safety of being "taken." Then the breakup with Othello, the illness, summer school.

ALL I CAN DO is hold on, preserve my sanity. Anyway, after this school year had begun with the rejection of my novel, I'm pleasantly surprised by an attentive man, who's on the same hall with me, who inquires after my MA. I talk in my most naturally giddy, abstracted way. I told him how I just wrote a story aimed for *Redbook*, and how I wanted a car, and an apartment. He says something—his humor is the pun kind, not the witty kind.

He offers to help me choose a car. I tell him how unhappy I am with the book list for the "Pursuit of Happiness" course. (Santayana, etc.) He tells how all the people in one department slept around, played musical beds. And I actually thought, from his expression of distaste, he meant married faculty—but no, he meant graduate students. Then, just before Kay Hammer came to get me for 8½, he blurted out forced-cheerfully, "Like to go out for a drink Friday night?" and then couldn't wait to get out of the office. Wednesday, he didn't come in.

OLD ENGLISH NOTES. Read *Sons and Lovers*.

At 6:10, he called. He said, "You haven't been in your office very much," and asked if I wanted to go swimming. I invited him to the play.

JULY 25

THE OLD SYNDROME: alone again, and grateful. A journal; a DHL paperback; a bed. A lamp. Enough.

Is everybody in hell, as well as myself? One of the professors has had a nervous breakdown. Cold A. came into my office and opened her soul. She had been having an affair with M. She was going to leave J., then M. dropped her. She's been suffering since February.

My problem is how to get my mental clamps sharp and tight. I don't know what to say about this week's crisis. Within one week, I fell in love then out again. We'd gone to the reservoir and watched the waters crash around six. He has not the play of mind I first suspected. He's tight about money, and somehow prim. He's not husband material. He's too hearty, he lets himself get sidetracked by people who don't matter.

At the Shaw play, how irritated I was with him for wearing the Pendleton jacket, for laughing so dutifully at all literary references, for being so tight about having to have his meal at a regulated time.

JULY 26

I'm overwhelmed by the absolute sadness of the lost ideal of the world. Once again, I created a dream and tried to stick it on to a real man. He should have been splendid, brilliant, gentle. I think I'll write my "Motes" story this weekend—pack the suffering into it. Show how one can change suddenly in the midst of life.

Excerpt from May 26, 1968, Draft of "The Legacy of the Motes"

—

[After taking the eye drops that Dr. Hunter-Hyde had prescribed for the motes in his eyes, Eliott walks to the park where he had seen visions. In Gail's early draft, they come in a dream; in her final draft, in his waking life. He never finds the park. In the final draft, he gets drunk, goes to the British Museum Reading Room, and is found lying besotted on the steps by Van Buren, a librarian. In the early draft, Eliott's withdrawal is more distracted and less painful.]

The examining drops had swollen Eliott's pupils and blinded him for reading. Knowing Van Buren would see to his stuff, he wandered the elegant vicinity around Hunter-Hyde's white-faced square and presently came upon another park. It was not his dream park, but it was one step nearer. It had a band concert. A Salvation Army lady with a tambourine sold him a program for threepence. What were they playing? His eyes traveled habitually down the list, which blurred and danced unreadably. He folded the program into a square the size of a small coin and put it in his pocket, next to the cool green bottle. Gazing for a long time at the banks of pink and yellow flowers, he finally made a silent bargain with the muscae [volitantes]. Then he closed his eyes, lay back in the grass, and opened his face to the sun. Beyond the music, he heard the approaching stampede of the beautiful white giraffes.

Excerpt from the Final Draft of "The Legacy of the Motes," Published in The Iowa Review (Summer 1972) and Dream Children (Knopf, 1976)

—

[There's no peaceful sun-gazing in the finished story. Following a dark night of the soul, Eliott faces his own identity, and faints.] Taking a small green bottle from his coat pocket, he squeezed two drops from it into each eye. "Keeping the li'l bastards in abeyance," he explained, winking at the perplexed attendant, who asked him, didn't he think he could do with a few hours' sleep, come in at noon, perhaps?

"Are you kidding? My whole life's in there on little slips of paper. You haven't thrown them away, have you? You haven't put anything back on the shelf?"

Van Buren took him by the arm, assuring him he had not. They went inside. Van Buren delivered Eliott his books and notes intact. Eliott settled himself unsteadily into his place at F5, opened to the title page of his dissertation, and began to scream. Van Buren made his way to him calmly, as though he were merely bringing another book. He led him whimpering past the discreetly lowered eyes of other scholars and out of the circular room, which had slowly begun to spin. He stood by in the Gents while Eliott vomited for a while, then carefully washed his face, looked in the mirror to check himself, and passed out cold.

JULY 27

I don't know how much longer I can endure this nauseating sensation about everything. Nothing to live for—afraid to die—a failure—unable to find sense among paltry humans. I washed my hair, and I don't have the strength to wait for it to dry. The words I'm writing seem useless and stupid. Everyone around me has problems.

JULY 29

I must get out. I want to leave clues for friends, in case it's necessary to trace my point of exit. I almost lost my mind twice—Saturday in Burger Chef. The presence of people doesn't help. The sensation is like the beginning of fainting—a vertigo—being on the verge of lapsing into a state where you have no control.

In Burger Chef, there were two young boys behind me, talking singsong, attempting to be sinister hippies, drumming their hands on the tabletop à la bongos. I was reading *Sons and Lovers*, the part where Mrs. Morel is hit by her husband with the edge of a drawer. The day lay flat, humid, and yellow outside. I knew that I was going to my office. Suddenly I began to slip away. I held on by concentrating on objects—the wall, a corner of the table. Then I went to my office and cried. Jane Casey came and scraped me up and took me home to spend the night at their farmhouse.

Today I got a rejection from *Redbook*. I spent all afternoon rewriting an old story.

JULY 30

Translating *The Wanderer*, a beautiful poem.[25] "Often he who is solitarily situated (the *anhaga*) finds grace for himself . . . Often alone I had to
speak of my trouble each morning before dawn. There is none now living to whom I dare clearly speak of my innermost thoughts . . ." I feel
close to him.

PORTION OF LETTER FROM GAIL TO
KATHLEEN COLE, JULY 30, 1968

The Old English exam is next Wednesday, August 7. Afterward,
I'm going to take the bus as far as Chicago, sleep at Lorraine's, and
maybe go out on the bus to Asheville the following evening . . . I
want to do some rewriting of the novel. I haven't touched it since
last summer and now begin to see what is wrong with it.

JULY 31

It's a race now. Can I get out of here without screaming, shattering? Old
Byron is on the warpath about Othello disturbing him. He lectures me
on "taking a firm stand." I can see what a pompous husband he'd make.

Othello called him and kept hanging up. So Byron, man of action,
has the phone company bug his phone. Then at 9:00 p.m., Othello goes
to Byron's office, apologizes profusely, and begins to "advise" him about
me. Byron calls me back. We get into a discussion about gentility, and
tradition and form. I find myself upholding things I long ago had
stopped believing in. Farther and farther we got away from each other.
Then he said, "Well, this doesn't have to be a soul-searching session,"

---

25. *The Wanderer* is a tenth-century Old English poem in which a warrior speaks of his
exile in a wintry sea following a devastating war.

cutting me off. He's shy and defensive. I'm shy and defensive. Will I ever get myself organized again, eating decent food, keeping decent hours, being able to read, and to write?

AUGUST 2

Lying fallow, they say. Dinner out at Yokums with Kent and Bev.[26] All year, I wanted to be friends with them, and was prevented by Othello's jealousy. The more I look back on that, the more unreal it is. I see him in the Union, and he is like a caricature.

These days, I collect married couples—the Caseys, the Hammers, the Dixons. They live vicariously through me; I shelter under the sanctity of their marriages.

These days, my thoughts veer from place to place—America, Europe, Iowa City, North Carolina. Let me remember how much I accomplished in the spring of '67, when I had decided to do one thing.

AUGUST 3 · *Saturday morning*

The writing business is eating away my skull. I feel it's the world against me, murmuring, "Not good enough, didn't quite make it." Everything else is peripheral, I want it so much. I have no way of knowing: Am I there? Almost there? Today, I'll finish "The Angry Year," send it to *Redbook* tomorrow. Just write honestly, sentence by sentence.

Saturday night

The taste of bad sausages at the Union, the blaring party next door, and a sense of the inelegance of life. All feels tawdry, indiscreet, and sloppy-minded. Just had a forty-five-minute argument with Byron about wealth, welfare, etc. We do not want the same things. He would drive me nutty in no time at all.

26. Kent Dixon was a Writers' Workshop student, married to Bev. Gail's story "Interstices," published in *Dream Children*, took its kernel from them.

AUGUST 4 · *Sunday*

Alys Chabot has accepted "Liza's Leaf Tower" for publication in *North American Review*—should be in print within six months. Already, the liberating feeling has set in. I feel I can slow down, write as I want. Byron and I lay on the riverbank by the English building and watched the lightning flash in the clouds.

I have ceased regarding him as magnanimous, and think of him as parsimonious. I don't feel he is benevolent, though he thinks of himself as trying to be a good person. He was going to come back for me tonight, late, but somehow, it seemed so cut-and-dried, prescheduled. So I left him a note and came home to share my triumph with the one who has stood by me through dark days: myself. Wednesday, I get out of here and Greyhound it home. Next fall, I can come back with one publication credit, get myself organized, eat good food, exercise, and have Byron as a squire.

AUGUST 5

No, not even that. I picked him apart like a chicken tonight: the false-hearty laugh, the tight-lipped, closed-teeth grin. The beady eyes. Oh, God, what is it about me that hurls myself at such unworthies only to recoil violently afterward? I only want to write, get a good start on the novel at home—write with Coover in mind. I have never felt so bankrupt, so blah about everything.

Fall
1968.
The leaves die—the days shorten,
And I come alive.

SEPTEMBER 17

Back from North Carolina, recharged for the winter, in a nicer new apartment in the same house that Lorraine and Chap lived in. The spirits are friendly at 501 North Dubuque. *Confluence* took "Dandelion."[27] Welcome back to sanity, relined with a stable madness consisting of many unseen, but more and more friendly, presences. Breakthrough in writing.

PORTION OF LETTER FROM GAIL TO KATHLEEN COLE, SEPTEMBER 17, 1968

Dear Kathleen:

It was a wonderful visit, something I won't forget. Thanks for so much, but mostly for just being what you are.[28]

Redbook *didn't accept the story on account of its being set in England and also [the editor] had seen it last year through Lynn Nesbit, but she was full of praise for its style, the characters, etc. Then I was crossing the street this morning and a man who edits a new magazine called* Confluence[29] *(very small, mostly student writers) said he wanted to buy "Dandelion" (only $100). I had sent them an earlier draft. I decided to sell because what I want now is to get myself published as many places as possible. Talent scouts search out these magazines, then offer fellowships, etc. So I told him I had changed the end; he came back to my office, and took the new end, which he liked better. So now I will have two stories in print. The main thing this is doing for me is releasing my ego so I can write what I believe in without so much looking to the "public" for my guideposts. I shall try* Redbook *soon again; she says she is hungry for student stories set in America. I will probably be able to cook up one with no trouble, since she obviously likes my writing and the content is her only problem—what will* Red-

27. "Dandelion" is the story of an American girl who works in the artificial-flower department of Harrods department store in London. The dandelion becomes a symbol of her desire for an ordinary, native life in the sun as opposed to the world of social posturing.

28. See Gail's account of this visit and her relationship with her mother in Gail's preface to this volume.

29. *Confluence*, started by Peter Neill, lasted for one year.

book *readers read?* Confluence *comes out in October, I'll send you a copy. It will hit the stands on October 1, your birthday.*

Wrote about forty pages of beautiful stuff at the Freemans' (I was released); will send you a carbon as soon as I retype . . . could be a new form.

er time with the Freemans in Chicago led Gail to write "Some Side Effects of Time Travel." The story exemplifies what she called a new type of writing for her, a free-flowing chronicle. Published first in Paris Review *and later in* Dream Children, *it is one of the key works of Gail's late 1960s period. The heroine awakens in her friends' apartment, not knowing where she is. Her mind goes to thoughts about experiments in narration.*

Excerpt from "Some Side Effects of Time Travel,"
Published in Paris Review *(Summer 1972) and*
Dream Children *(Knopf, 1976)*

—

Then she remembered. "Ha, I'm improving." And rose and began writing on a rickety old Remington belonging to her hostess, who had gone to work. Last night she told the host and hostess, "I've finally hit upon a method of chronicling myself which won't bore me to death. I'll be me at my most entertaining with friends and wine after dinner. I'll tell it like the Icelanders told their sagas, just narrate, *This happened, Thor felt this,* and so on, before the dawn of the writer's self-consciousness. Forget H. James, God love him, and the rules, the expectations of the clever reader, and go searching for myself all over the printed page, like an old-country granny spieling her life, skipping around the years, sidetracking into the really choicy operations, the gall bladder, the hysterectomy, anecdotes about Ebenezer's drinking and how Maud was never the same since menopause, following her own infallible train of intuition like one does on long bus rides or just before falling asleep."

JUNG SAYS: THE WORD HAPPENS TO US; WE SUFFER IT . . .

Gretchen had this typed on a note card. Note cards are her way of tabulating and taping a madcap inner and outer world that shapeshifts and self-destructs by the second.

Whenever she gets bored with plotted, pared stories that restrict, leave out, scale down, distort, she shuffles through her vast collection of note cards, written over the heady years, which have no form, no system, no end and no beginning, no one subject or single style, no unifying principle.

These note cards are the nearest she has come to getting outside of time.

SEPTEMBER 19

"The First Diary." Acts as genesis of a writer and as the Genesis story. He becomes aware of himself—creates light, etc., creatures, fables; gets more preoccupied with effects. He exhausts all possibilities, even if it means letting the other one take over. Evil is born. Describe. Then he finally gets compassionate, tries to stop it, wash it out, start all over. But even the ideas, people, he keeps are "infected." He decides to go into my story to see how I set them straight. In my story, I call to myself—a former, nobler self—"Why! Why have you forsaken me?"

WELL, I AM nice and solitarily situated again, without recourse. The last comparable time was right before I married Ian. Generally, it's not bad. Yesterday I allowed myself to become more and more like Aesop's "The Miller, His Son, and His Donkey." Kent said, "Oh, did you hear?

Scholes has let Aukema count Old Norse for four requirements."[30] Byron said, "You're a fool to take Chamberlain, he tells you how short to cut your toenails before coming to class."[31] I went looking for motorbikes with Kent, remembered Jane saying, "John was unhappy about your getting a motorbike. They're dangerous." The tide turned when I went out for a beer with Byron and was finally driven by boredom to stir something up. He retreated, Johnny Panic. Now that I think of it, fear was sparkling in his eyes, and his lips went thin as the edge of paper.

Anyway, I went to sleep feeling totally confused about my academic career.

Should I see Scholes? Or should I go on and take Chamberlain? I went to sleep and my friendly dreams diminished my fear of Scholes by having me have an affair with him. So, I was able to go in today, fix it up to take two courses which would count as four, one of them being Chamberlain's.

Lunch with Kent, who praises Aukema's inhuman computerstories. There is a real vogue for this sort of thing, but I'm still going to try for the essential dimension of feeling. That was what was so shortlived about Byron. So diabolically cold because he was frozen in fear.

SEPTEMBER 21

Lorraine is thirty-four; Ian is thirty-seven today. I went to the office, wrote an eleven-page story, talked to Kent, and walked home, dead tired. Ate perfunctorily and am now in bed at 8:30.

My two stories coming out in *Confluence* and *North American Review* mean little; I now want a national magazine. Then I'll want a novel out. Then I'll want to start getting a name. Then I'll care for the critics. Then I'll start wanting a place for myself in the halls of literature. So the best thing seems to me now is to skip all these intermediate stages

30. Robert Scholes was a professor of literature at the University of Iowa. By 1968, he had published *Elements of Fiction* and books on James Joyce.

31. Gail enrolled in David Chamberlain's class, "Medieval English Literature in Translation."

and try to write something truly meaningful and original. As for companionship, I'd like a husband, yes, but the wrong husband, no.

SEPTEMBER 22

Finished "The Apprentice—Fates,"[32] may refurbish and start sending out to magazines. *Mademoiselle*, then? I think I've had a breakthrough in writing—back to the intuitive, what interests me first.

Tomorrow: first day of teaching.[33] Am preparing to collapse from exhaustion. I think I might as well give up on finding a companion-lover.

SEPTEMBER 23

Jane today: "We've switched roles. It's me who's perturbed and you who sit there calmly chewing your gum and fiddling with your glasses."

New novel form. Letter about Gaert with dramatis personae at bottom.[34] Good thing about this, it can continue changing and growing as I do.

SEPTEMBER 25

Ten till eight, and I'm in bed. New opinion of Coover. That whole experiment-for-experiment's-sake school. By itself, it's arid. Something like E. Underhill's distinction between mystics and metaphysicians.[35] As

---

32. Gail wrote "The Apprentice—Fates" for Robert Coover's workshop. In it, a writing instructor, Miss Olga Slade, tells her students to fashion a true character from bits of information, representing the process as a kind of witchcraft. One student uses such magic on the instructor herself, capturing her in her drama, and then contemplates creating a further outer shell by writing about herself writing about Miss Slade.

33. Gail taught "Greek Drama for Freshmen Engineers" in the spring of 1967, and two Core Literature classes in the fall of 1968 as part of a teaching fellowship.

34. Gaert had been a friend of Gail's in Copenhagen in 1961–1962 and was to be a character in a Lawrence Durrell–like novel that Gail considered writing about that city.

35. Evelyn Underhill's 1911 book *Mysticism: A Study of the Nature and Development of Man's Spiritual Consciousness* distinguishes between a kind of mysticism that is philosophical or occult, and that which is practical and leads to a more creative life. "Where the philosopher guesses and argues," she writes, "the mystic lives and looks; and speaks, consequently,

I told Jane, I feel Coover is using God to get further with his own mind and art.

I am divided now about what I want to write—the Saga experiment or a straight Gothic novel about two metaphysicians searching for more knowledge. It's so bloodless, and that's why it can't succeed. Got to have my weekends for writing alone, whatever else happens. Get fifty pages and maybe try to get an option for it.

I miss only one thing now: somebody to eat with at the end of the day. Next story: "Somebody to Eat With."

OCTOBER 1

One of those days when I feel at the mercy of the world.

Got home and found a $24 bill for library fines and books. Better borrow more money from NDEA.[36] Kent, Ace, Jane, all have their own lives. Kent says he's lonely anyway. Jane is basically happy and pregnant. Ace dabbles in the daytime among the flowers, has his anchor at night. Yet at least I have three fairly akin spirits to talk to, even if it's no more than fifteen minutes a day. My tendency is to withdraw, withdraw until I get okay again.

OCTOBER 2

I dreamed there was a house where my future was. It was horribly dirty and sooty. I went down a hall and right into a living room—substandard furniture, filthy, no books—a young boy there. Blond. I said, "Do you know if there are any books here?" He said, "No, but downstairs." He showed me how to climb downstairs, and there was a library of boring, old books—just one bright one, about ducks or animals by Casey. I went into other rooms. Each got cleaner till at last I found a neat study, and in there I found a thin book that was mine.

---

the disconcerting language of first-hand experience, not the neat dialectic of the schools. Hence whilst the Absolute of the metaphysicians remains a diagram—impersonal and unattainable—the Absolute of the mystics is lovable, attainable, alive."

36. The National Defense Education Act of 1958 provided low-interest loans to students.

Unpublished Prosperity: Nine Essays, which somebody in the preface said I'd agonized over. Now there is this busybody woman following me. She has something to do with me—a sort of mother-landlady figure. In search of more books, I go into another room where a huge man is lying on the bed slantwise. He gets up. He is about seven to eight feet tall, a faded athlete. I say, "Are you my husband?" He says, "Yes," and wearily, affectionately comes toward me. It is as if he can't understand my tenderness. I think I ask him, "Have I been a bitch?" And he says, "Yes." We lie down together on a chaise lounge. I discover his false teeth lying on the arm of the chair and, although he has some in his mouth, I want to leave him again. Then the woman comes in. It appears I took her hairbrush. I give it back. She tries to stop my search. She has taken books out of my hand when I was trying to memorize the titles to take back to now. I asked her to write them down, and she wrote them down wrong. There was also a book I wrote about a computer.

Then I go to another room, climb out the window, run across the grass, feeling pursued, and climb into the window of an elegant house. A young Jewish man is in his study writing. He knows me, after being startled. I ask him what else I've written. An older woman comes in— his mother, a maid—and tells me, "Oh, that study of Nathan Allen (I think she meant Ethan), and the thing on London," and she begins to cry. Nathan Hale.[37]

G ail is searching for a literary form that is of her making. The Writers' Workshop environment complicated the effort with its mind-set of cliques and literary fads. On June 27, she'd noted that Montaigne had invented a form to suit himself—now why not she?

Repeatedly, she writes of having made breakthroughs, which involve writing that is intuitive, writing that is warm-blooded, and the creation of a design that doesn't parrot but makes use of the episodes in her life.

37. In the dream, Gail rejects the connection with Ethan Allen (patriot of the American Revolution, but also the namesake of the modern-day furniture manufacturer), to assert the connection with Nathan Hale, America's legendary spy.

When she wrote her mother on September 17 that the forty pages she'd just written—presumably the "Gretchen Saga"—"could be a new form," Gail was attempting an honesty of presentation through a fictional chronicle. She would employ that approach to some extent in 2004 with the Christina stories in the Ballantine edition of Evenings at Five.

The "Gretchen Saga" did not find publication, except in part in the short story "Some Side Effects of Time Travel." But the other major work on which she was working—her rewrite of "The Beautiful French Family"—did. This novel represents her breakthrough in warm-bloodedness. As she will write on October 14, she is conceiving the novel to show the characters' "growing awareness in the full flower of their failure." The new approach necessitates a new title: "The Perfectionists."

The neurosis—"flowering within failure"—is everyone's grand, contradictory, transformational design. And it might lead to solving a great mystery in Gail's life, the suicide of her idealistic father, evoked by Gail on July 26 when she wrote, "I'm overwhelmed by the absolute sadness of the lost ideal of the world."

OCTOBER 3

I seem to be the third everywhere I go. All my married friends, couples: Hammers, Dixons, Caseys, and Ace Baber, even though he's with a shadowy stay-at-home. Hammer's pregnant.

They like to talk about one's current boyfriend. One doesn't have one. Ace says: "You're alone right now, aren't you? I saw you coming across campus all by yourself at nine thirty this morning." He said: "You won't be alone for long." How many intervals have there been when I was without a man?

The thing is: Get as much done as possible while I am free. Ace said: "What were your husbands like? How long did it last each time? That's funny, because I can't imagine you ever leaving somebody. Walking out on them. Saying, 'We're through.' Like with me, even if you stopped liking me, I can't imagine you ever saying, 'I don't want to see you anymore.' Not with anyone you'd ever liked. You're too gentle somehow."

I give notice to this journal. How long will it be before the next man? Think I'll go to the MLA conference if it's in Chicago. That's where one meets intellectuals. And it's at Christmas, so those who go will be, some of them, loners. At times I think: If one can just be charitable, that's what counts.

OCTOBER 4

"It's the end of the week. Everybody's gone away to lick their wounds. That's why you haven't been able to make contact with anybody."—Ace

NOW, BACK TO WORK.

"THE ANGRY YEAR" at *HJ*.[38] Very little chance. There's just a hex.

"The Man on Sofa" at *McCall's*.

"Time Travel" at *NAR* [New American Review]. This was, I'm pretty sure, a mistake, and I will probably get a very cold rejection.[39]

WROTE PART OF "Sorrowful Mother,"[40] which I got from talking with Kent. Next: Write "George." "St. George" is a pregnancy metaphor. The girl is single, self-sufficient. Scene opens in bed. "He's growing. He'll change my life." Look up dragons.

---

38. *Ladies' Home Journal* (*HJ*) did not publish "The Angry Year," but *McCall's* later did. The story is included in Gail's collection *Mr. Bedford and the Muses* (Viking, 1983).

39. "Some Side Effects of Time Travel" was eventually published in *Paris Review* and is included in *Dream Children*.

40. "A Sorrowful Woman," Gail's most anthologized story, would be published first in *Esquire*. It is included in *Dream Children*. In 2009 a short feature film was made of it. (See gailgodwin.com for the link to this film.)

OCTOBER 6

I've been behaving like someone who's been told she has six months left to live. Got up, researched dragons. It may be my best yet. Went to office. Talked to Kent, finished "The Sorrowful Mother."

Tomorrow, write the agent John Hawkins, send him glowing rejections from *New Yorker* for "Illumined Moment" and "Dandelion," plus "Angry Year" rejections from *Cosmo* and *McCall's*.

OCTOBER 9

Tomorrow, a bit of freedom for writing—the Dragon. Haven't quite got my girl yet. She's set up—say she somehow has a house. She rents rooms, has slept with her tenants in the past, but they had gotten too involved. I think she should be working toward some goal she doesn't want upset—I'll probably have her be a graduate student, for lack of anything better.

OCTOBER 11

Jules and Jim[41] scene yesterday in the parking lot with Kent and Ace. Something to remember when contemplating the lies we tell each other, and the lies we tell ourselves. I have learned much about writing from Kent, and he's able to do a little bit of what Ian could do, explain me to myself. Some of Ian's phrases now come back: "Another person's love can be terribly helpful." I miss Ian now, but not in a way that would make me go back to that watery sunshine.

OCTOBER 13 · *Sunday*

At last I am able to set myself a job and do it. Finished "St. George." Next project is: Get fifty pages—excellent ones—of the novel ready to

41. *Jules and Jim* is the classic François Truffaut movie, released in 1962, about an ill-fated love triangle between two men and a woman.

send to John Hawkins. I am thinking of putting in an odd scene: visit with Ian's mother and the Jesuits in the ruined garden. I can afford to do surer things now.

Interesting development, it would make a good story. The Kent-Bev thing. After my believing him to be the intelligent, sensitive one, he gives me a piece of work she's written. Lucid—no, pellucid. Hot-honest. Intelligent and sure.

OCTOBER 14

Awful indigestion. Dinner with Ace and Kent. All sorts of interesting personal politics in which we are less than perfect.

Tomorrow, write novel, now *The Perfectionists,* a book about intellectuals seeking the illumined life. They make provision for everything but love. The novel shows their growing awareness in the full flower of their failure. About lack of love, Yeats: "Man can embody truth but he cannot know it."

Dane is a voyeur, wants to have a front-row seat in the awareness theater, but does not wish to get implicated. She is painted into a corner, where she is compelled to do something.

OCTOBER 23

So exhausted these days. Came home, smelled egg-rot in the sink from unwashed dishes. Am saving up energy to change the sheets. Am building up my pinnacle of works on which I will later stand. Vicar story in spring 1965. Liza first in summer 1965. These were the seeds.

Coover said he felt "Sorrowful Mother" was my peak, and I had gone to the final shape for that sort of thing. That story is now complete—yet that story was first conceived on a walk with Ian in the summer of 1965. I later wrote the first draft, which is back at 1 Argyll Mansions in London. I have needed this much time to develop my writing.

I want so much to write something thoughtful, warm, strung out— like, I think, my father. The synchronicity aspect. "We'd been on Canto

XIII of *The Inferno*[42] in my sophomore lit class when my father, that incorrigible playboy of fifty-one, drove home one snowy afternoon and put an end to everyone's envy of him."

The most meaningful experiences:

DATE	Story	Area of Experience
	Elegiac—still to be written	St. Genevieve's[43]
SPRING 1967	Illumined Moment	Peace College; Father Webbe; London
	Liza's Leaf Tower—sold	Mavis;[44] Ian
	Dandelion—sold	Gordon; the Caseys; Harrods
	Wonderful Story	Father
	Beautiful French Family	Majorca
SUMMER 1967	Angry Year	Chapel Hill
	Dollar's Worth of Hygge	Copenhagen
FALL 1967	Sacrificium	Aukema
	Dream of Insurrection	Jack;[45] Embassy
SPRING 1968	Man on Sofa	Ian
	Uncle	Ian
	Motes	My neuroses, my eyes, my MA final exhaustion

42. In Canto XIII, Virgil and Dante encounter the spirits of suicides, who have lost their human forms.

43. Gail's 2010 novel *Unfinished Desires* would eventually explore this material.

44. Mavis is Ian Marshall's sister.

45. Jack Malone, the homeless man whose memoirs Gail typed when she was working at the U.S. Travel Service in London.

DATE	Story	Area of Experience
SUMMER 1968		
	unfinished manuscripts:	
	The First Writer-God	Coover
	Sarah's Gothic Marriage	Ian
	Where Does a Tornado Convalesce	Jane and John
	The Sunday Calyx	My breakdown
FALL 1968	Time Travel	Bus trip; Freemans; finding form for the complexity of my experience
	Apprentice-Fates	Story in sci-fi book; Irene Slade; Borges
	Sorrowful Mother	Ian; Kent and Bev
	Dragon	Kent; me at 501 N. Dubuque; medieval lit.
NOV. 1968	Blue	Gaert; Bluebeard; H. C. Andersen's "The Shadow"
	Morningside	Denmark story, "Mrs. Fönss"; Mayview Manor; my mother and Milledge

OCTOBER 24

Your stories pick you.

WENT TO SEE *Magician* tonight.[46] It was a comedy, and anything sinister had to be put in by you. Deposit this in bank.

The magician, the preacher, the charlatan, [L.] Ron Hubbard, the Svengali-Rasputin type interests me. The power of silence and watchful

---

46. *The Magician*, Ingmar Bergman's 1958 film, depicts a charlatan, played by Max von Sydow, who can be seen as comic or menacing.

eyes is this: People see whatever they want to see. I may now be able to do this with my book.

A PANTY RAID in progress outside.

OCTOBER 29

I'm just beginning to see, and am glad I haven't had my "success" yet. I fall to pieces with praise. Went to the Union for breakfast. There in the newsstands was *Confluence*. I had apoplexy, was sure I'd been left out. No, there I was, illustrated with alien photographs—except the first, a field of dandelions. Typos, a sudden intrusion of an alien sentence, a paragraph left out. Father Webbe's words return: It's down there now in the naked light of day, for better or worse, to influence our brothers. Then Workshop applauded my story "A Sorrowful Woman" until I was embarrassed. Jane there to steady me. Coover is good to me, sending out my stories, pushing me to the limit. He may publish a book of very short stories with Kim Merker's Stone Wall Press here. This means, rewrite "Uncle." The thing now is to be selective.

OCTOBER 31

Well, there's a new star on the horizon, and again I'm not going to gobble him down only to find he gives me indigestion—or ptomaine poisoning. This one compliments of the Caseys—older, haggard, deep voice—a hand printer, with who-knows-what sad and shameful story to tell. Anyway, we got drunk at dinner, said all the background material straightaway, held hands under the table, walked in the yard, kissed. He said, "Let's not be drunken about this. There will be other evenings." And now there's titillation again in hearing the footsteps come down the hall.

Kim Merker—Vulcan. He came here as a published poet—now he's a printer with his own press. But slow down, what I wanted was something to keep it from being bleak while I worked. I think I'll work myself to death for the next three weeks—midterm, then grade papers, then Dragon. If I do everything, there won't be any time left.

Gail's search for a lover and companion who would not distract her from her work—or trap her in another conventional relationship—led to her creation of a medieval studies–inspired fantasy, "St. George." The story begins with a perfect relationship. In Gwen's life, her lusty, uncomplicated boyfriend Silas, a printer, "had served as her antidote against Love, the disease that had felled all her friends in the midst of whatever they were pursuing and left them handicapped forever after, trapped in mortgaged homes with rather ordinary men, all their grand possibilities extinguished."

Excerpt from "St. George," Published in Cosmopolitan (September 1969)

—

But tonight, as Silas stood over her bed, buttoning up his shirt, his usual blond, untroubled countenance clouded over and he said, "This isn't much of a relationship, is it?"

"Of course it's not!" exclaimed Gwen. Imagine Silas using a word like "relationship." "It's not supposed to be one. Relationships take too much libido and right now mine's all booked up." She was getting her master's degree in English next June. Then she could go out and make her demands on the world. Then she could begin to look for someone, her equal or better, with whom to fall in love. Silas was her Now man. She had picked him up in an all-night coffee shop. Having cleared her life of bearded graduate students who wanted to latch on to her psyche like leeches or lie in bed afterward discussing D. H. Lawrence, she had been on the prowl for a simple man, a truck driver, perhaps, a non-soul-sharer she couldn't get serious about, but who would stand between her and loneliness in this impersonal city.

Silas understands, he says, but then vanishes for days, without calling. Subconscious instincts and needs emerge in Gwen's life. "St. George" crosses into fantasy, as Gwen symbolically gives birth to an impossible child. Cracking an egg for a midnight omelet, she finds a red embryo embedded in the yolk. She discovers that it is a tiny dragon, and she nurtures it until it grows large enough to cause great havoc and needs to be granted its wildness.

NOVEMBER 3

November is never my good month. Gemini fights the removal of light and shudders at the thought of the settling down that winter brings. These last few days I've been at my unhappiest. Why? There is not even the astringent honor of being alone. I have Kent to lean on and subsequently torture. I have work to do, and the sooner the better. When I'm writing, the images lift me out of the mire.

Rewrite the Dragon as if Vulcan might read it. I'm engaged in my usual pre-new-affair sickness.

If I were smarter I'd learn a few things: first, not to try to read the minds of strangers; second, not to put my own thoughts into their minds; third, to *balance* between worship and disgust.

The thing is, I'll be here for two to three more years, so will Vulcan, so there's time to find out about each other. Whereas there's not as much time to break through in the writing—and I'm so near now. See what I can get out of Coover while he's here in the way of advice, good graces. If he does do the little book with Vulcan's Stone Wall Press, I can put "Uncle" in, maybe something else short—

A METAMORPHOSIS, PERHAPS—

Part seven

THE VOID AND
THE VALIDATION

Iowa City

NOVEMBER 3, 1968, TO DECEMBER 11, 1968

Bloody Marys for Jane's baby shower. I came back and slept on the river-bank.

What would make this place a home? Liquor, music, hospitality. 415 South Capitol was shabby, but I made people comfortable there. Some great parties! The curries with the Casey-Plimptons. St. Patrick's Day, when Vonnegut and his wife actually made costumes. Jane was William of Orange; Kurt, St. Patrick. Now, 501 North Dubuque, a step up in the rental world, just needs tall candles, the smell of good food, the smell of me around; but my heart isn't here. It's in getting published and being entertained by somebody else.

I studied on and off, 5:00 to 8:30 p.m., down at the office. Kept getting distracted by Vulcan going to and from his printing shop. Trying to read his mind. So I did the *I Ching*.[1] What is the state of affairs? ENTHU-SIASM. Then I asked, "What should I do to win him?" Threw six times, was on the verge of looking up the answer, when he stuck his head around the door and said, "How was the baby shower?" He came in and sat down this time. Regarding the Condés,[2] he said, "I couldn't take that kind of life. I have to have some serenity."

"Ohhh. DO you?" I said.

He said, "Shut that up or ..." something.

He said, "Have you ever seen the shop? Would you like to see it?" So down we went. Me and Vulcan. Nerves. His gorgeous yellow suede jacket.

---

1. When consulting the *I Ching*, the questioner throws three coins six times to produce a hexagram (six lines) that matches up with any of sixty-four universal conditions. It indicates the present state of the matter being inquired about. A hexagram that has one or more "changing lines"—lines containing three yins (6) or three yangs (9)—generates a second hexagram that predicts how the situation will evolve.

2. Miguel Condé, an artist, and his wife, Carola Schisel, loved to entertain.

Black beard, dignity. Nerves. I talk about his work till he says, "I'm not making much sense, I just got up from a nap."

I entertain him about Uncle William: the last Godwin, how he had to give up cigarettes.[3] I talk some more—about scholars, and how I hate the thought of being one. About the new agent, John Hawkins, and the novel. I say, "I'll let you work." He walks me to the door of my office. I say, "I'll walk you to the Coke machine." He buys himself a second drink within fifteen minutes. Then he buys me one, so, he says, "you can work better."

I: "Actually, I was doing the *I Ching*." "The what?" He's interested. Really, no skepticism. Wants to see it, wants to be shown. I show him. Shaking. He asks: "Will I get the ten-thousand-dollar grant from Urbana?" We throw the coins. He comes and stands behind me. He gets ACCUMULATION. He borrows the book. He comes back fifteen minutes later. "That's a scary book," he says. "I'd like to know some of the things you asked it."

"Maybe I'll tell you sometime," I said.

"Maybe you won't," he said. Left. But he has my property, something in which I've invested myself. Why not believe in something good? He has enough dignity to cover a multitude of flaws and it is so good to feel excited about someone again.

NOVEMBER 4

At 11:00 p.m., he comes to the door, says, "You'll never make it."

"Yes, I will," I say.

"I was going to ask you out for a drink, but the *I Ching* said no, that there would be an obstacle. And there was. Some friends called from out of town. So I have to meet them for drinks."

"What an original approach," I said. "Well, I want to do well on this test, so ask again."

---

3. Gail's uncle William had looked after her following her father's suicide in 1958. William suffered from depression, for which he underwent electroshock treatments at Duke Hospital when it became unbearable, and then returned to work. He had recently given up smoking, "cold turkey."

"I will," he said.

I think his eyes are blue. And he wore short blue shirtsleeves. Now I know I am in his intentions and can let it happen. For my own peace of mind, I must not design my days around it. It has only been the sixth day since meeting him.

NOVEMBER 5 · *Tuesday*

Shambles of a day. Must subvert ego or die. Don't talk to people sloppily, keep something sacred. Oh, God help me.

NOVEMBER 13

Nothing since November 5? Where to start?

"Your star is in the ascendancy, I'm sure of that," says Jane.

11:00 p.m.

But I have wet hair and a lot to say. Even in the midst of achievement, excitement, and hard work, there is a great void, and I cannot fill it by myself. At the end of it all, I am lonely. I want to touch, but not indiscriminately. There is someone who interests me, but he is no savior. He's a wounded bird. If he's a rock, the rock is built from pain and defenses and might not be hard enough to lean against. I want it all now, but that's not the way it goes. Things build and fall, shape-shift, grow, metamorphose into new forms. How can I, who have benefited through change and growth, fear or push it now? Last Wednesday night, he took me home to his house for drinks. He told me about his dogs, his Prussian ancestors, his family motto ("Break but don't bend"), his rebuilt Jaguar, and his best friend's wife, who'd just committed suicide. He replenished my drinks and did not try to ravish me as surplus entertainment. Kissed me as much as I wanted to kiss him and knew, without my telling him, where I lived.

Friday a letter arrived from John Hawkins in New York telling me he's interested in representing me. Apologized for asking, but wanted to know how old I was and whether I was English or American! Vulcan was the first to read it.

Vonnegut on a whirlwind reading tour blesses our union in the hall. Saturday night I want to talk with Vulcan so bad, I snub him at a party. He leaves at once. I despair. Kent and Lorraine both crawl on my bed, hang their wishes over me, and despair of me. The next day—Sunday—I see him in the hall and nervously make known my goodwill. He says he's going to a party after Coover's reading, and I am miserable because I have not been invited. I think I decided then to go anyway.

I maneuver it, practically collapsing from a resurgence of childhood anxieties. After a terrible initial period, I am befriended and saved by Mrs. Scholes.[4] Then he comes over and I'm with him for the rest of the evening. He says, "I know you've been dying to talk to me. Now is your three minutes."

We sit in a corner by the fire. He tells me he goes to a psychiatrist. He tells me I'm dangerous; he can sense it intuitively. "You are a pusher," he says. "Success is not in my dictionary." His psychiatrist has a clubfoot.

I say I hope he can talk to me. "I'd like to," he says, "but how objective can you be? Suppose you fall madly in love with me."

And later I slipped and said "I love you"—in a context, of course—and then, like a neurotic, was sorry. I think it impressed-scared him. "Let's go to bed," he said. Once or twice at the party, he held my hand. He betrayed me to a friend—"She's dangerous!"—and then said, "I want to walk outside and kiss you." But he got busy with people. I left with the Foxes. Vulcan comes out on the porch and calls me back. "Gail!" He kisses me on the porch.

ABOUT THE CHEMISTRY

He says, "I'm my own bottleneck."
Is tired, driven, pushed, black-coffee-drinking,
& still prefers to collapse at the Condés'

4. The wife of English professor Robert Scholes.

to being energetic with me.
Maybe he's afraid it will go too fast and
he'll be stuck down in the basement with me for
another three years. I don't blame him.
Can I condemn his caution? How can I expect him to suddenly
shift me to center stage, spotlight me, dim the lights on all his past
habits, past loves, acquaintances, loyalties? The most I can do is
do what I have to, intersecting weekly at free crossroads
in his life, dropping a smile, an idea,
an inspiration when I do see him. The
real thing is, If I'm the sort of
person who interests him, he'll show
interest. About the chemistry, that
is a matter over which we have no
control. There is or is not the attraction.

Oh yes, one more thing. He wants me to read his novella. That is no small thing.

Friday, John Hawkins comes to Iowa to visit clients Willie Nolledo and Kent Dixon and to look for new talent. Saturday I do the laundry.

NOVEMBER 14

Rain. And I am angry and depressed with circumstances. Write away, little loner, suffer, suffer, suffer. "Ah, to be great, you have to suffer." Damn rain. Iowa City. I want Vulcan to pour me drinks, talk with me, take me to bed. I want it now that I've finished "His House," no small achievement.[5] Backing off, he is perhaps playing subtle games for self-preservation, instigated by his psychiatrist.

---

5. In Gail's story "His House," a man tells a woman about his house, and they visit it. It's the middle one of three identical structures on a city block. The front door is locked, so they look over a wall and the woman sees that the man's house is a façade between two substantial structures. Below the façade, a train roars through a tunnel. She feels "cold, wise, lonely, old, and clean." "Why?" she asks. "I didn't build it," he replies. This story was published in *The Stone Wall Book of Short Fictions*, edited by Robert Coover and Kent Dixon (1973), a hand-printed limited edition of 325 copies.

I meet him as I rush to class. "There she is . . . the picture of . . ."

"Late as usual" is all I have time to say. So he echoes, "Late as usual."

At the coffee machine, late afternoon. I say, "Are you still working hard?"

He says, "Yes, but last night I got snockered at home. It was fun."

I wanted to ask, "By yourself?" But was stunned, and mumbled something about what I was going to do next. "Let me get you some coffee, I hope," he says.

Damn it, here I am cataloging with great interpretation a meaningless exchange at the EPB's equivalent of a water cooler! Shit. I refuse to play those games. Can't. He's so jaded-looking, those circles under the eyes. He's a mean, sleek animal, sharp-toothed when in danger of being attacked. He says, "I'm a sadist when I have to be." He has a beautiful secretary, young and flawless in the flesh. It is nice looking into that world-weary, sarcastic face, but knowing my own penchant for unhappiness, I am not going to lie down in front of him. He would probably run over me.

10:30 in the evening

It's so true that one has nothing, really, except what one makes of this vast black void. This is a short-term lease among the stars.[6] All right. Work, then, but it must be meaningful, generative work. Work for work's sake is not enough.

At the moment, it's bad because: I have finished a span of work and now wish to rejoice, and I can't. And, I have no way of knowing what's on this man's mind. So why not act as I did before there was anybody?

I feel paralyzed till I know whether anyone will want the novel. At such an edge of my life.

6. This existential expression about sense of purpose is brought to the understanding of Theo Quick, the noble, despairing, suicidal brother in Gail's novel *A Southern Family*. He says, "Look up there at all those stars . . . Some of them are so far away that they stopped burning thousands of years ago, only we don't know it yet . . . What if it doesn't add up to anything? What if there are no patterns or meanings? What if there's nothing to understand?"

NOVEMBER 16 • *Saturday, 11:50 a.m.*

More excitement than ever, best and worst kinds. Every one of my childhood neuroses is blooming. Jane calls at 9:30 a.m. and we talk for an hour—John Hawkins was at their house last night, Bill Keogh brought him by, and, furious not to have been invited, I say all the unsaid things about their "snobbery" and "jealousy" and she cries. She excuses herself to get a Coke and comes back and I lambast her some more. We both go at it. She: "But you're my friend. You're not my *best* friend, but . . ." I think we both learned a lot.

So much I could write here, but very little that I need to write for the purposes of my book. I have to focus on the book and write two hundred more pages, and it's got to be top quality. Dane has got to be everything. The book must keep readers on the edge of their seats. It must not be a word too much.

Excerpt from The Perfectionists
(Harper & Row, 1970), Chapter Five
[Dane criticizes her husband.]

—

"Would it be compromising our perfect marriage if you spent more time displaying your attractive qualities and left the inner mess for yourself, to tinker with in your spare time?"

"You don't seem to distinguish between mess and the natural disorder that precedes growth," he retorted angrily. "Where is the girl who wanted visions, who could cite with such relish the crises of great saints? What kind of mess was it when Saint Paul fell off his horse and writhed in the dust and stood up a transformed man? I suppose that disgusts you, too."

"You have all the saints on your side. I know that. Intellectually. But I still feel disgust. And it separates me from you. Saint Paul knew better than to come home and tell his wife. He knew better, for the sort of man he was, than to take a wife."

12:05 Sunday morning [November 17]

I want to hibernate. So much meaningless drivel. I can't talk to Vulcan without being shy, jittery, falsely cheerful. I'd rather give it all up.

Hawkins is back to New York with my forty-eight pages and it's up to the higher powers. I'm so sick of the English-Philosophy Building, the classes, the whole rigmarole. Everybody's in the same boat, sick of themselves and everyone else.

NOVEMBER 17 · *Sunday night*

Wrote fourteen pages today. I know this woman Dane now. I know the man. I can keep control.

Tomorrow: Xerox pages for Coover; do *Antony and Cleo,* Act II, for my Core class; read *Tristan* for my medieval course.

NOVEMBER 18

The mighty oak toppled with virus. Or else my body, a *bon gourmet,* has refused to put up with any more junk. Rallying now. Such odd half dreams all day: pedestrian, long, boring conversations with people over the mechanics of things.

Rosenthal[7] called, gave me some news which explained things, about Vulcan's former marriage. He propositions when drunk, wiggles out of an assignation when sober. He works like crazy, long hours alone at his job, then goes home and drinks himself to sleep. The tension is taken off. Now I know it's not me, but his own fears.

NOVEMBER 19

I'm so woeful, I have to smile. Fingers chewed to bits, face broken out, hair lank and greasy, legs unshaved, fillings about to fall out.

---

7. Lucy Rosenthal, author of several novels, including *The Ticket Out,* had been a student, like Gail, in the Writers' Workshop.

Coover gave me the greatest compliment, considering who he is: My imagination is so alive. These days—when my hallucinations under fever are so dull and mechanical.

Jane Casey hurt with me, possibly I eat Thanksgiving dinner alone. That, my dear, is the price you pay. Vulcan bounces in twice today, once in the morning in his printer's apron, once in the evening all cocked out in his russet turtleneck en route to a faculty drink-meeting, coming in, dancing out, leaving me with nothing.

NOVEMBER 20

It's been two weeks almost and he hasn't repeated his invitation. Maybe he's not for me, and how nice it never got off to a rip-roaring illusion of a start. Naturally, in a dearth like this town's, everything fairly attractive and suave is going to become a minor god. Remember my own incredible lapses in taste. I do know I need a change from that terrible English building—paper cups thrown on floors, sinister noise of floor waxers bumping off elevators.

LETTER FROM JOHN HAWKINS: Morrow upped the $250 offer of an option, but too late. John thinks we can do better somewhere else.

NOVEMBER 21

From suicidal back to human via Kent. I can't discount those people who are always there when I need them. Coover didn't like my novel; he read the whole thing, not just the forty-eight rewritten pages John took back to N.Y. He was afraid it would get published and read by the wrong people and that would be the end of me.

Robert Coover was the advisor in the Writers' Workshop with whom Gail had a love-hate relationship. He also taught a graduate course titled "Ancient Exemplary Fictions," in which Gail was enrolled in the fall of 1968. Gail remembers him as "a formidable little magician who encouraged us to play games; he loathed realism in fiction, particularly anything to do with interpersonal relations." One assignment for "Ancient Exemplary Fictions" was to write from the point of view of a seventh-century Irish monk who had just discovered an ancient manuscript that turns out to be: Scheherazade's last tale! Coover's end-of-course test question was: "If the original leap from interjectional language to objectification was based on magic, is the search for reality behind language still based on the same impulse? How does language communicate the ineffable?"

The question represents a gauntlet through which Gail had to pass to gain acceptance in her writers' community. It also reveals a way of looking at things that had enchanted a generation in the 1960s. Stanley Kubrick's movie 2001: A Space Odyssey, then just out, exemplifies this worldview. Based on a concept from Arthur C. Clarke's 1953 novel Childhood's End, it embraces the idea that humans are evolving from one stage of living (functional, with language used as a tool of communication) to a higher one (transcendental, with language helping people get above matter). In the future, the idea goes, humans will become more consciousness than being, and will connect with a universal mind.

"Childhood's End changed my whole way of thinking," Gail wrote in her term paper. But still there was a problem with going along Coover's path. It involved reducing characters to symbols. Gail eventually sought to reveal the design of universal consciousness through something more character-based, the personal problems of identifiable individuals.

In a letter that she would write to Coover on January 29, 1969, Gail pinpointed the technique that would bridge his and her methods. "I am not afraid of crossing the boundaries between what our age calls 'fantasy' and what it calls 'reality,' " she stated. "I also see the things gesture can accomplish after all the interpretations are dead and gone. The Green Knight can pick up his severed head and stalk out of Arthur's hall as many times as he likes and all the interpretations of all the sensibilities in the world will not lessen the charm of his action . . . I believe the gesture may be the way I can express the ineffable."

૭

NOVEMBER 22

Five years since Kennedy died. Dear old England. It was on a Saturday the day after, when we went beagling—Gordon L., Gordon W., and I—and I was finally able to break the Gordon W. spell.[8]

Rock Island today.[9] I bought wines, liqueurs, whiskeys. Saw Vulcan briefly this a.m. in the basement, told him I was spinning off to R.I.—offered to get him something. He accepted—one Compari. I told him just enough about Coover, and he was actually involved in a conversation with me—then he was called to the phone. I disappeared before he got back.

Tomorrow: groceries, writing, read *Tristan*.

NOVEMBER 23

There are some nice wineglasses in Younker's for $1 each. Have spent some money since yesterday to make my life bearable. A long note from Jane left by her in my typewriter. It's okay. I think I can even stand Thanksgiving alone. Read all weekend at 501 North Dubuque. I've broken my habit of not staying here. Booze, food, books. I'm making a stew.

NOVEMBER 24

Leisured late—Bloody Marys—and ambled off to my office to read *Antony and Cleopatra* for my Core class. Beef tartare at Kent's with banana daiquiris and wine. Back. Read fairy tales for Coover and started writing one.

Condense through use of imagery.

8. The Kennedy assassination coincided with and may have precipitated Gail's awareness of the apathy into which she was letting herself sink regarding her unsatisfactory relationship with Gordon W.

9. Iowa City had a state liquor store where, Gail recalls, "you could buy only the basics, and the staff frowned at you if you asked questions about the qualities of a wine." Rock Island, across the Mississippi River in Illinois, had all the fancy stuff. The island is the site of the former village of Saukenuk, birthplace of Black Hawk.

The washed-out greeny horror of supermarkets, the piped-in music. I'm what comes after Whiter Than White. Our "religion" of cleanliness corresponds to hatred and fear of the Negro.

She's the one that gets the shadow's extra kick. It only talks when she bathes in it. New sensations, and not all of them nice. She wants whiter than white at the beginning—celestial.

Almost back to my old self. It's taken me almost a month to get over the man in the basement. Dentist tomorrow. Reminds me of pain and death and getting old. Nervous about Hawkins, about the book. O God, let something nice happen soon.

NOVEMBER 25 · *Monday*

Came home at four—drank, ate, slept, read *The Painted Bird*.[10] I dreamed I was not invited to another party. I'm not on the faculty, and this leaves me to the mercy of friends who remember. I feel so trapped in my situation, I could cry out in despair.

NOVEMBER 26

The Phoenix reborn. Wrote first good draft of "Blue,"[11] which may be a milestone. Silence from New York.

Shortly before twelve, Vulcan reentered my life with renewed vigor. I was able to speak with no giddiness about something serious—the Coover problem, how he admires my "great imagination" but deplores the kind of novel I am perpetrating—and he sat down, read another letter (from the editor at Morrow to John, offering more $, but saying how he'd change things in the novel), and went away promising more.

Tonight he came again, sat down, talked about several more subjects. I told him dentist stories. We talked of Kafka's suffering. He's off to play bridge with the boys, says he'd rather have cocktails Negrita with me.

I say, Let me ask you five questions about yourself. Do you take

10. *The Painted Bird* by Jerzy Kosinski, published in 1965, depicts a Gypsy boy who learns that humans are essentially violent.

11. The story "Blue," about a failed artist, is lost.

sleeping pills? No, I drink. Do you read science fiction? Do you take basically an optimistic or pessimistic view of the world? He backs out of the office in his chair. He says he wants to keep *I Ching* to ask it a few more questions. I say, "If you'll give me a Xerox copy of the questions." He says, "You!"

He says, "Are you going to be around for the holidays?" Yes. So there.

NOVEMBER 28, THANKSGIVING

In a few hours, I go to the Dixons' to drink banana daiquiris and eat dinner and drink wine, and I'll be bored by all but Bev, who is at least making an attempt to be interesting by losing her mind.

Came home, couldn't read Kafka or *Frankenstein*, could only lie in bed, insomniac, and think petty thoughts. What thoughts I think—of God, my novel, words, love, discipline, meaningful despair. Listen to my thoughts (I tried to derail them, but they came back, whistling on that endless track): I thought of all the people who would have Christmas parties and not invite me. I went on to think of all the things the faculty and local Workshop crowd would say to me and then behind my back in the halls of EPB. (See how limited the area, even?) Then I caught myself practicing false little conversations with Vulcan. And then thoughts of me getting older and unattractive and ending up alone. These thoughts don't do anything but keep me awake—and drain my self-respect. I've got to finish this novel, stick to the original premise of exploring this woman's personality. About the insolubles—age, disease, death—use them as motifs in the writing, but don't dwell on them.

NOVEMBER 29

This was an exemplary day during which war waged within me, and the artist emerged in the heavy hours. But just. Did not want to wake— I somehow knew what was destined to go into my mailbox.

I dreamed of leading Coover astray in an elegant bookshop. He was dressed in tights, like a court jester. We had gone there because, after lecturing me on piecing short fictions together with a long one (he thought this a good idea), he admonished me for getting behind on the class bulletin board. Apparently, he took pride in this. It was an extension of his identity. I said I didn't want to do it till I had beautiful porcelain colored letters, and I knew where we could get some. I enticed him into going to this place I'd visited before. He became entranced by a little glass elephant with a rider. He saw this figure as an emblem of himself. I encouraged him to buy it. We giggled. I went off, came back, and he was still entranced. I talked him into buying it, then we looked at the price—$11. "That can't be right." It wasn't. The parts were priced separately, and when added together, totaled something like a fantastic $183. Of course, he could not buy it. I was embarrassed. Then I saw some new bookplates with the pictures of authors on them. I decided to buy Professor [Gayatri] Spivak[12] the Yeats one, and maybe also the Valéry, if the shop carried them.

In the morning mail: the letter I dreamed I'd get. Hal Scharlatt at Random House waxes to Hawkins over how beautifully I write—a born storyteller; intelligent feeling—but feels the subject and location of my book are too remote. He's afraid we can't sell enough copies.

Bless John's heart, his upbeat letter accompanying it. He is so good, I hope he doesn't go cold on me as Lynn did.

Went to the office, couldn't do anything. I am beginning to learn secrets about how to ward off breakdown. First of all, I am more neurotic in the daytime. Today, my muscae volitantes[13] (seen against the white wall) were driving me to distraction. I felt removed from my concentration because of the intervention of faulty eyes. The building is deserted. I go see Kent, who is cool, to say the least. He walks out and leaves me to go to Hamod's office.[14] I realize I didn't want to see him anyway; he is

12. Gayatri Chakravorty Spivak, born Gayatri Chakravorty in Calcutta, India, taught at the University of Iowa while completing her PhD at Cornell University. She was then married to Talbot Spivak. Later she gained international prominence as a scholar and translator of the philosopher Jacques Derrida, and she authored a founding text of postcolonialism, "Can the Subaltern Speak?"

13. It's the condition that Eliott, the metaphysical scholar, has in an extreme form in Gail's story "The Legacy of the Motes."

14. Sam Hamod, now a published poet, received a PhD from the University of Iowa, where he attended the Writers' Workshop.

only something to chafe against. I go back downstairs. All I can manage is the *I Ching*.

I ask how to get Vulcan. It says PEACE. I ask how to behave now regarding my life in general. It gives that horrible ABYSS reading: six in the first and in the last place, which is not only misfortune, but misfortune for three years.[15] I ask how I shall act today, and I get ABYSmal again. I leave, utterly defeated, go to Whiteway, buy food, come home—eat sandwiches, drink beer, and read *The Owl and Nightingale*.[16] Back to office at 5:30 to begin the painful sixth-chapter rewrite. Did four pages, polishing, repolishing, then typed up "Blue" on a stencil.

Came home. Brisk cold, stars; a truck in distance. I'm alone with my companion: me. Whenever I start to go to pieces, it's because I'm looking outside and trying to guide myself by the charts of others.

With my studies and teaching the novel, plus whatever story comes up, I have enough to put me to sleep at night without a social life, too much alcohol, or Vulcan's caresses. If anything happens that is pleasant, it belongs to the periphery, where all things perish, change, fly, disappear.

"THE ILLUMINED MOMENT"—revisions.[17] Focus in on his personality at the beginning. The vicar is a young man, thirty-one last June. Physical description: eyes that have seen things. He's suited best for country roads, gratefully munched-over scones in a parishioner's drawing room. He's going to pieces over his picture in *Time* magazine. His rib cage might be protecting a little bird. His bishop keeps hinting he should marry.

Metaphor for artist who has just published his first book. He sees that it will never be so simple or so quiet again. He's on to something new.

15. "Abyss" encourages diving into a situation that is, at any rate, unavoidable.

16. *The Owl and the Nightingale,* composed in Middle English circa 1200, is a verse debate between two birds about moral philosophy.

17. "The Illumined Moment" became "An Intermediate Stop" and was published in *North American Review* and then in *Dream Children.*

Excerpt from "An Intermediate Stop," Published in
Dream Children *(Knopf, 1976)*

—

The vicar, just turned thirty-one, had moved quietly through his twenties engrossed in the somewhat awesome implications of his calling. In the last year of what he now referred to nostalgically as his decade of contemplation, he had stumbled upon a vision in the same natural way he'd often taken walks in the gentle mist of his countryside and come suddenly upon the form of another person and greeted him. He was astonished, then grateful. He had actually wept. Afterward he was exhausted. Days went by before he could bring himself to record it, warily and wonderingly, first for himself and then to bear witness to others. Even as he wrote, he felt the memory of it, the way the pure thing had been, slipping away. Nevertheless, he felt he must preserve what he could.

Somewhere between the final scribbled word of the original manuscript and the dismay with which he now (aboard a Dixie Airways turboprop flying above red flatlands in the southern United States) regarded the picture of himself on the religion page of *Time* magazine, his tenuous visitor had fled him altogether. The vicar was left with a much-altered life, hopping around an international circuit of lecture tours (the bishop was more than pleased) that took him further and further from the auspicious state of mind which had generated that important breakthrough.

NOVEMBER 30

December may be better. Struggling with the novel. I know I'm beyond this story, this woman, now. But I think I can make an honest novel out of it, and one with some black punch to it. After that, I want to try something completely fanciful, break away from the Gwen-Dane woman-in-the-single-room syndrome. Like Lawrence after *Sons and Lovers* saying "This is the last of its kind." Tomorrow I'd like to get into the torture of the riding ring scene[18] before the onslaught of my classes.

It begins to occur to me that Vulcan is painfully shy, that his social life about equals mine, that he, too, hopes for a savior, but is not about to lose his pride. He came down, worked till about nine. He made the long journey down to his office by going by mine, rattled keys, unlocked, locked, came back, knocked, came in and looked rather pale, his hair washed and flying away again like I like it. He was limping, said he sat down on a Condé chair and reslipped a disc. Said, "I called you Wednesday night. I was going to invite you for a cocktail or even invite myself over for a Bloody Mary." So I do know he's trying. I invited him over tomorrow morning. Instead of morbidly expecting the worst, I shall expect him. The trouble with being lonely is, I tend to forget that other people are lonely, have barricades against disappointment, too. So, I admire Vulcan's caution; it is charming, honest. It is as if he is saying, "I am coming as fast as I can." I think he needs encouragement, but no games; he would recoil from games. And this, after all, is a not-bad stage: a potential companion in the mead hall. I think one has to go the rest of the way alone.

DECEMBER 1

This apartment. The radio. Enough to eat. Drink. At least my husband was not sealed up in the West Virginia coal mine catastrophe. Mother just called: "You've still got us. Come for Christmas." This morning Monie told her: "I dreamed last night I lost my horse, Jim." Mother: "That's funny! Last night I dreamed I found a horse. I gave it to Rebel. It must have been Jim."

---

18. This occurs in chapter 6 of *The Perfectionists*. Dane, the disenchanted wife on vacation with her husband, John, and stepson, Robin, in Majorca, gets an invitation to go riding at Count Bartoleme's stables. John has her take Robin with her. Miraculously, the count coaxes the resentful, withdrawn boy to ride a horse, and is successful until he lifts him to take him back to Dane. Robin has a tantrum and kicks the count in the groin.

DECEMBER 2

Hit bottom last night. Cried, drank, sobbed, cursed, prayed. The solitude. Nothing to hope for. Then Old W.,[19] of all people, called at ten and
I went over there, stayed till three listening to his stories of broken marriage. How his wife made him drive straight from the church to the
cemetery, where she laid her wedding bouquet on her father's grave.
Smelling of Guerlain men's cologne, he begged me to spend the night,
and I noticed he'd put fresh sheets on the bed. His hands were clammy
and he was going on about how he'd failed to get it up with some girl
last week. I had a difficult time getting out of there.

I had six to seven hours' sleep, woke hungover, prepared my class,
barely made it. Have felt sore-throaty all day. Cold feet. Went to see Bev
in the psychiatric ward. She's holding out for perfection, and she still
thinks she'll get it. Even when she's telling me about her breakdowns,
screaming, wanting to die, I have this eerie feeling she's dramatizing it all.

Back to the EPB—Jane had read my note, all's well there again. Encountered poor Vulcan limping along with his back ailment—had been
to the doctor, who'd prescribed hot pads, and if that failed, a corset. I
wished him better. He said he wished himself better, as it was separat-
ing him from the mainstream of life. No mention of Sunday. Mother
called again. Christmas at home.

DECEMBER 3

Composing myself at the bottom of the abyss. If I go home, it will be
with the promise to myself to write the Chamberlain paper there and
prepare to teach *The Canterbury Tales*. Rewards today: an A on McDowell's[20] midterm with notes like "Excellent work" and "A pleasure to
read." Vulcan still scarce and limping. I said, "Better?" He said, "A little."

19. W. was an English professor.

20. Frederick P. W. McDowell was the chairman of Gail's doctoral committee. She says that
in retrospect he was the most valuable of her teachers, "because he let me know what was
available in literature and kept his ego out of it."

I learned a good lesson from *Tristan*. At the moment I don't really want to suffer.

> *Now when the maid and the man, Isolde and Tristan, had drunk the draught, in an instant that arch-disturber of tranquility was there, Love, waylayer of all hearts ... [Tristan] at once remembered loyalty and honour, and strove to turn away [but] love tormented him to an extreme ... He fixed his mind on escape and how he might elude her ... But the noose was always there.*
>
> —GOTTFRIED VON STRASSBURG, *TRISTAN*, translated by A. T. Hatto

DECEMBER 4

Night before last: a dream—a nightmare—from which I awoke in despair. I dreamed Vulcan came to Kathleen and Frank's house. It was the present temporary one, very cramped.[21] Everyone in the family was on their worst behavior. My mother went around in a dirty girdle. We were all going out, and I became so ashamed, I couldn't go with them. I stayed home and cried. Next day, I asked my mother about it. She said, "He was very formal and thanked me for dinner. He left with another girl." Mother showed me the girl's picture. She was that rather homely but sincere type. I woke up saying, "Oh no."

This afternoon in the graduate bitch-session: listening to the women PhD candidates. One blond divorcée who tried to kill herself last year; and poor Winifred, whose comps start tomorrow, and whose office is overrun with mice!

DECEMBER 5

Vulcan knows what he likes and wants, and is discreet and cautious. He will not have his credentials trod upon. Tonight was the first time I saw

---

21. While Frank Cole, Gail's stepfather, was building the family's next home in Asheville, the Coles lived in a rented house.

him show enthusiasm for something—his hand-printed books. He doesn't want to reprint anything. He has interesting ideas. Jane had said he hadn't shown up at a Condé dinner party. His place had been laid. He apparently disappeared for two days.

Tonight, he was having a late dinner at Jane's. She was stooping to put a casserole in the oven. "There's a woman!" he said as he spun and pointed.[22] He said he'd been drinking less. He likes *Nightwood*.[23] He told me he'd read my professors' comments on the PhD sheet. Coover had said: "Outstanding writer. I only hope she doesn't get the PhD and writes instead." I grow more and more attracted to Vulcan and refuse to deny it.

He was explaining to his mother about modern art: "the landscape as seen whizzing by in a car. Grandfather never saw it like that." I told him about *Philobiblon*.[24] I think I'll just regard him as a male friend. If he is a man of habit and security—and all points that way—then I slowly will become more important to him.

DECEMBER 6

I feel like a mouse that a cat has been toying with for several hours. That foxy Prussian knew damn well every effect and side effect he had on me. I must acknowledge the fact that, for his own good reasons, this man is not interested in me. He has his freedom, a fantastic car due in two weeks, lots of friends. He's invited to a dinner and three parties tonight. There is no room for me in his life. All he likes to do is peep in to see me working. The way he kept playing with the *I Ching* tonight and reading out terrible answers: "You should not marry such a maiden." And then asking: "Will I find romance at the party?"

---

22. Jane's pregnancy was well advanced.

23. *Nightwood*, by Djuna Barnes, published in 1936, is a novel that has achieved long-lasting acclaim and cult status. Its heroine, attracted to her bestial self, has three doomed love affairs—two with women—and cannot accommodate a doctor's counsel to unify her civilized and primordial selves.

24. *The Philobiblon* is a book that Richard de Bury (1281–1345), who served as bishop of Durham and high chancellor of England, worked on until the end of his life. In it he explains his love of books and the principles of book collecting.

If only I could get a fix on him, but he's foxier than I am, and I can't fathom him. I can't go on with this dragging, lackluster hope. The *I Ching* says SPLITTING APART: take no action. OUTSIDE CIRCUMSTANCES. All I can do is refine my character, hope for greater understanding, and put this energy into writing.

Maybe I can work this out tomorrow in my "Morningside" story about Mrs. Pedersen and her daughter. The daughter is young, demanding of love. The mother is the stoic who accepts love in whatever shape it comes. Use this frustration about the Prussian to put power into this story. Write a high-quality Virginia Woolf story.

DECEMBER 7

No nonsense on weekends. They're my only time with no duties other than to write. I see, in the morning's clearer light, that with him it could be worse. If he started taking me out secretly, then I'd want to go out with him publicly. I'd start wondering where he was every night. The more familiar I became with his habits, the more they would trap me. I'd much rather carry on this sort of flirtation. I thought for a while I was abnormal, but one can't close down. Because then when something does come, you're cold to it. If I could work out my premises on this subject in that story, then maybe I could go beyond it both in life and art. Also, I want to rewrite Ambrose—make it more mythical.

THE FUTURE VULCAN

He is a man pretty well settled in his life.
He will live here. Be near his children.
Have his press. Work himself and others
hard in the shop. Go out with his cronies.
Be invited everywhere as the extra man.
Drive around in his rebuilt Jaguar.
Put out elegant little books. Be good at
what he does. Be fashionable.
Dapper. Prussian. Humorous.

And maybe or maybe not he'll miss something.
He goes on and on about women
being serving, gentle creatures. He said
once, when drunk, "She was a fine woman,
it's just that she had nothing of her own."

Almost midnight

Wrote three single-spaced pages of Mrs. Pedersen, somewhat losing it at the end.

Got a step further this evening through Kent's idea about paradigms in psychology. If a certain evasive type of man appeals to me over and over again, it may be I'm asking my father to desert me over and over again.

DECEMBER 8

Hold on hold on hold on. Wrote six and a half good pages of "Morning-side."[25] The people are becoming real. Will write more tomorrow, and several nights through the week—send to John Hawkins next weekend.

Ace came by. He said he knew when women were after him. "The first sign is when they're always *around*." Two more years in this place. Ayyyeee . . . I live in a world in which people get married. As a single woman graduate student, I will not be invited to parties of couples. Single men faculty will. That is a social rule. Don't say I'm going away for Christmas. Just disappear.

---

25. "Morningside" was published in a rewritten form, as "Last Summer on Pelican Island," in *USA Today*, August 4, 1995. The magazine's Summer Fiction Series also included stories by Stephen King, Alice Hoffman, Rita Dove, Julia Alvarez, and Walter Mosley. Gail's story begins with a young woman, Evvie, breaking off a marriage at the last minute and then having her grandmother, "Van" (for Evangeline), take her to an inn on Pelican Island, where Van's family had taken vacations. Van tells Mr. Mayberry, a friend, about the time she'd realized with surprise that her island nanny—a woman who she'd felt had been a part of her—was black like the servants back home. Evvie, as it turns out, elopes with and marries her fiancé, having witnessed the pleasure that Van had conversing with Mayberry.

Excerpt from "Last Summer on Pelican Island"

—

"What were you thinking?" Horace Mayberry presently inquired.

"Goodness! About someone who was very important to me as a child. An island woman named Flavia who took care of me while we vacationed at the inn. Flavia and I spent our days and nights together. She slept on a cot in my room. We were so close, I believed she was partly me. At night I sometimes felt sure I could hear her thoughts. But then—oh dear. Daddy took some movies of our vacation one summer, and when the family was watching them at home the next winter I went into hysterics. When I saw Flavia in the movie I realized she was just like our other servants. She had dark skin and was wearing a uniform. I felt they had done something terrible to her. I was completely bereft; I felt I'd lost her.

"And I had. The war started that same winter, and my father was killed in it, and we never went back to Pelican Island. But I just realized Flavia may have been the person who taught me what might be expected from love."

"My late wife would have been absolutely fascinated by that story," said Horace Mayberry.

"Why is that?" asked Evangeline, who had been obliged to accept his handkerchief to dry her eyes.

"Because it's about, oh, the mysterious things. The ones that truly turn us into human beings."

"You must miss your wife terribly."

"Our marriage was like one long conversation."

DECEMBER 9

Jane has a girl. Horrible labor—twenty-four hours almost.

I hereby give notice. How long, little book, is this to go on? Really, I am dying.

Peter Ellis, a Workshop student, came in, read aloud from his work, said I fascinated him, said, "*You* are the dragon." Vulcan calls after me in the hall. He waits till I come back. All friendly. "Gail, you know what happened to me the other night? ——— left me at the party." He comes again to sit and talk. Round and round we go.

What is killing me is the trudge, trudge, trudge, with no reward. One day follows the next, my hair gets dirty every Wednesday, I can hardly stand myself, I can't see any way to get out of this damn trap. Except, in times when you can't do anything about the external: Refine your patience, your work, sentence by sentence.

*O*n December 10, 1968, Gail's agent, John Hawkins, took the editor David Segal of Harper & Row to lunch at the Brussels in New York City. Having admired the first forty-eight pages of "The Beautiful French Family" along with Gail's outline for the rest of the novel, Segal made an offer of $1,250 for an option on the book. Hawkins told him how much happier his client would be with an actual contract for $2,500, part payment on signing and the rest on delivery. Over dessert Segal agreed. Delivery date was set for May 1969. Though Segal was willing to work with Gail during the intervening months, he also offered her the freedom to complete the manuscript without consulting him—the choice she ended up taking.

DECEMBER 11

EPIGRAM: AND STILL PEOPLE GET TOOTHACHE...

I find it almost impossible to put this down (Why? Am I really, then, conditioned for failure, so that when success comes I hardly know how to handle it?):

I SOLD MY BOOK.

Hawkins called me at home at just slightly before 6:00 p.m. yesterday. I can't write any more now.

Later. I found: (1) I could not believe what he was saying; (2) could not concentrate on hearing the things I wanted to hear most.

Afterward, I made $100 worth of calls: Mother, John Bowers,[26] Lorraine—and Ian.

Then Vulcan called to say there was a note on my door to call New York collect. I told him come round. He came about 11:30, was terribly charming, appreciative—kept saying, "I knew it was too good to be true. Just before I get the relationship started, she goes into another sphere."

"Not so," I said. "Still here, but going my own way more."

"That's what I mean," he said.

He's taking his kids to Chicago, Friday or Saturday. Said he felt guilty and sometimes thought of going back to his wife. Said he liked his children in the abstract, but not all that noise. Then he said suddenly, as if to say more, "Oh, so many people are in love with me."

I said, "Who else is in love with you?" And he kissed me. He kept looking at me and kissing me. I would say, "What are you looking at?" He would say, "Just smiling at you." He rubbed my back. He kept saying, "I know now we're going to end up in that double bed, though

26. John Bowers was an aspiring writer whom Gail had met in London. He went on to publish novels, as well as a memoir titled *The Colony*, about life in an all-male writers' colony established by James Jones's mentor, Lowney Turner Handy, with proceeds from *From Here to Eternity*. Bowers married and kept a weekend cabin in Phoenicia, New York; he and his wife were good friends of Gail Godwin and Robert Starer in Woodstock.

maybe not tonight." And when he stood up to go, he put his hands on me, and kissed me for a long time, and said, "You're nice. I like you." And all this, dear reader, was like being hot and twenty-one again, but with new wisdom and appreciation. Several times, he started abasing himself, saying he had to "make something of his life." There was some Virginia–Leonard Woolf conversation, too, though I can't remember it, and him saying, "You've got to have money, of course you know that." I told him how I thought he had everything—a business of his own, pride, respect from everyone—and he would just look at me and kiss me. The effect of all of this plus codeine from the dentist is to make me float like a feather.[27]

HARPER & ROW

Phone ringing. People coming up to me in the hall. "Congratulations." And yes, I love it, though in a subdued sort of way.

Yes. I know what they mean about love. Yes, it does ache. It limits one's freedom. (All this in "Morningside," which I hope to finish before Christmas.)

I am teaching and looking out my window, and I see Vulcan coming across from the Union—and wonder how I ever could have preferred big men. He's so small, erect, dapper, and, as Pitty Pat[28] remarked, "so *pure* in his printer's apron."

We go out Tuesday in his new rebuilt Jaguar. All this pulls at the soul. The feel of his hair, I know it. The white stitching on his blue shirt. He's so intensely drawn for me. I suppose he now eclipses all other styles for me. All I can do now is show the affection I feel, keep my own boundaries, and let the seasons take their course.

HARPER & ROW

27. Gail awakened on the morning of her triumph with a throbbing jaw. She rushed to the dentist, who, she says, "looked and looked and x-rayed and found—nothing. He gave me a few codeine tablets and off I went to get used to this new thing I must have despaired of ever happening."

28. "Pitty Pat," whom Gail had recently met, was Patricia Hampl, poet and memoirist, who would become a longtime friend.

Part eight

THE
WRITER'S CONTRACT

Iowa City

DECEMBER 13, 1968, TO MARCH 11, 1969

DECEMBER 13, 1968

I am glad for this calmness. Jordan said, "Kim told me you'd sold a book. He said something about celebrating."

Bitter cold. Face still sore from phantom toothache. Real deep winter. Coover wrote in my file that I had a brilliant mind.

Vulcan is taking his children to Chicago this weekend. I thought he'd gone today, but I saw his car. I'm going to read tonight, rewrite the rest of the vicar story. Relax.

Byron heard. Came in and invited me for a beer. A nice thing is my stability when nobody comes or calls. I have me and my book and confidence in myself. Relax and listen to people. Relax. Relax. Relax.

DECEMBER 15

I don't think I'll ever again be unconscious of adversity and fate, even in the midst of something good. Four more days—at last, I'll go home in triumph, like Faulkner wanting the man at the grocery store to hear about his Nobel.

DECEMBER 16

I was profoundly disgusted by everything today. Coffee machine out of cups, coffee pours out on the floor. Hong Kong flu on the periphery. Bernie, my ride to the airport, has deserted me. The airlines charge $5 tax, I'm totally broke, and will have to overdraw. I hope I get away with it.

Bernie's friend Jeremy is taking me to the airport—smooth, cool, decadent Jeremy. And Vulcan, poor he, with haggard Monday face—no joy—he meets me in the hall, up all weekend babysitting with his kids. I think he's preparing to renege on tomorrow night.

DECEMBER 17 • *2:00 p.m.*

Let's see: Where to begin? Tonight is the night Vulcan's supposed to take me out to celebrate. Why do I think he won't? Because his car was broken down, and is being fixed. Because he had sat all weekend beside his sick child.

So I came home, I suppose, so that I would not have to confront him, so he would not have to face me. He can call and say, "Look . . . ," and I can do whatever I please with my face, and be charitable with my words. It is conceivable that he will not call. His way of keeping the world at bay may be to flee and then apologize when it's too late. He can do things on impulse, but if he has a space in which to think it over, he retreats back into the known. The things that won't give him pain: his work, his routine.

He asked me to dinner on an impulse. Then postponed it the next day. I'm glad I came home so that he can call here if he remembers. If he does not call, then I won't be quite as charitable. At least, through all this, I will know more about him.

I wrote. I turned the light off and imagined how I would feel if I were in his position. Trying to imagine this took all my energy, and I fell asleep.

At three he called, and I expected the worst, but he still wanted to come, even without his car. So, he's bringing food here, which is much more relaxed.

It's been so long since I scrubbed the toilet for anyone. The place looks comfortable, nice.

I told him I dreamed I was looking in the window at him, and he was sitting at a desk, his head buried in his hands. "God, you understand me subconsciously," he said. I told him about Holger Danske.[1] Such ha-

---

1. Holger Danske is a major figure in Danish folklore, emerging in early historical sagas, and widely popularized by Hans Christian Andersen in his fairy tale "Holger Danske." To the Danes, Holger Danske is the great ancient warrior, aroused from his ages-long sleep at Kronborg Castle by military invasions. To Gail, who spent an impressionable time in Denmark (see *The Making of a Writer: Journals, 1961–1963*), Holger Danske represented the dark side of the Danish soul, holed up in a dark cavern, grim, depressed, and potentially savage.

ha-ing you never heard. I told him about Coover coming down to my office to congratulate me for selling my novel then saying it might not be good for me, and me bursting into tears.

Vulcan said, "If you'd done that to me, I'd have been out of there in a shot."

I said, "That's because you know more about women, you're experienced with women."

He said, "I'm not experienced with women. In fact, I think I'm impotent."

Ha, ha, dear reader.

I said, to cover my surprise, "Well, I'd be impotent, too, only I can get away with pretending."

He said, "Well, I'll go now and bury my head in my hands."

"And I'll hurry over and look in the window."

All in all, it's been a good week. Thank you, God.

DECEMBER 18

I've got to turn this into art (or notes for later art) before it turns me into life. Has anyone discovered where the true focus lies in romantic love? Today I thought: Might it not lie in one's own mirror reflection? (I went and looked into the bathroom mirror and watched myself cry.) Or in one's own temporary needs as dramatized through the imagination and then projected upon a suitable person? I'll make a story of these last twenty-four hours. First, I must write it personally so that in the finished form it can be left out. It's my salvation: to strain it free from the impurities and pain of individual experience and give it over to myth.

I wonder if there are two people in me: the woman and the writer. The woman comes back to her apartment after the night of the affair, counts his cigarette butts in the ashtray and prolongs emptying it, goes into the bedroom, puts her face into the pillow he slept on, locates the faint oil-smell of his hair, weeps then at: his absence? The passing of time? The vulnerability of humanity? The mystery and poignancy of being in this world?

She weeps and knows she is nothing when judged on this basis, and yet she is most strangely alive. She goes over his words, which she has saved from the edge of her drunkenness last night to sort and sift and interpret today.

I'm glad you're a good writer.

Why can't you be natural with me?

I'll tell you. There are many reasons. First of all: animal attraction. Second: You can't tell me you let me come here like this and lie in this bed and have not given one thought to a future. And there are three thousand and eighty-eight reasons why it wouldn't work, and you've thought about these, too.

I'd turn you into a painter again.

Don't you see? While it's this way, it's all right. But if it turned into something else, I'd start eroding you. Why? Because I can't be good to anyone while hating myself. I'd start chipping away at you. I don't like myself and therefore I don't like anyone getting superior. I'd keep undermining you. You're a masochist and I'm cruel, and that's why it's bad.

You're better than me.

Do you mind if I stay here and sleep?

AND YET: BE SENSIBLE. Be a writer for a minute, the cataloger of loves. Remember how you loved the mortality in the spent face of Sandy, cherished the green circles under his eyes. Remember the agony of nostalgia when contemplating Claude's slim, small, taut body. Where are those feelings now?

The coffee cup—not yet emptied—stands by the ashtray.

All night, the light shining in the window, the dog barking. The garbage men came.

"What? What?" He jerks awake.

"Nothing. Just the garbage men."

I can reach out in my own bed and touch him. How can I sleep and waste my consciousness of the time when he is next to me? When the light begins to come in stronger, I sneak looks at his face. Arm flung up and across his head. Hair, dark brown, thin, mashed down on his forehead. Beard is shaggy, straight, and has gray in it. He is a youth in his innocent sleep, an old man laid out on his bier. He is here, now, beside me.

Now? As I write? No, but perhaps more now than then. All those human things we grow weary of in those we love, I loved in him. The choking snores, the age creeping up on his face, the slackening of muscle tone. A mole on his back. The morning breath. Even our failed attempt.

And, you know, he's probably right. He's offering you his defenses, warning what's behind them. Will you persist?

Yes. But with importunate advances, wordiness. How he hates my wordiness at the wrong time. Hold tight to yourself. Love and dignity. Quiet affection.

LATER, WORKED LIKE HELL from 6:30 to midnight. Started rewriting "Drive Back"—no, it's not sorted enough—went on to "Uncle," rewrote that; and rewrote "Liza," which is, was, and always will be an incest story. I did this so that I could leave these stories with him: "Sorrowful," "Uncle," "Liza," "Illumined," "Blue," "His House," and "St. George."

I think this is the best thing I can do. He asked. So I give him my seven best pieces. In doing so, I give him the themes that mean most to me. I'm in effect offering him a sort of spiritual dowry, which he can either accept or reject. If he can't stand the themes of my work, better to know it now because I can't thrive on adverse criticism. If he likes them, all the better. He admires quality; he's strict with himself.

He told me how he came to Iowa and suddenly stopped writing. He took some academic courses and dried up. At dinner, he kept getting up, coming around to my chair, kissing me. I can't complain of his lack of affection.

He told me how, when he came here twelve years ago, he realized he didn't fit in anywhere. "I didn't have a business," like the husband-and-wife owners of Things & Things. So he decided to "create [his] own circle." He and his wife entertained a lot. "We gave two lavish parties a year." His work is his identity.

I remember the October morning when I saw his picture in the DI^2 and wanted to keep it, but threw it away as a good-luck omen toward getting the man instead.

2. *The Daily Iowan,* the student newspaper of the University of Iowa.

Jane Casey brought us together at a dinner party. He took it from that point. He is pursuing slowly, cursing himself every step of the way. But it is progressing.

His work. It's what he has, and he knows it. When I asked what color a certain book was, he thought I meant the paper and said, "Buff," proudly. Also, he prides himself on being a bit of the mystery man: "They try to figure out what I do with my spare time." He hangs out with Bender, Kelly, Irwin, Harper.[3] Goes to committee meetings. Plays bridge. Has lunch with the faculty. I suppose he's bound to feel something about all those PhDs.

This much I've finally realized: My worth resides in me and not in the man I "catch." I'll leave him the stories with an affectionate note. Major themes: Men have let me down, and I construct my meaning in the emptiness they've left behind. Imagination—art, religion—triumphs over reality.

If he is to be a good critic for me, he must have areas in which he is my superior. I must go on being superior in my own areas so that he can be proud.

JANUARY 2, 1969 · [After returning from a visit home to Asheville for Christmas]

I'm back. With more energy, it seems, more taste for the household chores I couldn't do before. Good to be alone. Mother: "How awful, that you can be that far away in so short a time." Tomorrow, get my house in order, start to write.

Wind rattles the windowpanes. The smell of My Sin. Flowers on pillowcases.

Keep busy—I am trying not to give in again to yearning, howling for a man I hardly know. Think of Claude, of that evening in an Albany bar when he leaned across the table and said: "You know, I really love you. I see you." And he meant it. And I didn't think I could contain my joy. And it passed. I stopped loving him as soon as I went out of his mi-

3. Members of the University of Iowa English Department: Paul Bender; William Robert Irwin (eighteenth-century English literature); Robert E. Kelley (Samuel Johnson scholar); John Brammer Harper (an administrator).

lieu and he tried to fly his plane to Iowa to see me and got stopped in Chicago by bad weather and had to arrive on a commercial flight, his pride grounded.

If there is any resolution, it is to dampen down the ego. Stop fantasizing gratifications. Stop talking about yourself, exaggerating, and feeling "hurt." Shyness is a form of selfishness.

JANUARY 3

What have I done today? Bought food. Traipsed around in minus-ten-degree weather, gotten frostbite on my face. Oh, God. Let me stop and get a drink. I see why anchoresses had to have handbooks written for them.[4]

I spent three to seven in the EPB answering correspondence. Then I wrote two more pages of the "final" novel. I don't like this chapter yet, but will not stop until I capture what I want. I'm not going after anybody this damn semester. All I want to be is self-contained.

Queer letter from Solotaroff[5]—very warm, but then said, after much hemming and hawing, he'd decided it was not the story of mine he wanted to buy.[6] He said that I would be in *NAR* "before either of us is much older."

John Bowers called. He's coming to see me on the way back from San Francisco. He met the Harper's editor who bought my novel, David Segal.[7] He said he was "brilliant, world-weary, Jewish. Taciturn. Tired of words. Tired of politics." John said: Do your thing. It's going to happen big for you. I can just tell by knowing you. You have a sixth sense about things.

---

4. In the Middle Ages, particularly in England, religious women sealed themselves away from society and protected their inner lives from external temptations and threats. The *Ancrene Riwle*, or *Ancrene Wisse*, written in early Middle English, was created as a guide for a small group of anchoresses.

5. Theodore ("Ted") Solotaroff founded the *New American Review* in 1967 as a way to offer general audiences current, high-quality fiction and cultural journalism. Ian McEwan has called him "the most influential editor of his time," one who shaped "not only the tastes, but the direction of American writing."

6. Probably "Some Side Effects of Time Travel"; see October 4, 1968, entry.

7. John Gardner called David Segal "one of the best editors America has ever seen, far better than Maxwell Perkins, for example." Segal had gotten his start with Ted Solotaroff when Solotaroff was at *Commentary*.

I am bogged down with Dane in the riding ring scene. It doesn't have what I want it to have—that hurt that nonphysical people can feel at seeing something physical done beautifully.

Excerpt from The Perfectionists
(Harper & Row, 1970), Chapter 6

—

Count Bartolome came and sat beside her. "A splendid sight, two beautiful animals in agreement," he said.

"Yes, that's true," she replied.

"Do you ride, senora?"

"No. My father gave me lessons, but I never could learn. The horse and I never seemed to get together."

"Ah, that is a shame. I am sure I could teach you. I would first get you to feel the extensions of the horse: the way he moves, the way he *is*. All the technique, that is second. Anybody can teach the curve of a leg, the holding of the reins, that's nothing. One must first get in harmony."

JANUARY 4

For the past half hour, I have been extremely happy. First, I contemplated writing a letter to Solotaroff, and decided to do it. Second, there's Bach choral music on the radio. And I know that this religious, mystical, spiritual thing is very much a part of my "calling." I feel near to that. I'm happy to pursue, almost single-mindedly, what gives me most satisfaction. My small, local passion brings me nothing but defeat. And there is so much to do.

Later

I wonder if I will go through life with a headache. Wrote seven pages, thus finishing the dread riding-ring chapter.

JANUARY 5

Well, I wasted another night in hopeless melancholy over my local passion. Ah, if I must persist, I will.

I came across an Ian remark I had written down. He said that you could judge from the emotional relationships a person found most vital what sort of state he was in.

I am not going to let this passion affect my life. If it becomes difficult, I shall move my typewriter here and buy a floor lamp, and work at the desk. I can learn from this passion.

I have gotten fairly adept at waiting out my loneliness. I was thinking how outraged I'd be if I went to the EPB and heard he had died. So much left unsaid.

Lady, what do you want to say to him? Is it to him or to all the men who have failed you? Most remarks, I admit, are: How much I can do without him. How little he means to me. How very much I would love him if he gave me half a chance.

Who is the first man in my life I would wish to have made those statements to? Three guesses. Even I know.

Speaking of him, his brother[8] just called. Said he's sending me a twelve-pound something that I'd like. A ham, a hair dryer, a typewriter? God knows.

I'm writing the novel. I think I am going to like this chapter. I added a new scene: Dane goes into a church and is frightened by a priest.

JANUARY 6

Came home at five in a taxi, sat down, and read J. C. Oates's new novel straight through.[9] I am envious. Her scenes of anguish, violence: just right.

8. Gail's generous uncle, William Godwin. Recalls Gail: "It turned out to be a small television set."

9. Joyce Carol Oates's 1968 novel *Expensive People* was the second in a quartet of novels—sometimes called "The Wonderland Quartet"—about changing American values in her parents' generation and her own. It tells the story of a boy who, in the 1960s, violently reacts against his parents' affluence and suburban existence.

My local passion, it appears, has been felled by the Hong Kong [flu]. I'm scared of getting it, hallucinating by myself. Jane today said: "What's wrong with you? Why aren't you talking about yourself?" I get more satisfaction out of this new way. I would like to reach the point of not depending on anyone. Let's face it: If I get the H.K. flu, who can I depend on? If I find out tomorrow that old Vulcan went back to his wife because she came over and took care of him during his illness, I'll be disappointed.

This snow makes it difficult to get around.

I want to do the Polly chapter next weekend. I see how few people I want to have around, time-wasters, and I haven't the time, I've wasted too much already. I'm like a house in snow.

My favorite student dropped by today, her play of mind so much wider than the others'. She's in love with her father. She's living in a Gothic-Victorian trap. The tale about her doctor father sewing up her grandmother on the stairs, while she, a girl, held the split forehead to-gether.

I NEED TO dramatize my writing, one scene after another.

CHAPTER VII: The church with the spying priest
Dane applauding Polly when she beats one
    of her twins
The talk
Dane going back as to a new husband,
    the one she'd told Polly about

JANUARY 9

Letter from John Hawkins: "It is a joy to receive a manuscript from you."

My crazy-intelligent student stopped me in the bathroom. "Guess what?" she said. "I found my grandmother dead." We started laughing. Another girl in the bathroom was shocked.

People started nicking away at me last night and today. The slow eroding away. Jung's words come back: Every man must have a secret, something he cannot tell anybody. If you give it all out, soon everything is gone. When people go away, you feel yourself going with them, off in all directions, and feel alone without yourself to go back to.

JANUARY 12

Yesterday the contracts came in. The stark icy night is not so cold.

I'm having a slump with the rewrite. So, fittingly enough, at the Caseys' farewell party, I achieved a shallow ambition: to go to a party and be admired by peers. Coover and I go over the contract. Vulcan and I doing our foxy flirting. He'd drift by throughout the evening, and we'd jab at each other.

Next semester, I just want to write. *Beowulf* and write.

JANUARY 15 · *1:20 p.m.*

Where do I begin when probably more has happened than I'll ever re-member or comprehend? I suppose I'll begin at the end.

I got up on this iciest of days—radio announcers begging people not to go out—and I kept resetting the alarm clock. I finally got up to pre-pare my classes. Gael Hammer called to say he and Kaye were iced in.

I started out, saw ice on the doorstep, on the streets, coating the snow. I saw people losing control—sliding, precariously twisting their poor upright Homo sapiens backs.

I came back in. I canceled my classes. I totally cleared Jeremy from my house,[10] mopped floors, shook rugs out a window, threw away

---

10. Jeremy Shaw, a graduate student in the Writers' Workshop, was from English landed gentry dating back to 1465. Gail was immediately attracted to his grace and kindness, fasci-nated to go with him to the university library and find his name and family lineage in *Burke's Landed Gentry*, but increasingly troubled by his recklessness and self-destructive be-havior. However, after a tumultuous attempt at a love relationship, they ended up peacefully sharing a house in Iowa City from 1969 to 1971 with a growing family of Siamese cats. "If it weren't for that fortress of a house," Gail recalls, "I might not have done so well on my doc-torate. Jeremy provided me with a sort of monastery and I hope I did the same for him. He also did excellent graduate work. We dated other people, but never brought them to the house."

whiskey bottles. Bernie called and said that, after he left me, Jeremy rammed his car into another car and stumbled around, falling on the ice. He couldn't remember where the car wreck was.

Then John Hawkins called. How pleasant it is to hear his rich, deep voice, his taking-care-of-Gail's-property voice. We talked about the not-making-more-than-$15,000 clause. "I have to protect you against success," he said, laughing.

Jeremy came back and apologized. His hands shook, his eyes watered, his reddish hair curled and dripped water. He dirtied up my clean ashtray. His socks (I made him take his shoes off) were so wet he left his prints on the rug.

Coover is right. Gestures came before the word, and can sometimes be more interesting.

I told Jeremy I was going into hibernation for a while. I may stay home tomorrow. I'll get my classes completely prepared and read *Piers Plowman*[11] and *Gothic Image*.[12] Somehow, I'm not so interested in contemplating myself as I am in noting people's gestures.

Lorraine called back to say, re Jeremy: "Forgiveness is beside the point. What is important is having pity for ourselves as well as others."

I must write Ian for the journals. Send him the money.

5:00 p.m.

More about the gesture—Jeremy: a study in gesture.

People's ideas about why other people do things must be subjective. Say, Jeremy's performance last evening. I interpret it my way, Bernie his, the Cooleys theirs, Kent his, and Jeremy his. But which is the most "literary" aspect of all this: my discussion of the events with Bernie, the words changing with each rendition? Or the Jeremy performance itself—Smirnoff in hand, cigarette in other; weaving around in thin, wet shoes; falling in the frozen snow once and again; forgetting where

11. *Piers Plowman*, by William Langland, is a fourteenth-century allegorical poem about a man seeking the true Christian life in a dreamworld.

12. *The Gothic Image* (1958), by Emile Mâle, looks at the mind of the French world in the thirteenth century through the iconography of its churches.

he'd had his accident; ramming his car into another; insulting his friends, having gotten them up in the first place to go chasing him in the sleety snow? Vomiting in the snow, making little puddles of warmth in the treachery of the ice. If only he can vomit enough times, he can warm the world!

Andrew, or The Importance of Gesture

—

"We are a bunch of writers." Open with a few vicious anecdotes. Then work up to the question. And describe the gesture and end with a question mark.

THE RADIO JUST announced that garbage collection will be postponed because of the ice.

"Any community where writers congregate is bound to have its special hang-ups. Also, I think, writers will do anything to get new material."

"Recently, there was a tragedy among us, which taught me something really important about the craft."

THE CURRENT RIFT among us over sensibility vs. gesture.

For though myself be a ful vicious man,
A moral tale yet I you telle can.
—CHAUCER, *THE CANTERBURY TALES,* The Pardoner's Prologue

Andrew St. Victor, our colleague and companion, has died in his final contact with the ice.

Andrew, like J., is hooked to the yoke of his formidable history. I want to select a suitable name that can stand by itself. The pragmatic mystic Hugh St. Victor wrote, "Learn all you can. You will find later that nothing is wasted."

Another character, Regie, suffers more integrally than any of us. He is the only Jew in the group, but transcends it utterly in his writing.

GREAT THUNKS in the night outside—pieces of ice breaking loose from corners of eaves and crashing to the ground.

DEMANDING READERS expect you to spread a foundation of facts upon which you then construct the wildest fantasies.

It is all ice here today. Andrew is dead. He died instantly, face down, on the ice.

"He looked," Regie told me this morning, "like Hamlet must have looked when he was drunk. God, Clare, you should have seen him, just before he crashed, weaving [along] the sidewalk, bottle of Smirnoff's brandished like a family standard, shirt collar open, jacket unbuttoned."

"He weaves even when he's sober," I said. "It's because he walks with his legs so close together. He bought that jacket at Harrods when he was fifteen. Do you realize he had it half his life? I tried to patch the elbows. It was a really nice houndstooth, but he abused it."

"A metaphor for himself," put in Random, who had come over to my apartment to help me clean up the violence and begin making the whole thing into art. Hating ourselves as we went along.

"I heard that," said Regie, disgusted. "Can't Random stop that? Christ, can't he ever stop? Today. Of all days. I'm getting out. This place is sick."

"I know. You're right," I said. "God, I can just see him navigating that treacherous ice."

"We couldn't get to him in time. We weren't drunk enough to be as cavalier. He was rather magnificent. You should have seen him."

I want to take some classics and personify them, such as *The Wanderer*—make the old warrior the hero of my story; or *Beowulf*—what really happened down below.

"Andrew, or The Importance of Gesture in Fiction"—it's also an answer to Coover, and an answer to why pure gesture is boring. You have to know who's playing first.

JANUARY 16

Well, that's the end of that story. Andrew doesn't die, after all. Clare needed what he has. Also, it hurt me to hurt him.

I get free tuition next year as well as the scholarship.

This weekend, I'll give my all to "The Motes." I don't want to write about me at the moment. Vulcan of the black shirt came in and solved my dragon story, "St. George," for me. I still can't talk to him completely straight, but I can see him much more as he is. The fact that I don't follow "he is" with a colon and a typecasting is a hopeful sign. He'll knock and enter now, and can give good advice, perhaps because he is removed from me emotionally, and can judge the writing.

"I can't give advice on that. I can only give advice on matters of taste, like telling a woman how to cook my meals," he says, fetching the ashtray, in which his cigarette butt joins four of Jeremy's.

I wonder when his spell fell, or did it slowly work itself out of my system like a drug? First his warning, then our failure in bed when our defense armors clanked like mad, then my going away at Christmas, then his not being well, and his simply not asking me out. Necking at a party is not the same. Then Jeremy who really did touch me, my guts went out to his kindness, he took time with me, and we didn't need to make war. The turning point came, I think, when on Tuesday, having lunched with Jeremy and seen Vulcan eating alone, I was able to approach him familiarly in the hall, pat him on the back, and talk to him without wanting anything from him. Vulcan said he was reading my stories slowly, and he was having his assistant read them. "She made me promise not to give them back until she'd finished." He said, for the first time, "Oh, you *do* have a sense of humor." I actually think what we have will last: a steady, uninvolved kind of low-key relationship spiced with a bittersweet flirtation.

JANUARY 18

The light in libraries.

I finish "The Legacy of the Motes" tomorrow. I am getting back my touch, my style. The unconscious world is mingling with the rational. I must go terribly gently on the transition. He decides to take the summer off. He can't stand reading. Say how he feels psychologically at this time, as if the balance had accrued on the other side and shifted the weights entirely.[13]

JANUARY 20

Vulcan comes to my office today: "I saw you get out of that car. What are you doing? How have you been?" I give him "Motes." He brings it back at 1:30 and tells me, "I'm learning a lot about you from your stories." "That's all right," I say. "You're valuable to me. I can stand giving myself away for that."

JANUARY 23

Jeremy's long legs in Wellingtons, standing in a snowdrift beside the car. It's hard for me to comprehend someone born at the top who spends the next thirty years climbing down.

FEBRUARY 3

Jeremy and I are two of a kind: wanderers, dreamers, snobs, neurotics, the kind who at one time or another, for different reasons, has been

---

13. The draft of the "Motes" story on which Gail is working devotes a couple of pages to the time her protagonist spends between giving up reading and having the muscae volitantes in his eyes clear up. "Eliott became a park-hunter," she relates about this interval. In the final version, published in *Dream Children*, Gail provides only a brief glimpse of his transition, and jumps ahead to a coda that reflects on what had happened to him.

threatened by extinction. He wrote an outline for his novel. It was stunning, and I believe he may be better than I know.

FEBRUARY 4

On M-W-F, I teach a Core class at 12:30 and have Professor Spivak's at 1:30. Jeremy has his at 1:30, so maybe 2:30 lunch? I write till 9:00 at the office and go home. On Thursday, I have nothing, except Workshop at 4:30. On these days, write from 9:30 a.m. to 4:30. Use the evening to prepare for classes or write.

I'm finishing up "Motes." Difficulties. Here is a young man who has known nothing but scholarship his whole life. There is a security in this. Scholarship is conquerable. Then, just as he's rounding out a future for himself, he gets these things in his eyes. The point is: They are not dangerous. But they are limitations on his vision that show/lead him to correct the limitations on his vision, figuratively. They act as correctives to his vision as well as hindrances to his scholarly habits. But it is a violent changeover. He has to learn a whole new way of seeing. He sees a better world through the motes than he did before or will after them.

For the next month, my novel is my only responsibility. Jeremy will be thinking of his novel. I'm learning so much about why I failed in the previous drafts—my perfection thing turned against me. So, this is the novel I can write. It could be a great book.

Rewrite the first five to six pages of the novel: more electrifying—hook the reader—more Gothic. Don't name the places.

The opening of Gail's novel, ultimately published as The Perfectionists, *kept going through changes. The earlier drafts begin in the taxi from the airport, and they dwell a good bit on Penelope, John's patient, who's come to help with nanny duties. The final draft starts in the airport and moves quickly to a mini-crisis: Dane momentarily losing sight of Robin, John's little son, in the crowd. Here's a comparison of opening paragraphs.*

From the May 1967 Draft, Titled
"The Beautiful French Family"

—

"All this light. One could easily drown in it, after London," Dane said, frowning. She rebalanced the stiff little boy on her lap. "It makes you feel exposed."

"Oh, I want to bathe in it," said Penelope dramatically. "Absolutely bathe in it."

The Spanish sun baked the little island, poured boldly through the rear windows of the taxi and impartially touched the four of them. The pale, preoccupied doctor moved his lips silently and constructed something in the air with his long, tapered fingers.

From the Second Draft, the One Rejected by
Gail's First Agent, Lynn Nesbit

—

"All this light. One could easily drown in it, after London," Dane said. She stuck her head partly out of the window of the moving taxi and let the dry golden warmth touch her face for a moment. "It makes you feel—"

She stopped, wanting the exact word. She shifted her weight a bit, so the stiff little boy sitting aloofly on her lap might be more comfortable. But he drew up sharply, looking inconvenienced. She turned to John beside her, to see if he'd noticed his son's latest snub. He hadn't. He sat staring straight ahead, moving his lips soundlessly and constructing something in the air with his long, tapered fingers.

From The Perfectionists
(Harper & Row, 1970)

—

The island made her feel exposed. Its colors were raw and primeval: scalding azure sky, burnt sienna earth, leaves of dusty green. The scrutiny of its noon light rooted out the skulking shadow, the secret flaw, and measured these ruthlessly against the ideal. It pained them at first, the people coming from London, which was still sealed in the gloom of winter. They edged sidewise from the cool, dimly lit charter plane into the spotlight glare. They blinked, became conscious of their pallor.

FEBRUARY 13

The novel becomes more and more Dane's. I may retitle it "The Perfectionist." I'm trying to catch those exact psychic vibrations. Those sickening quarrels. She is, as Jeremy says, magnificently destructive. She must refuse every attempt John makes at psychological closeness. Why? I understand the dangerous idealism—the acute criticisms because she wants him to be without fault, so that she'll have him to hide behind.

Talked to Vulcan for over an hour. The freedom is immense. Now, where? When did it change? Perversely, when Jeremy became a possibility. We talked about our crass respect for money, the way we nitpicked at those we were close to, my masochistic fantasies, his sadistic ones. The thing Vulcan has left for me is his wonderful dignity. I do think he knows his dimensions and has accepted them.

I keep seeing Jeremy differently—now bits of the real him, now bits of my fantasy.

How can Coover be bored with interpersonal relationships?

FEBRUARY 16

Once again, the Lucifer bitch has been called in to save my skin. I'm trying to be fair to myself, as well. Uneasy night—anticipating drunken J.

redisturbing my sleep; a dream about my students finding me unpre-
pared and going on to educate themselves.

Vulcan teaches me how to behave socially at the country club. J. is
in Waterloo, staying with the policeman who'd named his son after
Jeremy. I talked with this man on the telephone. Infinitely strong,
cool—a Rock of the World, a survivor. Yet, I'll bet he's impressed with
J., wobbly as he is.

Do I prefer an aristocrat who poses as a down-and-outer, or a
middle-class unsteady like myself who has developed an impeccable social manner?

What happened?

I took Jeremy with me to a party to which I'd been invited, given by
the secretary to the chairman of the English Department. We sit down
by ourselves, not wanting to crush into the mob. Vulcan comes in, remarks audibly: "There's Gail Godwin, Girl Goddess." He meets Jeremy.
"I'm sorry, I didn't get that last name," Vulcan says. "Gail, I'm going to
get another drink," Jeremy says, "would you like one?" To Vulcan,
"Would you?" We begin to have more fun. Kent comes over. He and
Jeremy get along.

Sitting in a corner, I start playing with a puppet hanging up. I set
him down—he's a cowboy—and I aim the pistol in his hand at his head.
Vulcan, who is standing quite close, suddenly reaches down and hits the
puppet, disengaging its suicidal pose. A gesture—in the finest Coover
tradition.

We get to the car. Jeremy says, "Oh, hell. Let's go back." I say no,
we've already left. On the way home, I give a pep talk on the Henry
James lifestyle: keep your dignity, etc. He was drinking that awful Cal-
vados brandy. I tell him to throw it out. "I'm out of control. Can you
help me?" he says. This makes me irritable and I start trying to reason
things out. He says he doesn't like my attitude. Says he has to get away.
At this point I am

 — scared I'm losing my security: the capable Jeremy;
 — bewildered as to why he's "out of control."

I say: "You'd better not let me see too much more."

"Okay," he says, and stumbles out.

HOW FAR AM I ready to commit to this unknown substance?

I can use last night as a withdrawal point. If Jeremy can take care of himself, THEN is the time to consider can he take care of me.

week later, Gail and Jeremy set up a new schedule. Though she's still keeping her apartment at 501 North Dubuque, she sleeps at his house on Rundell Street and writes all day in his study while he sleeps. At this time, he was working four nights a week as a hospital orderly. In mid-March, Gail will give up her apartment and move into Jeremy's house.

FEBRUARY 23 · *Sunday*

The writing going well. I work at Jeremy's. There are no distractions, except for Jeremy's cat, Virginia, who occasionally jumps smack into everything. Novels mean nothing to HER. J. sleeps all day. So on Tues., Thurs., Sat., Sun., I get up around 10:30, stumble around, [have] coffee, etc., and sit down to MY NEW TYPEWRITER around 11:00, and then write till 3:00 or 4:00. I averaged seventeen pages [a day] this week. I'm going right ahead, *intelligently*, meanwhile polishing up some of the roughage in the transition chapters, where I went to pieces after I sold the book. I want to go back and do the scene where Dane stays alone in the room, contemplating.

Oh, I wish I understood relationships. I suppose I have one with Jeremy. But there are no illusions. Maybe there shouldn't be. He is kind. He comes off well socially. He is pretty good at getting along with me. I realize I'm a bitch. I think independent people who keep to themselves a lot don't need to get a lot of things from someone else: amusement, etc.

They have learned to amuse themselves. It is in the other realms—the things you *have* to share—that a partner comes in handy.

FEBRUARY 24

Ian used to say I was as expedient as a Nazi. At times like tonight I'm not sure. Am I too rough on Jeremy? Or am I "good" for him? So often now I hear echoes of those Ian-me impasses, only now I can understand slightly better. The Jeremy relationship combined with writing the final draft of this novel is really fortuitous. At times we "fight" the chapter I've just written.

MARCH 4

These next two months are too vital to mess up with my untalented love affair behavior. The thing is this: I'm behaving wildly, badly. Dramatizing old patterns. It looks as though I'm doomed to some of this throughout my life, but the essential thing is to understand why. Then if I want to go on and do it, go on and do it. J. only goes mad periodically—and that's so minor compared to mine. I think I'll finish out Lent with a bit of austerity. My side in the thing with J. is too, too shaky. Maybe there's no hope for me in relationships. I've learned over the years to balance by myself, but am not so good with someone else.

I screamed at Jeremy. Somehow I "acted" an anger I didn't really feel. J. rose to the occasion, held my arm while I was having a tantrum in the kitchen. He looked good, healthy and whole. Always, there comes this lack of restraint on my part, this testing of the other. This dramatizing . . . of what?

MARCH 4, 1969[14] • *3:00 p.m.*

Five pages of Dane in four hours—about a page an hour, with time out to eat a grapefruit, go for a bicycle ride, prowl around the house. This is

14. Gail wrote this long entry, also on March 4, on loose-leaf pages, which she tucked into the back of her journal. It is an inventory of her behavior over the past few months.

about my maximum. I have approximately a hundred more pages to go. At the present pace, it will take two months, not one, to finish, then another month to type and polish. It is choppy in the new parts. Virtually all I have written this month is not only new, but difficult. I still don't know what it is. If it has appeal, I guess it's the kind of appeal *Women in Love* has. In spite of its flaws, it adds dimensions to man-woman relationships in the Western world. I've been told by John Hawkins that it is the woman ("You have gotten right inside this woman's skin") who carries the book. If so, then my prime function is to tell her truthfully. ("A magnificent destroyer," in Jeremy's words—a frightening phenomenon, but she is what she is, and what happens must happen as a result of it. Her actions can't be judged morally.) Coover felt that my best direction—considering what he felt were the limitations of the novel in this form—lay in providing interesting incidents, one after the other, to keep the thing going. I am in pretty fair control now. I know these characters, what they are supposed to do for and to each other, how they act as foils.

What I wish I did understand better, although it doesn't worry me unduly when I've been producing, is my perversity in personal relationships. Maybe I'm making too much of an issue of it, but some quality of it escapes me, and maybe repetition—making an issue of it—is the only way to get at it.

A pattern such as this: September to December 1968. Dreadfully lonely, lots of writing done, an unbalanced desire for comforts of home, never really comfortable in human terms except when in the tub. Hurry away in the morning: work, work until ten or eleven at night. Walk home, drop. Preoccupation with Vulcan begins mid-October, planted by Janie, who says he'll do. And now a bit of sexual-interpersonal tension to alleviate the workday. AND an impetus to come early, stay later at the office. How I listen for his footsteps. How I grit my teeth. Curse. Ask the *I Ching:* Now? Is it now? I get used to being alone. Then angry one day—everyone but me going "home" to supper. Kent to Bev, Ace to Beth, Kim to the Condés—and hovering eternal and ever out of reach: the Caseys, the Caseys, Perle Mestas of the Midwest. At this point, I develop my "mead hall" image. And I take security in being the true *anhaga*[15] out there in the astringent night amid Van Gogh's swirling stars.

But decide to increase my creature comforts. First, sulfur bath salts. Then to Rock Island for $62 worth of liquor. Then a $16 pouf to rest my weary feet on. Sipping my morning Bloody Mary, I am gratified. And here comes Coover, saying, "You—you of all people!" And the gossip drifts back he has said I was one of the three or four best, a brilliant mind. And there was Vulcan, who said, "Put on your jacket and I'll take you to my place for a drink—if you promise not to attack me." And Janie to tell it all to. And Hawkins, who, as an agent, has loved me. And the Morrow editor who wanted me but had only $250 to spend. And then popularity. I am "at home" in 68 EPB and sooner or later everyone finds me. Dinners with Kent, who drops nuggets of insight. Fights with Kent, who calls me a ball-crusher. I begin to think I'll never be attracted to anyone physically. Except possibly Vulcan, who will only neck.

I begin to achieve an exquisite balance as the lone girl who doesn't belong to anyone and therefore is anyone's property. There are rumors. I'm a lesbian? Can't have relationships? (Look at her latest story, "St. George." Who the hell do you think Gwen is? She's busy raising dragons, maybe. Wait, she *is* a dragon!) But she qualified for a PhD and sold her novel (Harper & Row, you can't sneeze at that), so who cares what perversions she has.

And now: giddiness. Incredulity. It is WORKING. I've been accepted in N.Y. and Iowa City. Janie has her baby Maud, and I have a contract. And Vulcan says, of us, "Sure it would be nice, but you're better than I am and it wouldn't work in a thousand years." So I'm still balanced in the single-star state, but the new air is intoxicating. Hurry home and be praised. Collect those debts owed from people like the stepfather, who has said for years to company, "Oh, she writes but she hasn't *published* yet."

---

15. In her diary entry for July 30, 1968, Gail quotes from the Anglo-Saxon poem *The Wanderer*, in which a solitary warrior, the *anhaga*, "finds grace for himself." She says she feels close to him. Sorry-hearted, the *anhaga* in the poem wanders, mindful of hardships and the downfall of kinsmen. Occasionally, in exile, he finds one in the mead hall who knows his people.

Over Christmas in the Coles' winter-rented house on Country Club Road while the latest of their brand-new houses is being built, I decide: Romantic love does not exist, except by collusion between two deluded idealists. ("If I could once, just once, perceive a person for himself and not in terms of what I needed from him," said Lorraine at the Holiday Inn.) So, I think, I must mobilize. And at Christmas I talked myself out of Vulcan by writing loose pages and pages like this until I wrote him out of my system.

Back to Iowa, glad to be back, and the writing went soggy on me. Still interested in Vulcan—but now also Jeremy, who had driven me to and from the airport. I'm also irritated by the circumspect silence of Jeremy. Dissipated, you can tell. He is most likely hiding some unpalatable secret, just barely covering it up with the strange routine of his life.

So that is how it stands—the single star contemplating her satellites. But who should I bump into in the elevator, as I'm on my way to Kent's office? Old Jeremy himself, really looking a mess. So far from my standards of neatness it's not even upsetting. I consider him beyond repair and determine to explore the wreck. He is nervous, smokes, says he has no roots. He asks me mine. I think about it, and tell him, and I sound pretty good. After he goes, having (and it's about time!) asked me to "see him," I actually write: "I'm not neurotic anymore." Oh, I am so serene in my balance. The next thing to want is to get him to kiss me. What will it be like?

He doesn't. We float, poised, in our spaces. We pirouette, each for the benefit of the other. But each is wary, wants to prolong the tension. We make a further appointment to enjoy each other's company.

But prematurely he surprises me one evening in my nightshirt. He shows up at my apartment drunk, mad at his stepfather. I indulge him, thinking: Let him have this as his excuse to visit. I am not afraid of him. He has shown himself to me in his vulnerability. He unbuttons the nightshirt. I am pleasantly aroused. This one is good—in an intuitive way as well as being there in all his virility. But also I think: This strange shadow-eyed wreck might possibly marry me—and the danger is, we're both free to do it. I mention a farmhouse and he says he wants to send for his horse and live there with me.

He gives me his novel. I'm so afraid he won't be D. H. Lawrence or Lawrence Durrell that I have trouble reading it. Single spacing hurts my eyes. Some of the writing wanders. Other parts shimmer, but always behind a veil.

Next night: Dinner at a sorority house, invited by one of my students. All my old uptightness about sororities, yet I really like the conventions of such a place. I come home. There's J., waiting. He left a dinner engagement early because he was impatient to see me. Circles under his eyes are huge. Safety pin in his shirt. Maybe I can sew the wreck back together so that he'll appear a whole man. But, as in an evil fairy tale, the more I sew, the more there is to sew. He keeps saying, "Come over here, closer." I keep sewing. Holes keep appearing. Have another drink. Drink. Then *mirez le bitch*. I go into action, acting out the tenth year of marriage rather than the tenth hour of courtship. How can we hold up, this poor duo? How can we be a "we," me feeling like I do. I say melodramatically, "Ah, why couldn't it have lasted? The only reason you want to take care of others is because you can't face taking care of yourself." Oh, get rid of this wreck. Thirty years old and what has he got to show for it? Out, out. I talk on, mercilessly. He begins to cry. Goes. Comes back. Goes. I say, you can't drive, you'll have a wreck. But my heart is harder than Pharaoh's. I can't visualize him dead. Can't mourn for his passing. Just: Out of my life. Out. Next morning, I go around destroying traces of him. Shake the rugs out the window. Bathe. Yes. He comes back to apologize, gets another print on the rug, leaves his ash. Go out, do something complete.

Now he's out of my life. Better my phantom affair with Vulcan, my clean white walls, the bath. But it could have been nice. Bernie is sad, in that fulfilled way people always are—even the best of us—when their friends come to grief. He relates the gory details: the silent broken man, cat on his lap; remorse.

I try to write him ("Andrew, or The Importance of Gesture") as having died. I mourn for him through my own flawed art. How does he look when he's suffering? I want to see. Get him back. I call him. He hesitates. Last trick: I pretend to be crying, hang up the phone. Fifteen minutes later, he's there. What do I want from him? Who knows? But I don't want to give him up. We go to the Union for food. He looks ghastly, sleepless, like a mangled wraith. Failure. That destroyed countenance. If only we could have met as young and beautiful people. But where? He might have been at deb balls, but I wasn't a deb. Can we only come together like this—haggard, sag-faced, our best energies spent?

So, still on my own (more or less), I limp along as part of this flawed couple. The minute something goes wrong, I'll drop him. He has the advantage Ian had: He can show me to myself.

Schizophrenia sets in. Writing soggy. Can't get back to the novel. Lean on J. I'm tired of the English-Philosophy Building. I'm tired of solitude. J. can help me hobble through the novel. Maybe he'll make something of himself. If not, when we reach the outer banks, he will get his word of thanks. Thanks. Splash.

Passion. Sitting on his sofa, I watch him cross the room completely enclosed in his own space. Beautiful. His hair has been cut to a thick red thatch. He walks lightly, elegantly, on the balls of his stocking feet. And earlier in the day I have noticed his legs—long, lean, in the Wellingtons. I begin to see him aesthetically.

A furtive between-semesters fling. I am completely in his space. Wrench myself from EPB. Now Vulcan is alive with interest. I prefer J. now, except for occasional relapses. Vulcan is orderly, finished; even though his dimensions are smaller, he has filled them out. Neat proud Prussian. Family motto: "Break but don't bend." Jeremy bends like a willow branch, but in his flexibility is his—perhaps ultimate?—strength.

Schizophrenia. I'm J.'s girl. I'm everybody's darling. I'm me and I'm his. Which? Can't give up my flirtation with Vulcan. I've worked hard at it. Isn't fair, I've put so much work into it and it's just coming to fruition and I don't want it anymore. As a token gesture of freedom-assertion, I let him kiss me in my office. Last stronghold of being everybody's darling. Twice a week at least he comes in; before he leaves, kisses me. I don't enjoy it anymore.

My friends, one by one, give their Good Housekeeping seal of approval of J. *Through their eyes* I am able to see: Jeremy's gentleness, his appealing remoteness, his perceptiveness about human behavior. Certain things become hard to do without—certain gestures of his, things he's unconscious of. Once I said to Ian, "Why did you fall in love with me?" "That," he answered, "is something I've never told you." He never told me. I'm glad he didn't.

I think my realizable self has gone beyond my conventions and neuroses. If I were to continue what I set out to do (get my perceptions in order, understand myself so I can be one step ahead of Dane), then all is not lost. I am still alone in the sphere that counts most.

Since I linked up with Jeremy, he has: gone to dentist to see what can be done about the two teeth he knocked out in his bicycle crash and didn't bother to go back and pick up, had his hair cut, got a tuition rebate, applied for a fellowship, impressed Professor Spivak, and been "recognized" at the Court of the Freemans. I've recognized where the strength lies in my novel and in Dane, seen why any relationship for me is going to be hard work, seen why it hasn't worked before, written fifty-eight difficult pages.

It is these things people can do for each other. The rest we must do for ourselves. We can't write each other's books. He can't give me a center when I've misplaced mine. We can enrich each other, sustain when one needs it. But the relationship can't, with us, be based on sustaining.

(Now it is ten past nine in the evening. Five hours and twenty minutes to get myself together. It takes some people twenty-five years of psychoanalysis; still others die separated from themselves; some are born magnificently intact; but I must work with what I have.)

MARCH 5

Incredible: reading over the Polly villa scene I wrote July 1967, and rewriting it according to my present standard. Now, I hone in to what is relevant. Before, the whole thing ricocheted like a squash ball. I kept veering off the interesting stuff. Also, I think I was under the influence of the show-not-tell trend. Now I feel no scruples about charting Dane's thoughts as she thinks them. I want to tell the truth about this marriage, these people.

A sophomore came in today. She'd read three of D. H. Lawrence's stories, and she didn't really understand what was going on. "In 'In Love,' there's this girl who stops loving this boy because he says he loves her. Then he says it was all a joke, so she decides to marry him after all. So did she love him or didn't she? What was she doing?"

I am playing to the audience that is interested in working out these strange nuances in human relationships.

MARCH 6

I'm doing Roger Rattigan.[16] His dialogue will have to be redone. He's a combination of Robin,[17] Merker, and something else. Coover came by my office tonight, like a little boy, to tell me of his latest publishing and cinematic exploits. I was touched and flattered. Vulcan and I fantasized some more about a Virginia–Leonard Woolf future. I can be so *awfully* honest with him. He with me. Say outrageous things. I talked to swarms of people today—I only hope it hasn't affected my writing. Kent is so wise, intuitively. He's a master of nuances. He loves people so much more than I do. The Roger scene can be symbolically strong—the boutique of shabby clothes he runs, etc. He brings up the question: Would people rather have the genuine shabby article or the artifact? The real aristocrat or the phony, who does a so-much-better job?

MARCH 11

Page 153 of the final draft. It seems plodding: Dane gets up, Dane sits down, Dane thinks. From February 20 to March 10, I did sixty-five pages of the rewrite. I want this book to be good. But, God! Sometimes it's such a chore. If I could sell a story, I might believe in myself again.

16. This scene is neither in the early drafts nor in the published book. Gail had created an extra scene, involving a hail-fellow-well-met friend of Dane's, in order to represent Dane's life before her marriage to John. Though Gail had been pleased with the writing, she determined that the scene took away from the thrust of the novel, and she kept it out.

17. Robin Challis was Gail's friend at the U.S. Travel Service office in London in 1963.

COMPLETION

Iowa City

MARCH 12, 1969, TO JULY 6, 1969

MARCH 12, 1969

603 Rundell Street. (Trust J. to choose a house on a working-class street with no trace of university faculty or students!)

GOOD NEW BEGINNING. A novel to finish which is already sold. Moved in with the man. Whatever has to be taken care of under this roof will have two to work on it, not one. I hereby make a promise to stop being a middle-class worrywart. To organize this household so we can live elegantly on little (for instance, Gallo Paisano poured from a decanter).

MARCH 13

Housewarming all day. Plenty of space. Page 157 of the novel. Dane has cut herself off from further help. The reason it's better this time is that Dane is responsible, not little acts of fate. The rest of the book consists of her cutting people off.

The house feels right. All I have to do from now on is write—the best I know how. Easter: can get a lot done.

From here on out, John is more interested in the ideal. His problem-solving scheme involves drifting away from human contact.

MARCH 15

Five and a half pages. I have a funny attitude toward this writing. There is preoccupation but no *joy*, like I felt in writing "Blue" or any of the fresh pieces. Bernie Kaplan came by and brought his new story, "A Sea Called Tranquility," written under tension of three weeks' love and hate. It was so damned good. So many signs of the true artist there. The complexities of character, the refrain of the baseball game, the harshness of the dialogue, the writing on the bathroom walls juxtaposed against the cosmic and poetic.

And I'm doomed to Dane another month. Still, she's earned $1,250 so far, so I'd better not shortchange her. Virginia the cat lying on the bed beside me in this bright white "writing room." Mail came for me at 603. (Rhymes.) It's almost four. J. still asleep upstairs. He'll get his eight hours. Boldts' party tonight.

"This woman—you've gotten under the skin of this woman." Page 160-something. About seventy more pages to go. The "closedown" begins after Dane's blackout. Bring in some weird stuff after this. A lot has to be understood, explained—cutbacks into Dane's background, more incidents of her marriage. Perhaps another change. Let chapter end with Dane going to bed as soon as they return. No, damn it. Why do little details mess me up so?

MARCH 17

Already? Has there been no change since Ian? Has my neurosis won, after all, by urging me toward this situation? What am I to do now if I am living in a house with a man totally unsuited for modern life? Is he some extinct breed having a last foothold in 1969? Well, I'm going to do my novel. What else? I may be the stupidest idiot who ever lived.

MARCH 21

He becomes a little more a member of his species, a little less a member of his local group: [Abraham] Maslow on self-actualized people.

PAGE 178 of *The Perfectionists*. Ninety pages of pica—27 lines x 12 words per line = 324 [words] per page. Ninety pages of elite—29 lines x 14 words per line = 406 [words] per page. Number of words now = 65,700. I have about twenty-four more pages to go to reach my 75,000-word limit.

I want the book to have thirteen chapters. Polly—Karma—doppelganger—TRUTH that Dane can't sustain.

Chapter XIII. In the restaurant Dane cleans out her purse, reads John's notes overtly. John writing and talking. She can no longer hear him. Their animals will always snarl at each other. Drinks at the bar. Frenchwoman writing letters. Dane sees gulf. Let reader see John as Gothic hero one more time to preserve the tension to the end. Penelope is reading The Brothers Karamazov. *Final scene: They have drinks, go up to the room. Dane looks below and sees Penelope stop to talk to the Frenchwoman. What did the two of them talk about? What did they have to say to each other?*

Easter vacation—forty pages, ten days, four pages a day.

As I was writing the lines about Penelope speaking to the French-woman, and Dane unable to hear the words, I saw where my power lies and the sort of thing I am able to do well.

The passage that ends with Dane becoming aware of Penelope's conversation with the Frenchwoman became part of chapter 12 in the published book (not chapter 13, as planned). Gail was engaged in several thorough rewrites of her novel right up to the deadline. Most of the ideas she jotted in her notes on March 21 did not survive a final edit. The chapter does end with Dane going out on the balcony after having re-tired to her hotel room with John. That passage, which Gail thought rep-resented one of her talents, reveals the process by which a woman comprehends a scene and slowly loses hold of an ideal.

Excerpt from The Perfectionists *(Harper & Row, 1970)*

—

She wandered back out on the balcony and leaned over the wall. The Frenchman was sitting on his towel, weaving some bits of straw together for the amusement of the two children. The woman stood some distance away, absently playing with her dark hair as she chatted with a handsome blonde woman. This second woman, Dane recognized with a shock, was none other than Penelope. The two of them were talking! Penelope and Dane's Frenchwoman. How could they? The Frenchwoman did not speak English. Did Penelope speak the Frenchwoman's language? Incredible. But there they were, down there together: gab-gab-gab. What were they talking about? It diminished the Frenchwoman for Dane. And there was old Penelope, breast-stroking in the warm sea of her life, unconscious of the Frenchwoman who had illumined Dane's dream. To Penelope, it was just another chitchat with a pretty woman with a husband and children from France. That should have been me down there, thought Dane.

MARCH 23 · *Sunday, 2:20 p.m.*

This is a time when I am extremely unsure about my writing "voice." It reads to me absurdly simple and flat.

The cat is being driven frantic by a treeful of birds. Purple and white crocuses are out in the front yard. It's a wet, cloudy, English-type spring day. Jeremy asleep. I went upstairs and looked at him sleeping on his stomach, his arm jacked up like a grasshopper's leg. And the shape of the arm, slender, curved, white, made me want to wake him up and say, Talk to me, play with me, hold me.

We went to a dinner party at the Foxes'. Strange interlude with Vulcan, who said, "I'm glad you've got something going for you," and really meant it. He was once the dark possibility and now he's the benevolent friend. Projections, one and all. What am I to write next? Must follow what is at the very frontier of my interest—I think more feeling for places might help. Inner emotions expressed by exterior landscape. But this book is the thing now. It's my debut and it's got to be good.

MARCH 25

Went to *Persona*, Ingmar Bergman film. I found myself coveting parts of it for the Dane-Polly scenes.[1] Next few days will be *Sons and Lovers*, and entertaining Lorraine.

Those bare statements and archetypal situations that move us in Bergman's films also do so in *Wuthering Heights*, which I finished again. I don't know how deeply my book lends itself to this. It's an analytical book. But I must make it reverberate as much as possible. As a particular book, its shape has hardened by now. I will have to finish the book that I began. It's a book that has slowly explained to me what happened to my marriage and how not to write a book (off the top of your head). I have to struggle with these last scenes and I ought to expect it.

Cat snores.

MARCH 30

Lorraine and Chap in and out, Lorraine being a regular dynamo power-figure and with not much to feed on this time. The power plays were interesting to watch—like her "not liking" Siamese cats. We had one fight yesterday and another at the bus, as it was pulling out. Her last words: "You are going to have to change. I am going to make you. You can't just be yourself." I was so glad to see her go. The night she was to come, I got the worst headache of my life—ran a fever. Jeremy is such a noble person. It's so easy to live with him. His way of relating to people—slowly opening up like a flower, not impinging like a sledge hammer. Had a small dinner party—the Dixons, the Freemans. I smoked pot and got really ill. J. came and lay beside me. Every time I woke and called out, he answered.

1. Gail will put a reference to *Persona* into a scene just preceding Polly's visit to Dane. Dane is contemplating joining her stepson, Robin, in judgmental muteness, and she recalls a movie: "One time she had seen an Ingmar Bergman film about a woman who wouldn't talk. She drove everyone around her mad—including the nurse."

APRIL 1

When Dane cleans out her purse, she finds the ball Mrs. Hurst gave to Robin.[2] Keep Dane's dialogue sparse. She's not an "oh dear" and "oh, well" kind of talker. Also, besides the creation of Dane (who, according to Jeremy, is a symbol larger than me and is capable of running away with me), I am saying farewell to John in this book, and therefore want to realize him for the companion he could have been (sexless companion). I want to enjoy in the remaining scenes in the book John's capability for entertaining someone on the metaphysical level. Like the little games Ian and I played for four or five days during the worst fog in London, when he took on my "education." The children-playing-together level. Again, sexless. No mother (which every adult wife has to be at times). No father (which every adult husband has to be at times).

APRIL 2

I've been letting the days drift by in housekeeping pursuits, listening to music. Finished *Sons and Lovers,* and went back to Flannery O'Connor. Too many excellences. Where do I fit in?

I feel I must suffer toward the end of the book. Take a lesson from Lawrence's excellent dialogue—the Baxter Dawes scene—unpredictable but right.[3]

Perhaps I write less in the journal because there's Jeremy to talk to. Robin is dead—dead to her. Perhaps he had never lived.[4]

---

2. Gail did include the purse-cleaning scene in her published manuscript. In one paragraph, she characterizes Dane's life through fourteen garbage-bound objects found in the purse, including the tennis ball she had forgotten to give Robin.

3. In *Sons and Lovers,* Baxter Dawes is the estranged husband of Clara, with whom the reeling hero, Paul Morel, is having an affair.

4. Gail is questioning her development of the seemingly judgmental, mute, tantrum-throwing boy in *The Perfectionists.*

APRIL 4

I have ten days starting tomorrow to finish the book, and I am worried, worried. I am going to probe for the experience of things, what is left in terms of scenes.

1. Polly-and-Dane confrontation. I have to know what each wants. John had written about her as if he'd given up hope. Polly says nice room. Dane says she was just reading something John had given her. Polly's dream—I have got to be Polly, and see what she'd try to do, say. Polly forces confrontation.

2. John brings Dane a little saint, wrapped up. He's agreed to go dancing, so Dane is stuck. She unwraps the present and sees what she can have with John. Penelope and Robin stop and talk to the French family. Dane is jealous. That was supposed to be me talking to the Frenchwoman.

3. The dance scene. Dane "feels" Karl.

4. The morning—the balcony and clean-out scenes. Robin's ball in Dane's pocketbook.

5. Beach scene.

6. Finale.

APRIL 6

The Pinter play displaced by the baseball game. I called the TV station in Davenport to complain, ended up shouting "Fuck baseball!" and hanging up in the poor man's face. Page 196 of the book. I think modestly: It's D. H. Lawrence at his best. Tomorrow I do the remainder of the saint scene.

Penelope and Robin and the Frenchwoman. Dane has almost a visceral jealousy for the child (and for the kind of woman she had wanted to be on the holiday). Like thinking you have a vicious, aloof dog, and suddenly he climbs docilely into a stranger's lap. From now until the end, she has to gravitate toward the child. Everything else must recede from her. She and he are the final couple.

Should finish the novel tomorrow. Can't say what it is. All I hope at this point is that it fulfills its own expectations. I go achingly, painstakingly carefully. Like a caterpillar. Am I a storyteller? Is it a good read? Are there a lot of deflections?

In the previous draft, there is so much archness. I am writing down to the reader. The whole thing is a novel being a novel.

Tomorrow: Dane idealizes herself to Polly for the last time. She decides that the swim to the fort with John will save her marriage. Have little notices of Robin from time to time. Karl comes (make this condensed). John comes. Dane decides not to swim. Lunch. The child humiliates her over the glass of water.

Rewrite "St. George" for *Cosmopolitan*.

APRIL 14

Page 9 of "St. George," with the Junius Adams[5] letter beside me. My people are evolving in the round. Without Coover to make me feel guilty for being clear. I shouldn't be afraid to give background, tell things, if necessary. Emphasis on having a pet—how it fills your life. "If she can find a way to make it work," writes Adams, "we would be very interested in it and I would certainly recommend it for purchase."

After her lover, Silas, leaves her, Gwen, the heroine of "St. George," finds that the dragon that she'd found in a grocery store egg has grown, through her pampering, and become a monstrosity. She tries killing it kindly with beer and a knockout clout, but falters halfway and succeeds only in making the dragon sick. Gwen calls her gone-away lover for help. The romantic hero arrives. The antic tone of Gail's allegory enabled her to incorporate the editor's wish for a romance ending.

5. Junius Adams had been the editor in chief of *Cosmopolitan*, and loved the "St. George" story. Yet he wanted Gail to add a human love interest at the end. Gail gave Silas his chance: he freed the dragon and came back for his reward.

⁊

Excerpt from "St. George," Published
in Cosmopolitan (September 1969)

—

The doorbell rang. At last! Gwen ran to open it and threw herself at six-foot-three of reassuring bulk. Silas was suntanned and smiling puzzledly. After she had mauled him for a few moments, he said: "Where's the sick animal? Did you get yourself a cat?"

"Listen, Silas, let me explain before we go in . . ."

APRIL 15

Jeremy is right: Don't *think* about the future, do what has to be done toward it, but don't sit around indulging in a lot of what-ifs. Finished St. G. It's much more coherent. The secret is knowing what you mean before you start, then throwing out the right hints.

J. is having a writing slump, unable to believe in himself. His style of dejection is an easy one to live with: he simply withdraws, goes remote, has a bit less to give. But remains polite and thoughtful. I am grateful for the lovely living conditions. I am able to give more to my writing. It's more straightforward and generous. Having fewer defenses myself, I no longer need to play hide-and-seek with a reader.

APRIL 16

I sat with a student by the river. He said: "I don't want to bloat your ego, but you and this Western Civ. teacher I have are the only people who ever made me feel like I was in, quote, 'school.'"

I talked with Coover about his movie. He is the most *un*personal man I've ever known. He never deals in personalities. I typed ten pages of the novel.

The student says: "Apathy waits for me to sit down in a chair. After that comes depression. When I'm depressed, I have a journal I write in. I never write in it when I'm happy." His father is an electrician. His mother is Irish Catholic. He's been athletic all his life.

Last night, alone here in the house, I dreamed I was having a nightmare. It got so turbulent, I decided to scream so that Mother and Frank would come. I screamed through the nightmare's nightmare, and through the nightmare, and woke up screaming. Only Virginia the cat. Did she hear or not? The awful disappointment when I realized no one would come to comfort me.

Virginia is snoring.

APRIL 18

Lucy Rosenthal called from New York. She met my editor, David Segal. Both drunk, they talked about me. She told him she thought I was a born novelist and that I had a "certain eye" for things. He wanted to know if I was academic—said my outline read that way. She said, "No, she must have been on a tear." Anyway, I really enjoyed talking to her.

I'm ruthlessly last-drafting. It must be sparse. It must fit together like a puzzle. It must be convincing and have intensity.

I would like to write a truly Gothic novel, the sort of thing I look to, find titillating. Somehow Uncle William might be the key.[6] Uncle William in that dream, growing younger by the minute.

APRIL 23

Moon outside at the top of the sky.
    Jeremy finished his novel. Terrifying last sentence!
    John H. called to say *Cosmo* had bought "St. George" for $1,000.
    Peculiar state of mind.

---

6. Gail has been contemplating a story based on Uncle William, the bachelor judge, for many years. The story would turn toward a young girl whose mother engages in a "protecting marriage" with the fictional judge.

Lawrence Durrell said: Art is easy; it is life I find difficult. I understand this.

It tears me apart, relating to people. Jeremy is relatively easy, because wherever he walks it's with ten inches of space around him.

Called Mother. A certain retentive note. Oh, God. That hurts. That tiny reservation.

APRIL 25

Keep the visceral tension between Dane and the child. Also, it's about time for a passage of good writing: the watcher theme. "I would have made a good God." Imagine John telling Polly.[7] Go back and get the feel of the island.

Went to Coover's film matinee in the old armory building. All the people who "mattered" were there—afraid they might miss the latest thing. He's really onto this gesture thing.

APRIL 27 • *Sunday—daylight saving time*

Four years ago, Ian and Audrey from Miss Slade's writing class came to tea. I should have this book finished next Sunday, May 4. Then devote myself to *Monsieur Teste* for Spivak's comp. lit. course. And teaching my plays for Core.

Page 153, final draft. From this point on, Dane is comforted more and more by the child so that the disappointment at the end really is disappointment. Hint that he sort of grows into her lover, then rejects her. The child becomes the center of her hope, her little god. He can resurrect her. At this point she cannot tolerate "the child" in anything.

He would speak in his hour. He would give her the word.

Levels of presentation. Statement (like those stories that can be expressed in a single sentence, and don't have to be written). Rendering,

7. Gail will not include the "I would have made a good God" line in her final work. Instead, she has John talk with Polly about astronomy and physics—collapsed stars and relativity. The second topic opens up Polly's wish for an alternate existence.

description, experience, metaphor, symbol. Find the intangible space beneath.

A new and very delicate development in *The Perfectionists:* Dane ends up with only the rejecting child as an object to venerate.

How could the child hurt her, humiliate her? He reflects whatever people want to see. They use him to achieve their own ends. Karl pours the water. The child shoots her a little look of triumph. Penelope: "Did you see that?"[8]

MARCH 28

Kent's little son Kevin tells this story: "A little boy lived alone. His grandmother had dived. His grandfather had dived. His mother had dived and his father was eaten by a giant. He lived there alone till the turnamites came . . ."

MAY 4

Last chapter. I simply don't know how it's working. She's tidying up now, like an automaton, no feeling left for John. She cleans her purse. Ticket stubs—goodbye to illusions. Unsharpened pencil—nothing wrong with it that sharpening won't fix (throw it out). Keys to her office and her old apartment. Tennis ball.

Evening

I didn't finish as planned but it was a mature gesture on my part. Approximately ten more pages to go. They have to clinch the deal.

As John goes off to sea, she thinks about him drowning—a substantial fantasy.

The child's *aha!* His spite-look must be eloquent so that what follows can simply follow action by action.

8. In the published book, it's Dane's task to pour the water, which she refuses to do for Robin because he's pointing and not speaking. Karl is involved in serving Dane a glass of Dubonnet and rubbing Penelope's leg under the table.

Somebody soaked poor Virginia. She's licking herself into shape.

Before a person like Dane breaks out—flowers—she pulls herself tighter and tighter. She throws excess baggage overboard.

The last-minute John-Dane conversation. Motifs: flower in her head. The circle—"Where am I in it?" Ramón Lull [the island saint]. Child's eyes.

In the final draft, John proposes that Dane accompany him on a two-mile swim to an island with a ruined fort. Dane gives no response, and when John splashes off she imagines the scene in which John's corpse is brought back. Karl breaks her reverie with an invitation for everyone to go up to the terrace, where Robin has his tantrum at not being obeyed in his mute demand for water. Dane takes him up to their room and spanks him for not saying, "Mommy, I want some water." She clamps her mouth on his to possess him, then comes "to herself in pure, perfect peace."

Excerpt from The Perfectionists *(Harper & Row, 1970)*

—

When she could gather her energies, she crawled from the small form, looking down at the mottled face at just the precise moment when the blue eyes hardened against her in a decision far beyond their years. She slid from the cot and made her way, dazed, toward the closed doors leading to the balcony. The hollow eyes of Ramón Lull watched her impassively from the dresser.

MAY 11

So that book is on its way back to New York.

I am trying to get my mind together for a paper—and then for the next book, which will take off in another direction: more symbolic, more fantasy, more chances. There is something deeper than relationships, a foaming swirl below them. This is not just a book about a white girl and a black girl.[9] It would be the exploring of a certain kind of synthesis. Can the one plant her dreams in the other? It is how the dreams would *fail* if replanted. I want to explore what I want to explore.

Eagdyth. Edith. Her name: Lenora. Lenore.[10]

My Copenhagen *Alexandria Quartet.*

A story about the relationship between two interesting women has more potential than same between two men.

Lenore: "I would hate to be on my deathbed and suddenly realize I hadn't known fully what it really meant to be me."

MAY 14 · *Wednesday*

I'm in limbo as I wait for another father figure's approval. David Segal.

Hawkins called first thing Monday to say he'd read the book, and it worried him that John didn't really have that much influence over Dane.

Then the check came from him today, via *Cosmo,* with a note saying he felt like a dog for having upset me so early in the day. Suddenly, this evening, I started writing again: "1000 Sunset Drive." That summer, when everything shifted and a young girl grew a carapace.[11]

MAY 19

I have been retreating into my little white bedroom. Hawkins due to call with Segal's reaction to my book. I feel and don't feel that this absolves me from doing anything. "1000 Sunset Drive" is telling me

9. Once again, Gail ponders writing about her friendship with Lorraine O'Grady Freeman and about Copenhagen.

10. In exploring the white girl's background in her new story idea, Gail goes to an eleventh-century woman, Eagdyth, granddaughter of Alfred the Great; daughter of Godwin, Earl of Wessex; childless wife of Edward the Confessor; and, later in life, a nun.

11. The impetus for this story will lie dormant until 2009, when Gail begins her fourteenth novel, *Flora,* about an eleven-year-old girl and her companion-tutor living alone on top of a mountain in the summer of 1945, while her father is away, engaged in secret work in Oak Ridge, Tennessee.

things I didn't know. That house on the top of the mountain! Children are like bombs that will one day go off.

MAY 23

Good, good day. Much to record. First, a few watchwords from thirteenth-century mystic Ramón Lull:

> *The Beloved revealed Himself to His Lover. Clothed in new*
> *and scarlet robes. He stretched out His arms to embrace him;*
> *He inclined His head to kiss him; and He remained on high*
> *that he might ever seek Him.*
>
> —RAMÓN LULL, *THE BOOK OF THE LOVER AND THE BELOVED*

Segal has taken the book as is and is sending it to the copy editor. It will be published in the spring of 1970. Must get a photo made and send my dedication.[12]

Vulcan read it. He wanted Dane to leave! So did Hawkins![13] I figure that the only men who have read the book right—Chap Freeman, Jeremy, Segal—are the ones who know me intimately or not at all. So good to see Vulcan. In a soft, spring green shirt. He suddenly appeared in the doorway of the English office. I was stricken. The old Romantic in me awakened. We went down to my office and talked—kissed at the end, with my student crouched outside the door. A hundred years from now people will accept the fact that we're not monogamous. I said to him (as he talked about whether to go back to his wife): I don't care because I feel I've got you, too. I feel we're bound up together somehow. He fulfills my requirements for the unattainable beloved—and with luck we can keep him unattainable.

He said the best writing in my book came when Dane was thinking of Penelope's swimming over the Caves of Atlantis. Showing the depths · of personality through metaphor.

12. The dedication is to Gail's mother: "To Kathleen Krahenbuhl Cole."

13. These two readers identified with Dane, a sympathetic protagonist, who, however, is presented as being monstrous.

MAY 25

Read Heather Ross Miller's *Gone a Hundred Miles*[14] and envied her knowledge of nature, her simplicity, her ability to make a fable.

That terrible feeling, in writing, when you know you're skimming the surface when there are millions of things crying out to be! The pondering of an object, then sending your rays around it. The apprehending of it without destroying it entirely.

MAY 27

John Hawkins sold two of Ace Baber's stories to *Playboy*. What a year! Pete Neill sold his novel to Viking.[15] Nolan Porterfield sold his to a subsidiary of Harper's.[16] I sold mine to H&R and a story to *Cosmo*. Will any one of us make a dent in the future? I'm worried about Jeremy. Things are happening all around him (I know how *that* feels) and he's bound to this terrible job.

> *October 1968: Got an agent for forty-eight pages.*
> *May 20, 1969: Book accepted complete.*
> *Seven months*

JUNE 16

Registered for the Faulkner seminar with Fredericks and for "Narrative Genres" with Spivak.

Jeremy took me to get the driver's license. I ended up in tears. They persecuted me for changing my birth date on my old license. I found a

14. *Gone a Hundred Miles*, published in 1968, was Heather Ross Miller's fourth book. A previous novel, *Tenants of the House*, won the top North Carolina fiction award—the Sir Walter Raleigh Award.

15. Peter Neill published the novel, *A Time Piece*, with Grossman Publishers, a Viking imprint, in 1970.

16. Nolan Porterfield published the novel, *A Way of Knowing*, with Harper's Magazine Press in 1971.

sympathetic patrolman and told him how I couldn't stand being over thirty. So it ended up a joke with all of them laughing. Dinner with the Dixons. They saw my old professor Walter Spearman in Chapel Hill and he praised me. I feel so free here—in spirit. I can pursue what I like. The writing: I'm dissatisfied with all that isn't valid. The novel will have to be reapproached. Next I'm going to do a short story. "Where Does a Tornado Convalesce?"

JUNE 17

A feeling like walking on eggs. It's all too good. Any moment the gods could send their thunderbolt. Why can't I accept the good times as easily as the bad? Read up on the characteristics of tornadoes.

JULY 5

"Tornado" turned into an abortive novel. Since my last entry, I seem to have been in the funnel of a tornado. Couldn't decide what I was interested in. Spent two weeks writing junk, autobiography. Finally, spent a day reading various stuff: medieval, mystical, Jung. Almost started a story about citizens' attacks on universities in the 1300s. It came to nothing. Then I decided I had to do something. I decided on the story of the mistress who is fascinated by the wife, and when the wife goes, the mistress's interest also goes. So I have worked for several days on that, a new frame growing in the form of the art of warfare: "Nicole: Highlights of a Memorable Campaign."

Woman next door mowing lawn. Is there any better smell? It would make one delay suicide.

ail then makes a list of her completed stories, seven of which will be published in magazines, and one, "His House," in Coover's anthology with Merker's Stone Wall Press. There is yet no inkling of what would be her second published book, the novel Glass People.

❧

Sorrowful Woman
Blue
Uncle
St. George
Illumined Moment and Consequences
Legacy of the Motes
Liza's Leaf Tower
The Dandelion, a Hardy Soul, Far from Its Proper Home
His House
Some Aspects of Time Travel

The notion of being dead, all except for one's mind and spirit—something I want to pursue.

RE "NICOLE": What things about an absent wife would fascinate me? Healthy ego. Someone who is supremely herself. She has ESP. She's a good mother. Plays with her children.

WATCHING THE "GIRLS" PLAY. Jeremy's Virginia and my new kitten, Flannery. The little one is like a cartoon cat. They provide our life here.

JULY 6

I try not to worry about this writing trouble. Maybe I am developing. Also, there is no longer Coover to impress and rebel against. Tomorrow, I must make some headway. "Nicole" is basically a good story. I'm just not sure about the form. Also the woman is not as fascinating as I would like. In addition, I'm terrified I won't finish it. I think I'd better get back to the source. What was truly interesting about the first story I wanted to tell?

Jeremy in to lecture me on my pessimism.

Rain . . . rain . . . rain.

I HAVE BEEN too damn lazy.

AFTERWORD

he final entry of Part 9, "Completion," ends with a self-scolding. The thirty-two-year-old diarist, whose first novel is now scheduled for publication, is dismayed that she can't plunge right into a second novel. She can't even begin a simple story. She's uncertain about the form the story should take, and the fascinating character has ceased to fascinate. Suddenly she is afraid. What if she starts a story and can't finish it? She concludes that her biggest problem has been laziness.

She will continue to scold herself for this failing during the next forty years of her writing life just as she will continue to keep diaries that chronicle the drama of a self trying to figure out how to live.

And so we come to the completion of this two-volume project, begun when Rob Neufeld agreed to help me shape the journals of my apprentice years (1961–1969) into something useful for other writers, not only those starting out but those committed for life. "I know with what kind of hunger certain people go to writers' accounts of their development," Rob wrote to me, after I had sent him the first two notebooks covering my 1961 waitressing summer in Blowing Rock, North Carolina, followed by the October freighter voyage and my first months in Copenhagen with a rented typewriter. "I can see that you offer a number of things—first an opportunity to identify with an emerging writer . . . and then there are the life choices, also critical and dramatic. There's so much more—commentary on other authors; examples of ways to sketch character portraits; good writing clues; witticisms; concerns about fleeting time, self-traps, and the writing market; insights into themes and motifs in your work; and connections to projects that might bear fruit in various forms in future works."

I hope these volumes have kept you company in all the above-mentioned ways and that they have emboldened you in your pursuits. I'll never forget the surge of resolve I felt, in the early 1960s, when reading some advice from Isak Dinesen. I can't quote it verbatim, but her message to other writers was this: If you keep working on something faithfully, *even without hope,* one day the work will get itself finished. And only this morning, I was heartened by this passage in Virginia Woolf's *A Writer's Diary* (the same paperback copy I was reading on the banks of the Iowa River in the fall of 1968): "I am old; I am ugly; I am repeating things. Yet, as far as I know, as a writer I am only now writing out my mind." She wrote this on Saturday, March 20, 1926, when she was all of forty-six.

I am only now writing out my mind. What a wonderful goal to reach!

Recently, after my friend John Bowers (whom you've encountered in these pages) gave a reading from his new novel, *Love in Tennessee,* I asked him how he had achieved such a fearless narrative tone. "You write," I said, "as though you weren't afraid of anything." Always the modest humorist, John replied: "It's simple, Gail. I'm old now and all these people are dead. They won't mind if I re-create them for the purposes of my story."

Four years ago, a Jungian analyst asked me, "What would you write if you weren't afraid?" This happened to be during the time when I was culling my 1963–1969 journal notebooks to put together volume two of *The Making of a Writer.* Browsing through the dispiriting fall days of 1968, I came across the October 2 dream of entering a house "where my future was" and discovering in its basement a single thin volume of my work entitled *Unpublished Prosperity: Nine Essays.*

This long-ago dream, recorded during one of the low points of my life, inspired me to begin a new kind of notebook, a dark sidekick to my traditional journals. In this notebook, which I call *Unpublished Desper-ations,* I practice "writing without being afraid." I pen umbrages and screeds, brazen out essays about things and people that haunt and baffle me, make up stories reimagining or exploding my past, coax dead people into arguments and dialogues. In these pieces ("Vicious and Holy," "Scared in Woodstock," "Your Loss, Not Mine," "Work on What Has Been Spoiled," "The Naked Nun"), I dig under rocks and find unlikely treasures, some of which I have been able to transfer, still wriggly and wet with life, into published work.

Thus the writing life goes on: the steady chronicling and keeping track, the digging and unearthing, the reshaping and the using up of the material that is yours alone, until you realize you have been—for how long now?—writing out your mind.

Gail Godwin

ACKNOWLEDGMENTS

I am deeply grateful to Rob Neufeld for his sagacious editing of the 1961–1969 journals for *The Making of a Writer.* If the diarist wrote an entry about a Dinesen story or a Camus essay, he wouldn't commit himself to a comment or a footnote until he, too, had read it. His footnotes are a cultural history in themselves. The Lord Mayor of London, Christine Keeler, Chief Spotted Back, the 19 and 22 bus lines, the Bisley shooting range: They meant something to the diarist, but the present reader needs to be apprised of the who and the what in order to appreciate the why.

When Jane Toby began transcribing the handwritten journals on to disks in 2004, I would go carefully through each notebook, marking in blue ink the passages to be typed and instructing her to "skip over" the rest of the material. But after a while we achieved such empathy of purpose that I started giving her the notebooks unmarked. I found that I got a better perspective on the project if she transcribed the entire notebook for me to edit on screen.

INDEX

GG refers to Gail Godwin throughout this index.
Books and stories are by Gail Godwin unless otherwise indicated.

Eliott (character), 192–93, 205–7, 242, 271
Ellis, Peter, 252
Ellison, Ralph, 170
Emma (character), 18
the Englishman (character), 122, 124, 127–28
Enrico (cat), 85
An Epitaph for Dixie (Ashmore), 49
Eva, 56
Evan (character), 18, 122, 127–28
Evenings at Five, 167, 174, 218
Evensong, 33
existentialism, 15–16, 25–26, 32–33
Exit the King (Ionesco), 29
Extensive Clean Air Act of Great Britain, 38

F
family of GG
 divorces, x, 92, 99, 171, 189, 191, 204, 220
 ex-husband Douglas Kennedy, 6, 17, 20, 48, 92, 99
 father. *See* Godwin, Mose Winston
 marriage to Ian Marshall, 132–36, 139–47, 151–52, 157–58, 161–64, 168–69, 187
 maternal grandmother, 67
 mother. *See* Cole, Kathleen
 siblings, 30, 37, 57, 81, 92, 135, 157, 169
 stepfather. *See* Cole, Frank
 uncle William, 38, 51, 129, 230, 265, 298
Farmer, Pat, 4–5
"Father Flynn." *See* "Mourning"
Father Melancholy's Daughter, 32
The Fire Next Time (Baldwin), 16
"The First Writer-God," 223
Flannery (cat), 306
Flora, 302–3
Fortune, Dion, 143
Francesca (character), 170
Frank (friend), 50
Fredericks (professor), 304
Freeman, Chap, 170, 181, 193, 212, 223, 293, 303
Frey, Barbara, 129

G
Gaert (friend), 24, 215, 223
Geoffrey Sykes (character), 122, 124, 127–28
George (friend), 50
Gian Carlo (friend), 21
Gianni Schicchi (Puccini), 10, 35
"The Gift of Insight," 172–74
Gilbert Osmond (character), 92
Gillett, Charles, 128
Gilmore, Voit, 136, 144
"Ginny on Sunday," 130–31
The Girl with the Green Eyes (O'Brien), 91
Glasgow, Ellen, 184
Glass People, 170, 305

The Goat (Albee), 105
Goddard, Dale, 189
Godwin, Mose Winston, 13, 17, 28, 117, 141, 218, 221–22
Godwin, William, 38, 51, 129, 230, 265, 298
Goldwater, Barry, 26–27, 49
Goller, Elia, 158
Gone a Hundred Miles (Miller), 304
Graziani, Simone Micheline Bodin (Bettina), 21
"Gretchen Saga," 218
The Group (McCarthy), 16
Guinness, Alec, 29
"Gull Key," 18, 63, 122–23, 124, 127–28
Gwen (character), 225–26

H
Hamilton, Chief Spotted Back, 21, 24
Hammer, Gael and Katherine, 196, 202, 204, 209, 218, 267
Hampl, Patricia (Pitty Pat), 254
"The Happy Couple," 12
Hardy, Thomas, 43–44
"Have Some Madeira, M'Dear" (song), 50
Hawkins, John, 185
 early contact with GG, 220–21, 231–33
 representation of GG, 237–38, 242, 250, 266, 268, 279–80, 298, 302–4
 sale of GG's work, 252–53
 visits to Iowa, 233, 235–36
Haydon, Mr. (colleague), 34–35
Heart: A Natural History of the Heart-Filled Life, 90, 151
heartfulness, 151
Henley Sailing Club, 6
Henry (friend), 25
Hilda (palmist), 10–11
Hinduism, 155
"His House," 233, 261, 305, 306
Høiass, Frowsy, 54
"Holger Danske" (Andersen), 258
Honest to God (Robinson), 32, 104–5
"The Honeymoon," 17–19
Hubbard, L. Ron, 141, 142, 170, 173, 174–75
Hubbard Association of Scientologists, International (HASI), 144, 147, 152–54, 156–57, 168
Hubbard Chart of Human Evaluation, 152–53
human-improvement movement, 151
 See also Scientology
Hurst, Andy, 53–75, 78–83
 engagement to GG, 84–85, 89–90, 95
 former girlfriends, 58–59
 friendship with GG, 91, 94–95, 96, 99, 103, 115, 131–32
 GG's doubts about, 61–62, 73–75
 on marriage, 68
 rugby world, 58, 70, 81, 82–83
 social skills, 59, 65, 68, 71, 116

ABOUT THE AUTHOR

GAIL GODWIN is a three-time National Book Award finalist and the bestselling author of thirteen critically acclaimed novels, including *A Mother and Two Daughters, Violet Clay, Father Melancholy's Daughter, Evensong, The Good Husband, Evenings at Five,* and *Unfinished Desires.* She is also the author of *The Making of a Writer: Journals, 1961–1963,* edited by Rob Neufeld. She has received a Guggenheim Fellowship, National Endowment for the Arts grants for both fiction and libretto writing, and the Award in Literature from the American Academy of Arts and Letters. She has written libretti for ten musical works with the composer Robert Starer. She lives in Woodstock, New York.

ROB NEUFELD is a librarian and a book critic for the *Asheville Citizen-Times.* He founded the Together We Read program for Western North Carolina.